MAINE POLITICS AND GOVERNMENT

KENNETH T. PALMER, G. THOMAS TAYLOR,
& MARCUS A. LIBRIZZI

Maine Politics & Government

UNIVERSITY OF NEBRASKA PRESS
LINCOLN and LONDON

Chapter 5, "The Constitutional Tradition," is a revision of Kenneth Palmer and Marcus A. LiBrizzi, "Development of the Maine Constitution: The Long Tradition, 1819–1988," *Maine Historical Society Quarterly* 28 (Winter 1988–89): 126–45, and is published here by permission of the Maine Historical Society.

Chapter 15, "Maine Documents and Sources," is a revision of Kenneth T. Palmer and Edward B. Laverty, "Maine Documents and Sources," *NEWS for Teachers of Political Science* 34 (Summer 1982): 17–19, and is published here by permission of the American Political Science Association.

The paper in this book
meets the minimum requirements of
American National Standard
for Information Sciences—Permanence of
Paper for Printed Library Materials,
ANSI Z39.48–1984.

Library of Congress
Cataloging-in-Publication Data
Palmer, Kenneth T.
Maine Politics and government /
Kenneth T. Palmer, G. Thomas Taylor,
Marcus A. LiBrizzi.
p.   cm. – (Politics and governments
of the American states)
Includes bibliographical references
(p.) and index.
ISBN 0-8032-3680-8 (cl: alk. paper).
ISBN 0-8032-8718-6 (pa: alk. paper)
1. Maine – Politics and government.
2. Local government – Maine.
I. Taylor, G. Thomas.
II. LiBrizzi, Marcus A., 1964– .
III. Title. IV. Series.
JK2816.P35   1992   320.9741 – dc20
92-6080   CIP

Other volumes in the series Politics and Governments of the American States include:

Alabama Government and Politics
By James D. Thomas and William H. Stewart

Arkansas Politics and Government: Do the People Rule?
By Diane D. Blair

Mississippi Government and Politics: Modernizers versus Traditionalists
By Dale Krane and Stephen D. Shaffer

Nebraska Government and Politics
Edited by Robert D. Miewald

Oklahoma Politics and Policies: Governing the Sooner State
By David R. Morgan, Robert E. England, and George G. Humphreys

CONTENTS

TABLES AND MAPS

JOHN KINCAID

Series Preface

The purpose of this series is to provide intelligent and interesting books on the politics and governments of the fifty American states, books that are of value not only to the student of government but also to the general citizen who wants greater insight into the past and present civic life of his or her own states and of other states in the federal union. The role of the states in governing America is among the least well known of all the 83,217 governments in the United States. The national media focus attention on the federal government in Washington, D.C., and local media focus attention on local government. Meanwhile, except when there is a scandal or a proposed tax increase, the workings of state government remain something of a mystery to many citizens—out of sight, out of mind.

In many respects, however, the states have been, and continue to be, the most important governments in the American political system. They are the main building blocks and chief organizing governments of the whole system. The states are the constituent governments of the federal union, and it is through the states that citizens gain representation in the national government. The national government is one of limited, delegated powers; all other powers are possessed by the states and their citizens. At the same time, the states are the empowering governments for the nation's 83,166 local governments—counties, municipalities, townships, school districts, and special districts. As such, states provide for one of the most essential and ancient elements of freedom and democracy, the right of local self-government.

Although, for many citizens, the most visible aspects of state government are state universities, some of which are the most prestigious in the world, and state highway patrol officers, with their radar guns and handy ticket books, state governments provide for nearly all domestic public services.

Whether elements of those services are enacted or partly funded by the federal government and actually carried out by local governments, it is state government that has the ultimate responsibility for ensuring that Americans are well served by all their governments. In so doing, all of the American states are more democratic, more prosperous, stronger financially, and better governed than most of the world's nation-states.

This is a particularly timely period in which to publish a series of books on the governments and politics of each of the fifty states. Once viewed as the "fallen arches" of the federal system, states today are increasingly seen as energetic, innovative, and fiscally responsible. Some states, of course, perform better than others, but that is to be expected in a federal system. Each state is unique in its own right. It is our hope that this series will shed light on the public life of each state and that, taken together, the books will contribute to a better, more informed understanding of the states themselves and of their often pivotal roles in the world's first and oldest continental-size federal democracy.

DANIEL J. ELAZAR

Series Introduction

The more than continental stretch of the American domain is given form and character as a federal union of fifty different states whose institutions order the American landscape. The existence of these states made possible the emergence of a continental nation where liberty, not despotism, reigns and where self-government is the first principle of order. The great American republic was born in its states, as its very name signifies. America's first founding was repeated on thirteen separate occasions over 125 years, from Virginia in 1607 to Georgia in 1732, each giving birth to a colony that became a self-governing commonwealth. Its revolution and second founding was accomplished by those commonwealths, now states, acting in congress, and its constitution was written together and adopted separately. As the American tide rolled westward from the Atlantic coast, it absorbed new territories by organizing thirty-seven more states over the next 169 years.

Most of the American states are larger and better developed than most of the world's nations. Maine is one of the smaller of the United States. In population and in area it ranks in the lower third. At the same time, it is territorially the largest state in New England, illustrating the point that each state has its own story and is a polity with its own uniqueness.

The American states exist because each is a unique civil society within their common American culture. They were first given political form and then acquired their other characteristics. Each has its own constitution, its own political culture, its own relationship to the federal union and to its section. These in turn have given each state its own law and history; the longer the history, the more distinctive the state. Maine's history is illustrative of this. Maine was originally a part of Massachusetts, and its decision to separate from the mother state in 1819 reflected how its people had developed a separate character as a civil society over the previous century and a half.

It is in and through the states, no less than the nation, that the great themes of American life play themselves out. The advancing frontier and the continuing experience of Americans as a frontier people, the drama of American ethnic blending, the tragedy of slavery and racial discrimination, the political struggle for expanding the right to vote—all found, and find, their expression in the states. The changing character of government, from an all-embracing concern with every aspect of civil and religious behavior to a limited concern with maintaining law and order to a concern with providing the social benefits of the contemporary welfare state, has been felt in the states even more than in the federal government.

Maine Politics and Government is the sixth book in the Politics and Government Series of the Center for the Study of Federalism and the University of Nebraska Press. The aim of the series is to provide books that will appeal to three audiences: political scientists, their students, and the wider public in each state. Each volume in the series examines the specific character of one of the fifty states, looking at the state as a polity—its political culture, traditions and practices, constituencies and interest groups, and constitutional and institutional frameworks. Each book reviews the political development of the state to demonstrate how the state's political institutions and characteristics have evolved from the first settlement to the present, presenting the state in the context of the nation and section of which it is a part, and reviewing the roles and relations of the state vis-à-vis other states and the federal government. The state's constitutional history—its traditions of constitution making and constitutional change—is examined and related to the workings of the state's political institutions and processes. State-local relations, local government, and community politics are studied. Finally, each volume reviews the state's policy concerns and their implementation from the budgetary process to particular substantive policies. Each book concludes by summarizing the principal themes and findings to draw conclusions about the current state of the state, its continuing traditions, and emerging issues. Each volume also contains a bibliographic survey of the existing literature on the state and a guide to the use of that literature and state government documents. The books in the series are not uniform, but they do focus generally on the common themes of federalism, constitutionalism, political culture, and the continuing American frontier.

FEDERALISM

Both the greatest conflicts of American history and the day-to-day operations of American government are closely intertwined with American federalism—the form of American government (in the eighteenth-century sense of the term, which includes both structure and process). Maine stands in an intermediate position in its relationship with the federal government. While not one of the original states, it was not carved out of the public domain as were the western states. Hence the federal government played no role in its settlement or founding other than to ratify its search for separate statehood. On the other hand, as a sparsely populated state whose economy was historically based on the exploitation of its natural resources, it has been more dependent on the federal government than some other states of New England with regard to its forests and fisheries. Its extensive border with Canada has also fostered close relations with the federal government. Strongly Unionist in outlook, Maine, for its size, played a major role in the Civil War. Its people's devotion to the Union led a very high percentage of Maine's men to volunteer for the Union army. Then and now the prevailing views in Maine have been sympathetic to those prevailing in Washington. This was true even when Maine was voting Republican against the national stream.

In recent decades Maine has been a major beneficiary of federal grants-in-aid. Moreover, it has been dependent on direct federal support in such areas as national defense. On racial issues the state has had a strong pro-black stance since its pre–Civil War antislavery sentiments when abolitionism was strong in the state. Maine has never had a sizeable black population, and it has had no serious problems of racial integration or other forms of white-black tension. Where necessary, Maine is institutionally alert to the realities of American federalism and has been able to mobilize its normally strong congressional delegation to secure federal assistance, even as it has preserved its distinctiveness as a state.

CONSTITUTIONALISM

American constitutionalism had its beginning in New England. Representatives of the Connecticut River valley towns of Hartford, Windsor, and Wethersfield met in January 1639 to draft a constitution. That document, the Fundamental Orders, established a federal union to be known as Connecticut and inaugurated the American practice of constitution making as a popular act and responsibility, ushering in the era of modern constitutionalism. Like the other New England states, Maine, too, grew from towns founded in the seventeenth century and, although not formed into a state until 1820, partakes of the same constitutional tradition as Connecticut.

The American constitutional tradition grows out of the Whig understanding that civil societies are founded by political covenant, entered into by the first founders and reaffirmed by subsequent generations, through which the powers of government are delineated and limited and the rights of the constituting members are clearly proclaimed in such a way as to provide moral and practical restraints on governmental institutions. That constitutional tradition was modified by the federalists, who accepted its fundamental principals, but strengthened the institutional framework designed to provide energy in government while maintaining the checks and balances that they saw as needed to preserve liberty and republican government. At the same time, they turned nonbinding declarations of rights into enforceable constitutional articles.

American state constitutions reflect a melding of these two traditions. Under the U.S. Constitution, each state is free to adopt its own constitution, provided that it establishes a republican form of government. Some states have adopted highly succinct constitutions, such as the Vermont Constitution of 1793 with 6,600 words, which is still in effect with only 52 amendments. Others are just the opposite; for example, Georgia's ninth constitution, adopted in 1976, has 583,000 words.

State constitutions are potentially far more comprehensive than the federal constitution, which is one of limited, delegated powers. Because states are plenary governments, they automatically possess all powers not specifically denied them by the U.S. Constitution or their citizens. Consequently, a state constitution must be explicit about limiting and defining the scope of governmental powers, especially on behalf of individual liberty. So state constitutions normally include an explicit declaration of rights, almost invariably broader than the first ten amendments to the U.S. Constitution.

Overall, six different state constitutional patterns have developed. One is the commonwealth pattern, developed in New England, which emphasizes Whig ideas of the constitution as a philosophic document designed first and foremost to set a direction for civil society and to express and institutionalize the theory of republican government. A second is the constitutional pattern of the commercial republic. The constitutions fitting this pattern reflect a series of compromises required by the conflict of many strong ethnic groups and commercial interests generated by the flow of heterogeneous streams of migrants into particular states and the early development of large commercial and industrial cities in those states.

The third, found in the South, can be described as the southern contractual pattern. Southern state constitutions are used as instruments to set explicit terms governing the relationship between polity and society, such as those which protected slavery or racial segregation, or those which sought to diffuse the formal allocation of authority in order to accommodate the swings between oligarchy and factionalism characteristic of southern state politics. Of all the southern states, only Louisiana stands somewhat outside this configuration, providing the fourth state constitutional pattern, since its legal system was founded on the French civil code. Its constitutions have been codes—long, highly explicit documents that form a pattern in and of themselves.

A fifth pattern is found frequently in the less populated states of the Far West, where the state constitution is first and foremost a frame of government explicitly reflecting the republican and democratic principles dominant in the nation in the late nineteenth century, but emphasizing the structure of state government and the distribution of powers within that structure in a direct, businesslike manner. Finally, the two newest states, Alaska and Hawaii, have adopted constitutions following the managerial pattern developed and promoted by twentieth-century constitutional reform movements in the United States. Those constitutions are characterized by conciseness, broad grants of power to the executive branch, and relatively few structural restrictions on the legislature. They emphasize natural resource conservation and social legislation.

The Maine Constitution of 1819 is an excellent example of the commonwealth pattern in that it reflects the underlying consensus that Mainers seem to have about political life. Though longer than the Vermont Constitution, the Maine charter is still, at approximately 13,500 words, one of the shorter state constitutions. It is confined primarily to matters of fundamental importance in the governance of the state. It is based on the pioneering Massachusetts Constitution of 1780, which stressed both strong political institutions and the rights of citizens. Most amendments to the Maine charter have won approval at referendum by large popular majorities.

THE CONTINUING AMERICAN FRONTIER

For Americans, the very word *frontier* conjures up the images of the rural-land frontier of yesteryear—of explorers and mountain men, of cowboys and Indians, of brave pioneers pushing their way west in the face of natural obstacles. Later, Americans' picture of the frontier was expanded to include the inventors, the railroad builders, and the captains of industry who created the urban-industrial frontier. Recently television has begun to celebrate the entrepreneurial ventures of the automobile and oil industries, portraying the magnates of those industries and their families in the same larger-than-life frame as once was done for the heroes of that first frontier.

As is so often the case, the media responsible for determining and catering to popular taste tell us a great deal about ourselves. The United States was founded with a rural-land frontier that persisted until World War I, more or less, spreading farms, ranches, mines, and towns across the land. Early in the nineteenth century, the rural-land frontier generated the urban frontier based on industrial development. The creation of new wealth through industrialization transformed cities from mere regional service centers into generators of wealth in their own right. The frontier persisted for more than one-hundred years as a major force in American society as a whole and perhaps another sixty years as a major force in various parts of the country. The population movements and attendant growth on the urban-industrial frontier brought about the effective settlement of the United States in freestanding cities from coast to coast.

Between the world wars, the urban-industrial frontier gave birth in turn to a third frontier stage, one based on the new technologies of electronic communication, the internal combustion engine, the airplane, synthetics, and petrochemicals. These new technologies transformed every aspect of life and turned urbanization into metropolitanization. This third frontier stage generated a third settlement of the United States, this time in metropolitan regions from coast to coast, involving a mass migration of tens of millions of Americans in search of opportunity on the suburban frontier.

In the 1970s, the first post–World War II generation came to an end. Many Americans were speaking of the "limits of growth." Yet despite that anti-frontier rhetoric, there was every sign that a fourth frontier stage was beginning in the form of the "rurban," or citybelt-cybernetic, frontier generated by the metropolitan-technological frontier, just as the latter had been generated by its predecessor.

The rurban-cybernetic frontier first emerged in the Northeast, as did its predecessors, when the Atlantic Coast metropolitan regions merged into one another to form a six-hundred-mile-long megalopolis (the usage is Jean Gottman's)—a matrix of urban and suburban settlements in which the older central cities come to yield importance, if not prominence, to smaller ones. It was a sign of the times that the computer was conceived at MIT in Cambridge and was developed at IBM in White Plains, two medium-sized cities in the northeastern megalopolis that have become special centers in their own right. This in itself is a reflection of the two primary characteristics of the new frontier. The new focus of settlement is in medium-sized and small cities and in the rural interstices of the megalopolis.

The spreading use of computer technology is the most direct manifestation of the cybernetic tools that make such citybelts possible. In 1979, the newspapers in the Northeast published frequent reports of the revival of the small cities of the first industrial revolution, particularly in New England, as the new frontier engulfed them. Countrywide, the media focused on the shifting of population growth into rural areas. Both phenomena are as much a product of direct dialing as they are of the older America longing for small-town or country living. Both reflect the urbanization of the American way of life no matter what lifestyle is practiced, or where. Although the Northeast was first, the new rurban-cybernetic frontier, like its predecessors, is finding its true form in the South and West, where these citybelt matrices are not being built on the collapse of earlier forms, but are developing as an original form. The present sunbelt frontier—strung out along the Gulf Coast, the southwestern desert, and the fringes of the California mountains—is classically megalopolitan in citybelt form and cybernetic with its aerospace-related industries and sunbelt living made possible by air conditioning and the new telecommunications.

Maine has an anomalous relationship to the American frontier. Because of its geographic location, its coast was among the earliest areas of the United States to be settled, while its interior fit the definition of a frontier almost throughout the nineteenth century. While clearly not part of the westward movement, Maine remained New England's far frontier during the same period. During the nineteenth century, conditions in the state were those of the land frontier, yet at the same time, it had an old, established population. The end result was a combination worthy of special study by those who are interested in the frontier experience. What came out was a situation in which the spartan conditions of the frontier were omnipresent and very influential on the lives of Mainers without the expansiveness and sense of unlimited opportunity generated in the West. Those Mainers seeking the latter went west, and many of them became important figures in the founding of greater New England, from western New York to the Pacific. Those who stayed behind helped forge the stereotypical "Downeast Yankee," frugal and tough as a result of scarcity and exposure to the elements.

The urban-industrial frontier in Maine also had its own special impact. Rather than directly changing the life of the Yankees, it led to the importation of great numbers of French Canadians to work in the factories generated by that frontier. They transformed Maine into a multiethnic, multilingual society with two classes of citizens, a change which Maine kept hidden from the rest of the nation for nearly a century until its worst manifestations began to dissolve.

That dissolution was in no small measure a response to the metropolitan-technological frontier, whose direct consequences mostly bypassed Maine, ending in Massachusetts or at most reaching southern New Hampshire, but whose fallout in the form of mass tourism generated by metropolitan America gave Maine a greatly expanded, if fragile and seasonal, economic base. Like the metropolitan frontier elsewhere, the new frontier partially melted down class and ethnic lines in Maine, bringing Mainers of French-Canadian extraction into the mainstream of the body politic and much advancing their assimilation into the Maine way of life.

The rurban-cybernetic frontier has only begun to touch Maine, mostly in the way of expatriates from the northeastern megalopolis seeking a rurban lifestyle in Maine's towns and rural areas. The extent and consequences of that movement cannot yet be foretold. For a decade beginning in the late 1970s, it began to be felt. On the other hand, as a result of the economic reversals which followed in 1988, it has slowed down.

THE PERSISTENCE OF SECTIONALISM

Sectionalism—the expression of social, economic, and especially political differences along geographic lines—is part and parcel of American political life. The more or less permanent political ties that link groups of contiguous states together as sections reflect the ways in which local conditions and differences in political culture modify the impact of the frontier. This overall sectional pattern reflects the interaction of the three basic factors. The original sections were produced by the variations in the impact of the rural-land frontier on different geographic segments of the country. They, in turn, have been modified by the pressures generated by the first and subsequent frontier stages. As a result, sectionalism is not the same as regionalism. The latter is essentially a phenomenon—often transient—that brings adjacent state, substate, or interstate areas together because of immediate and specific common interests. The sections are not homogeneous socioeconomic units sharing a common character across state lines, but complex entities combining highly diverse states and communities with common political interests that generally complement one another socially and economically.

For example, New England is a section bound by the tightest of social and historical ties even though the differences between the states of lower and upper New England are quite noticeable even to the casual observer. The six New England states consciously seek to cooperate with one another in numerous ways. Their cooperative efforts have been sufficiently institutionalized to create a veritable confederation within the larger American Union. It is through such acts of political will that sectionalism best manifests itself.

Maine is New England through and through in both respects. Indeed, as an outpost of New England, it has preserved much of what Americans associate with stereotypical Yankee ways long after those ways have disappeared in most of the other New England states. But even if there are those who make an industry out of cultivating "Downeast" manners and mannerisms, so much of it is real. At the same time, Maine is very much involved in the "New England Confederation" of interlocking and overlapping inter-jurisdictional cooperative programs, thereby giving it access to services which its small population would prevent it from providing for itself.

Intrasectional conflicts often exist, but they do not detract from the long-term sectional community of interest. More important for our purposes, certain common sectional bonds give the states of each section a special relationship to national politics. This is particularly true in connection with those specific political issues that are of sectional importance, such as the race issue in the South, the problems of the megalopolis in the Northeast, and the problems of agriculture and agribusiness in the Northwest.

The nation's sectional alignments are rooted in the three great historical, cultural, and economic spheres into which the country is divided: the greater Northeast, the greater South, and the greater West. Following state lines, the greater Northeast includes all those states north of the Ohio and Potomac rivers and east of Lake Michigan. The greater South includes the states below that line but east of the Mississippi plus Missouri, Arkansas, Louisiana, and Texas. The remaining states form the greater West. Within that framework, there are eight sections: New England, Middle Atlantic, Near West, Upper South, Lower South, Western South, Northwest, and Far West.

Maine both suffers and benefits from being at the furthest periphery of the greater Northeast. It suffers in the sense that it is off the country's main transportation routes and its economic growth has been retarded as a result. In benefits, it is able to preserve its unique ways, yet at the same is close enough to the great northeastern megalopolis to serve as a megalopolitan vacation land. It suffered more in the days of the urban frontier and has benefited more since the opening of the metropolitan frontier. As a New England state settled by Puritans and Yankees, Maine developed a classic moralistic political culture modified by some individualistic elements brought by those original settlers not of Puritan stock. Their individualism became a prominent feature of Maine's general culture while moralistic behavior came to dominate its political culture.

French Canadians who came in the nineteenth century brought with them a very different political culture. While the original Mainers were overwhelmingly Reformed Protestant in their background, the French Canadians were Catholic from a very traditionalistic society in Quebec that, when cut loose of its traditional anchors, turned to classic individualistic politics, seeking to protect the society and to protect and advance their interests as a group or through their families in the political system. Thus at the heyday of the urban-industrial frontier and during its aftermath, Maine's dominant political culture was challenged by a thoroughly alien one. The representatives of the dominant political culture were able to confine manifestations of the other to particular parts of the state. Since the opening of the metropolitan frontier, there has been a movement toward synthesis, more on moralistic than individualistic lines, as the descendants of the French Canadian settlers assimilate into the state's way of life.

In summary, Maine lives up to its image as a clean "hometown" moralistic state, full of spartan individualists, more than one would expect. Politics are mostly "amateur"- dominated and "clean." Maine politicians who have surfaced nationally, such as Margaret Chase Smith or Edmund S. Muskie, have attracted a great deal of attention for their reputations for probity and also for serving as consciences of the nation. Things are not much different back home. There is much of the freshness of the outdoors, the woods and the sea, in the Maine way of life, along with a lack of hesitancy to resist the encroachment and blandishments of outlanders. Needless to say, underneath the surface, Maine is a more complex place than that, but it remains its own place in its politics and government as well as in so many other ways.

THE VITAL ROLE OF POLITICAL CULTURE

The same locational factors place Maine squarely in the moralistic political culture area. The United States as a whole shares a general political culture that is rooted in two contrasting conceptions of the American political order that can be traced back to the earliest settlement of the country. In the first, the polity is conceived as a marketplace in which the primary public relationships are products of bargaining among individuals and groups acting out of self-interest. In the second, the political order is conceived to be a commonwealth—a polity in which the whole people have an undivided interest—in which the citizens cooperate in an effort to create and maintain the best government in order to implement certain shared moral principles. These two conceptions have exercised an influence on government and politics throughout American history, sometimes in conflict and sometimes complementing each other.

The national political culture is a synthesis of three major political subcultures. All three are of nationwide proportions, having spread, in the course of time, from coast to coast. At the same time, each subculture is strongly tied to specific sections of the country, reflecting the streams and currents of migration that have carried people of different origins and backgrounds across the continent in more or less orderly patterns. Reflecting their central characteristics, the three are called *individualistic, moralistic,* and *traditionalistic*. Each of the three political cultures reflects its own particular synthesis of the marketplace and the commonwealth.

The *individualistic political culture* emphasizes the democratic order as a marketplace in which government is instituted for strictly utilitarian reasons, to handle those functions demanded by the people it is created to serve. Beyond the commitment to an open market, a government need not have any direct concern with questions of the good society, except insofar as it may be used to advance some common view formulated outside the political arena, just as it serves other functions. Since the individualistic political culture emphasizes the centrality of private concerns, it places a premium on limiting community intervention—whether governmental or nongovernmental—into private activities to the minimum necessary to keep the marketplace in proper working order.

The character of political participation in the individualistic political culture reflects this outlook. Politics is just another means by which individuals may improve themselves socially and economically. In this sense, politics is a business like any other, competing for talent and offering rewards to those who take it up as a career. Those individuals who choose political careers may rise by providing the governmental services demanded of them and, in return, may expect to be adequately compensated for their efforts. Interpretations of officeholders' obligations under this arrangement vary. Where the norms are high, such people are expected to provide high-quality public services in return for appropriate rewards. In other cases, an officeholder's primary responsibility is to serve him- or herself and those who have supported him or her directly, favoring them even at the expense of the public.

The *moralistic political culture* emphasizes the commonwealth conception as the basis for democratic government. Politics, in the moralistic political culture, is considered one of the great activities of humanity in its search for the good society—a struggle for power, it is true, but also an effort to exercise power for the betterment of the commonwealth. Consequently, both the general public and the politicians conceive of politics as a public activity centered on some notion of the public good and properly devoted to the advancement of the public interest.

In the moralistic political culture, there is a general commitment to utilizing communal—preferably nongovernmental, but governmental if necessary—power to intervene in the sphere of private activities when it is considered necessary to do so for the public good or the well-being of the community. Accordingly, issues have an important place in the moralistic style of politics, functioning to set the tone for political concern.

The concept of serving the commonwealth is at the core of all political relationships, and politicians are expected to adhere to it even at the expense of individual loyalties and political friendships. Political parties are considered useful political devices but are not valued for their own sakes. Regular party ties can be abandoned with relative impunity for third parties, special local parties, nonpartisan systems, or the opposition party if such changes are believed helpful in gaining larger political goals.

In practice, where the moralistic political culture is dominant today, there is considerably more amateur participation in politics. There is also much less of what Americans consider corruption in government and less tolerance of those actions that are considered corrupt, so politics does not have the taint it so often bears in the individualistic environment. By virtue of its fundamental outlook, the moralistic political culture creates a greater commitment to active government intervention in the economic and social life of the community. At the same time, its strong commitment to communitarianism tends to keep government intervention local wherever possible. Public officials will themselves initiate new government activities in an effort to come to grips with problems as yet unperceived by a majority of the citizenry.

The moralistic political culture's major difficulty with bureaucracy lies in the potential conflict between communitarian principles and large-scale organization. Otherwise, the notion of a politically neutral administrative system is attractive. Where merit systems are instituted, they tend to be rigidly maintained.

The *traditionalistic political culture* is rooted in an ambivalent attitude toward the marketplace, coupled with a paternalistic and elitist conception of the commonwealth. It reflects an older, precommercial attitude that accepts a substantially hierarchical society as part of the ordered nature of things, authorizing and expecting those at the top of the social structure to take a special and dominant role in government. Like its moralistic counterpart, the traditionalistic political culture accepts government as an actor with a positive role in the community, but it tries to limit that role to securing the continued maintenance of the existing social order. To do so, it functions to confine real political power to a relatively small and self-perpetuating group drawn from an established elite who often inherit their right to govern through family ties or social position. Social and family ties are even more important in a traditionalistic political culture than personal ties are in the individualistic political culture, where, after all is said and done, one's first responsibility is to oneself. At the same time, those who do not have a definite role to play in politics are not expected to be even minimally active as citizens. In many cases, they are not even expected to vote. As in the individualistic political culture, those active in politics are expected to benefit personally from their activity, although not necessarily by direct pecuniary gain.

Maine's predominantly moralistic political culture has some individualistic and traditionalistic elements. Gradual urbanization has fostered a growth in the individualistic political culture, which may especially be noticed in centers such as Portland. Rudiments of the traditionalistic political culture may still be found in towns and cities primarily composed of persons of French ancestry. A central theme of this book is the ways in which contemporary changes in population and political culture in the Pine Tree State are modifying its long-established political practices, and the governmental process generally.

Authors' Preface

This volume seeks to provide a systematic overview of Maine politics and government. The emphasis is on primary themes that seem to be reflected in the state's political life. In some ways, Maine is best known for accomplishments remote from the realm of government and politics: its marvelous scenery, its quaint villages, and its native population about whom a substantial folklore has evolved over the years. But government has always been important in the Pine Tree State. We try to show government's significance in transmitting the values of the state's political culture into the work-a-day world of the political system. Accordingly, we spend some time on the evolution of Maine politics as a basis for exploring the institutions and policies of the present.

We are indebted to many people who contributed in important ways to the production of the book. Daniel J. Elazar provided the initial direction, and showed us how we could improve the first draft of the manuscript. John Kincaid reviewed the material as it neared completion, and provided much helpful editorial assistance. John N. Diamond, former majority leader of the Maine House of Representatives, read the manuscript from the vantage point of a political practitioner, and gave us useful suggestions as well as alerting us to potential errors. In carrying out the research, we had valuable help from several University of Maine students, including Michael Donovan, Paula Ashton, Steven York, Angela Vigue, Todd Jarrell, Andrew Robinson, Connie Massingill, Darlene Shores, Patrick Maxcy, and Danielle Tetreau. Librarians Muriel Sanford of the Special Collections Department of the Fogler Library, University of Maine in Orono, and Laura Goss and Robert Michaud of the Maine State Law Library in Augusta were unfailingly helpful in guiding us to appropriate sources. Several administrators, legislators, and faculty colleagues took time from their busy schedules to help us with specific problems and to read individual chapters. We are particularly grateful to Stephen M. Bost and N. Paul Gauvreau, members of the Maine Senate, to William Buker of the State Budget Office, to James Clair, Kevin Madigan, and John Wakefield of the Legislative Office of Fiscal and Program Review, to Sarah C. Tubbesing, executive director of the Legislative Council, to James Chute, chief clerk of the Maine Supreme Judicial Court, to Willis Lyford, press secretary to Governor John R. McKernan, Jr., to Robert Miller, former city solicitor for Bangor, and to Professors C. Stewart Doty, Richard W. Judd, and Eugene A. Mawhinney of the University of Maine. Finally, we give our special thanks to Julie A. O'Connor, Eva M. McLaughlin, and June W. Kittridge, who know much more about computers than the authors, and who provided fine technical assistance in preparing the manuscript.

MAINE POLITICS AND GOVERNMENT

CHAPTER ONE

State of the State

Significant changes have taken place in Maine during the last two decades. Its population and economy have become much more diversified, and its public policies far more complex. The state government is rapidly becoming professionalized, a process that is contributing to a growing centralization of state functions. Despite these alterations, the political attitudes of Maine's people show a remarkable degree of stability. As this chapter will show, some essential traits of Maine politics and government are being confirmed even as they are being challenged.

CURRENT TENSIONS

Change has accelerated so much in recent decades, especially when compared to the very slow development of Maine in the past, that it is sometimes easy to disregard the past and to focus only on contemporary events. To do this, however, would be to arrive at a distorted picture of the present. Maine's past is a vital part of its present. The state's constitution testifies to this fact. Not only does Maine operate under its original constitution of 1819, but the many amendments added over the years have largely maintained the original constitutional structure while making it more relevant to changing circumstances. The past is also helpful in understanding present events when they seem to diverge from tradition. Recently, Maine has been challenged by tension between its different regions. This phenomenon has deeper consequences in Maine than it might in another state because Maine has long enjoyed a politics based on consensus.

Maine's political heritage originated in a town-meeting politics that still exists, and that underscores the central role of local politics in Maine history.

The town-meeting tradition has helped foster a strong impression of the state as a community of like-minded individuals. This social and political unity has been threatened by uneven economic development in the state. When Joseph Brennan was governor (1979–87), the State Planning Office spoke of "two Maines" to explain the state's changing conditions. The idea was that the state has two key regions: a southern region undergoing rapid urbanization, and a northern region largely bypassed by development. The administration of John McKernan, Jr. (1987–), generally rejected that view, arguing that the state should be conceived of as having many different regions. Under McKernan, the state attempted to fashion a variety of economic development programs appropriate for different areas. Whether the Brennan view or the McKernan view is the more accurate is still debated in the 1990s. For an understanding of Maine politics, the larger significance of the controversy is that it takes place against a background of cultural and political consensus. The notion that there are now different "Maines" presupposes the idea that there was once only one.

GOVERNMENT PROFESSIONALISM

If state development is creating fragmentation, it is also producing new forms of political coordination and unification. A growing trend of state centralization exists, even while local governments retain much autonomy. The rather sudden appearance of a potent state bureaucracy owes its existence to many factors, including the rise of the Democratic party, innovative social policies, and the availability of progressive revenue sources. Another factor is diversification in the state's economy, population, and intergovernmental relations. The state government is no longer dominated by a few powerful economic interest groups, as it was in the past. Instead, many different coalitions, such as those representing women, workers, and the environment, are influential. Maine has developed some of the most generous social programs in the country. A strong state government is necessary to implement these programs because citizens are sparsely scattered over a large terrain.

The growth of bureaucracy poses a special challenge to the state's political heritage. Although professionalization of government is required by the current complexity of issues, it conflicts with the participatory politics of the town meeting. That tradition is premised on citizen involvement in government, and the idea that government should always be accessible. The state's citizen legislature, composed mostly of amateur legislators, has been a cherished symbol of Maine politics. The institution is currently turning into a

more professional body, one more competent to deal with modern legislation, but less approachable by the average citizen. In the state judiciary, centralization and professionalization have already attenuated the close relations that citizens once had with their courts. Citizen judges have become a
thing of the past.

Maine politicians are struggling to resist some of these trends. Members
of the state legislature and of the congressional delegation devote a substantial portion of their time to one-on-one relations with their constituents,
which requires that they travel extensively throughout the state. The McKernan administration initiated a "capital for a day" campaign in which state
activities are executed in different communities of the state. During the bicentennial of the U.S. Constitution in 1989, the Maine Supreme Judicial
Court held sessions in counties that it normally does not visit. Perhaps the
strongest force keeping citizens in touch with their government is a com-
monality of values in Maine. Public officials and citizens tend to agree on
most public questions. The legislature generally seems to enact the wishes of
the citizenry, which brings about a high degree of congruence between public opinion and public policy.[1]

DIVERSITY AND MODERATION

Maine's style is generally moderate in political discussions and in governmental arrangements. Unlike neighboring New Hampshire, which is very
conservative and very decentralized in its governmental operations, and Vermont, which is quite centralized and liberal, Maine tends to stay in the middle of the road. Personalities of candidates and specific issues have always
received more attention during elections in Maine than ideology. Candidates, even incumbents, who are identified with the ideological left or right
have been consistently defeated. This kind of moderation seems to extend
the town-meeting qualities of compromise and consensus building to state
politics. Until recently, Maine's tendency to settle difficult issues through
compromise permitted the state govenment to work effectively even though,
during much of the post–World War II era, one party had control of the governorship and the other party held majorities in the legislature. In the 1991
legislative session, however, a major shortfall in revenues created a budget
crisis in Augusta that received national attention. Republican governor John
McKernan and the Democratic legislature could not come to terms on a
1991–93 budget (the passage of which the governor insisted on linking to reform of the workmen's compensation system) until mid-July, more than two

weeks into the new fiscal year. The consequence was that during that period, most state services were sharply curtailed and most state workers were laid off. The persistence of serious financial problems is likely to continue to affect the moderate tendencies of state government.

Likewise, recent demographic changes have confirmed the state's participatory culture, even as they challenge it. New voices are heard in state and local politics from the in-migrants from southern New England and other states. Even more important, the rise of a two-party system in Maine helped widen the political forum. In keeping with the state's emphasis in governmental matters on representation and shared values, Maine's most prominent politicians reflect the new demographic diversity. In the past, political leadership was dominated by Protestant, Republican, upper-class males. In 1948, Margaret Chase Smith, of modest origins, defeated former governors Horace Hildreth and Sumner Sewall in the primary for the Republican nomination for the U.S. Senate. In 1954, Democrat Edmund S. Muskie, of Polish immigrant parentage, overcame a Republican party that had ruled for a century, and was elected governor.

Currently, Maine's congressional delegation reflects a broadly representative background in comparison with politicians of earlier decades. For example, William S. Cohen, currently a U.S. Senator, grew up in a working-class neighborhood in Bangor. U.S. Senate Majority Leader George J. Mitchell is the son of immigrant parents (Irish and Lebanese) who settled in Waterville. Olympia J. Snowe (nee Bouchles), one of the few members of Congress of Greek ancestry, became in 1978 Maine's Second District representative (northern part of the state) and second woman elected to Congress.

While social diversity has seemed to strengthen Maine's participatory culture, it has threatened it in other respects. Urbanization is altering the population distribution in the state and, consequently, is challenging some traditional political values. Maine's political culture evolved from very small communities where interests were shared and politics was conducted on a neighbor-like basis. Throughout its history, the state's patterns of settlement have reinforced this form of politics. Population has been distributed among nearly five hundred small towns. Despite considerable growth in the 1970s and 1980s, in 1990 approximately 70 percent of Maine's people resided in towns having fewer than 10,000 persons. Even the remaining 30 percent of the population was scattered over a relatively large number of communities; the combined population of the state's three largest cities (Portland, Lewiston, and Bangor) made up just 12 percent of the state's total population in 1990. However, as Maine experiences urbanization, the town-meeting tradition of governance becomes harder to maintain. In larger communities, town-meeting governance has given way to city councils and to career politicians, whose relations with citizens have become more formalized and sometimes distant.

Maine's identity has always been connected to its geographic separateness. On a map of the United States, its relative isolation is apparent. Maine is the only continental state to border on only one other state (New Hampshire). Geographic isolation was intensified after the Civil War when a long period of economic decline set in. Much as occurred in Appalachia, Maine's poverty helped isolate the state from the national mainstream. The sense of separateness has shaped the state's political culture in important ways. By identifying with the distinctiveness of their state, Mainers have sometimes been able to transcend demographic, economic, and partisan barriers, and to see their state as an autonomous community. Current anxiety over regional divisions in the state can be partly attributed to the importance that Maine has long placed on its cultural and political unity. That sense of oneness, in turn, has been greatly reinforced by the idea that the state is "a place apart."

Efforts to preserve the state's distinctiveness are noticeable in the actions of its public officials, as evidenced by their efforts to maintain close ties with citizens. Another example is the state's generous social programs, which reflect a communitarian attitude of "taking care of one's own." A third example is the great concern that Maine shows toward the protection of its natural environment. Over three-quarters of the respondents in a 1989 poll felt that "the natural beauty of Maine should be preserved even if it means spending more public money or interfering with private investment decisions."[2] In June 1990, the legislature approved a bond to help finance the purchase of 40,000 acres of public land, the largest purchase of public land in the state's history.

Although New England was settled early, Maine has always remained something of a frontier. It has considered itself rather different from the rest of New England for this reason. The state has a landmass nearly equal to that of the remaining New England states. Even today, nearly 90 percent of the land is wooded. Although Maine's frontier character contributes to the state's sense of separateness, in another sense that quality seems to connect the state to the rest of the country. The American frontier has played an important role in shaping the nation's values, especially the ideas of optimism and the possibilities of social betterment. The twentieth century has witnessed the drastic exploitation of the natural environment through industrialization and urbanization. That process has given rise, in turn, to a growing awareness that the natural environment must be protected. Although the challenges that Maine faces are unique, they also represent the same kind of dilemma facing all American states: the need to preserve what is cherished in an age of rapid change.

That problem is central in this study of Maine politics and government. We describe the various institutions and processes that comprise the way in which Maine people are governed. But the primary aim is not to provide extensive detail. Instead, our concern is to explore the role of government in a period that may be a watershed in state affairs. We are interested in how some traditional and important features of Maine—citizen government, political moderation, and a sense of separateness—are faring under challenge from some newer factors: government professionalization, economic development, population mobility, and budgetary crises. While the focus is on Maine, we keep in mind that similar clashes can be found in most other states. Indeed, this exploration of Maine politics may give some support to the saying that "as Maine goes, so goes the nation."

CHAPTER TWO

Maine's Political Culture:
The New England Frontier

Many of Maine's most distinctive features suggest a form of separateness. These include its geographic location, its decades of economic decline at a time of national growth, and its place as a northeastern frontier. Yet, culturally, Maine has much in common with its New England neighbors. In fact, the "Downeast Yankee" is often said to be the embodiment of old New England. A tension has always existed in the state between belonging and not belonging. Maine's political culture has originated and developed out of this tension. In some ways, the state's culture is unique; in other ways, it is representative of the political culture of its region.

A political culture is an orientation that a large number of people share toward politics. It includes the expectations citizens have of their government, and of their own involvement with that government. Geography, economy, and patterns of settlement are some of the major elements that shape a political culture. Daniel J. Elazar has identified three basic types of political culture in the American states: the moralistic, the traditionalistic, and the individualistic.[1]

Although the moralistic culture originated in the Puritan towns of New England, it should not be associated primarily with ethics. The moralistic culture is community-oriented. It stresses the idea of the state as a commonwealth, and the government as citizen-run. The traditionalistic culture, unlike the moralistic, is little concerned with popular participation. Associated with parts of the South, the traditionalistic culture tends to accept a self-perpetuating political elite, often drawn from a small number of families. The individualistic culture, on the other hand, grows out of an urban setting. It sees politics almost as a form of business run by professionals. As development continues in Maine, the individualistic culture may become more widespread. Right now, the state strongly retains its moralistic political culture. Maine shares this culture with New Hampshire and Vermont, as well as with other states in the northern parts of the United States, but Maine has some special variations, which are products of its history.

SETTLEMENT, 1700–1820

Separateness marked Maine in the early colonial period because it was an outpost between two historic enemies, the French and the English. Maine also was isolated from the rest of the Massachusetts Bay Colony because of the Indian strength centered in the region. Unlike the Indians in the southern parts of the Massachusetts Bay Colony, Maine Indians (Abenakis and Etchemins, members of the Algonquin nation) were not as quickly hit by plagues. Disease wiped out whole tribes in southern Massachusetts and made settlement for Puritans around Boston politically and economically much easier than it was beyond the Kennebec River in central Maine.

Even if they were not notorious for their military prowess, Maine's Indians could successfully attack English townships scattered throughout the remote territory. Between 1675 and 1760, over one thousand English settlers were killed and hundreds more captured.[2] Early on, this constant threat reinforced the importance of the local community, an importance that persists in present-day Maine. Localities depended on themselves for protection, rather than on the colonial government at Boston. The houses still huddled together in the oldest coastal towns attest both to communities' insecurity and to their self-reliance.

The hostility of the Maine Indians was sometimes incited by the French during the seventy-year period of the French and Indian Wars, which ended in 1759, the year in which England gained control of Quebec. By this time, sickness and warfare had reduced the many Indian tribes to two, the Penobscots and Passamaquoddies, who signed treaties with the Commonwealth of Massachusetts (treaties which Maine took over when it became a state). With peace after 1759, both the English population and its prosperity rose dramatically. From 1780 to 1790, the year of the first U.S. census, Maine's population doubled from 50,000 to 97,000. By the end of the century, the population exceeded 150,000.

Apart from renewing English prejudices—and, possibly, naming the state after a province in France—the French at this time did not extend great influence over colonial Maine. Creating permanent settlements was usually not the primary goal of most *coureurs de bois* (traders and trappers), missionaries, and explorers, whose families had often been left behind in Europe. The French who did attempt to settle the land had either emigrated during the chaos before 1759, or were later forcefully dispersed among the thirteen colonies and Europe, as were the French Acadians by Colonel Charles Lawrence of Massachusetts in 1755.

Because widescale settlement occurred during the latter part of the eighteenth century, the primary goal for most settlers was to carve out a livelihood, not to escape religious intolerance like their Puritan forebears. Pragmatism, therefore, had as much a basis in the settlement of Maine as idealism had in Massachusetts, in which Maine had been a district. The moralistic, participatory culture inherited by Maine was confirmed among its Yankees because settlement occurred heavily during the years of the American Revolution and because statehood in 1820 came at a time of growing democratization. By removing voting restrictions against Catholics and Jews, Maine's constitution provided more representation than the 1780 Massachusetts constitution, much of which Maine otherwise copied wholesale into its own charter.

The moralistic political culture was also reinforced by the rapid establishment of agriculture, which came to define the character of the state and its people. Reliance on the weather, especially in a climate as harsh and unpredictable as Maine's, placed great cultural importance on the relationship between the individual and his or her community. The town meeting, the staple of the moralistic culture, encourages a similar relationship. An individual freely participates, but usually in ways geared toward reaching agreements with fellow participants. The importance of the town, and its political forum, was established by the distribution of population over a large number of small communities. Those towns that became cities, such as Portland and Bangor, never had populations large enough to dominate the state.

Instead of being diminished, Maine's frontier character was enhanced by settlement. Not only was the state settled later than the rest of New England, but in a manner that was similar to the growth of some western states. To encourage settlers, Massachusetts offered one-hundred-acre plots free to out-of-staters willing to turn the wilderness into pasture or field. When Maine finally gained statehood, it was during a time of westward expansion. In fact, Maine was formed under the Missouri Compromise, whereby the balance between free states and slave states was maintained by letting one of each (Maine and Missouri) into the Union. Frontierism makes an important contribution to the moralistic culture by reinforcing the relationship between the individual and the local community. However, the civic emphasis of the moralistic culture is sometimes compromised by a kind of frontier individualism. In isolated parts of Maine, there is still an attitude that people can—and sometimes will—do whatever they want on their own land.

STATEHOOD, 1820–60

A new kind of separateness came to characterize Maine during the first years of statehood, summed up in one historian's statement that "Maine was being singled out as a place with a marvelous destiny, a place clearly of the future." [3] The attractiveness of Maine was entwined with all that the frontier had historically held for America—a promise of economic and social progress. In the mid-1800s, Governor Joshua Chamberlain told the Maine legislature that the state reminded him "more of the western states than the rest of New England . . . [she has] virgin soil, undeveloped powers, vast forests, and vigorous men."[4]

The state's resources were being developed at a spectacular rate. Maine dominated national ship construction, which was not surprising considering the state's vast forests and 3,500 miles of seacoast. By 1820, Bangor had become the world's largest lumber-shipping port. Quarrying and ice harvesting were expanding, along with the textile mills that were beginning to spread into the state from Massachusetts. The large-scale construction of railroads in the 1840s connected Maine's industries to a national market, while the construction of dams on several Maine rivers rendered them suitable for mill sites for the first time. Population growth responded to the prosperity, doubling to 300,000 in the twenty-year period from 1800 to 1820, the year of statehood, and doubling again to 600,000 by 1860.

The moralistic, participatory culture of Maine seems to have contributed to this success. Citizens strove to realize their vision of a government responsible for the direction of its society. In 1830, ethical opposition to state lotteries led to the discontinuation of their use. The harnessing of politics to social reform was sometimes a response to the environment. Maine could seem like a kind of Wild West in the middle of pristine New England. It has been said of the state that " 'there was little law or respect for law' in the early days; 'rum was the common beverage, and spirits were consumed on all occasions.' "[5] Exchange Street in Bangor was the scene of fabled brawls between sailors and log drivers.

In response to the problems associated with alcohol, the state was home to the world's first Total Abstinence Society. During the next decades, many more temperance groups sprung into existence.[6] These were effectively organized on a statewide basis by Neal Dow, a Portland businessman. In 1851, the temperance movement had enough power to enact a prohibition law widely referred to as the "Maine Law" because it was copied by many other states. This law, which would later become an amendment to the Maine constitution, was enforced until the mid-1930s when prohibition ended nationally.

The state's occasional frontier lawlessness did not always bring about ethical responses from representatives of the moralistic culture. The arrival of the Irish during this period, following the potato blight in Ireland of 1842, incited the natives to occasional acts of violence. One way to understand these acts is to see them as negative extremes of the state's culture. The town-meeting philosophy of consensus and participation, and the desire to shape the direction of society were all present, but in perverted forms. The basis of hostility was often economic, with natives believing that immigrants were flooding the job market and lowering wages. However, natives seemed to fear that their identity would be jeopardized by large-scale immigration. Natives objected to the Catholicism of the Irish more than anything else.

Maine's anti-Catholic violence paled in comparison with that of some other states, such as Massachusetts, New York, and Pennsylvania. Nonetheless, such demonstrations represented a severe compromise in the ideals of the state's political culture. In the 1850s, Catholic churches were burned in Lewiston and Bath. Ellsworth was the setting for a Bible controversy centering around public education. The Catholics, mostly Irish, resented the fact that their taxes supported a school system that required its students to read the Protestant Bible. When one citizen chose to educate his children himself and then billed the state for the costs, the Protestant majority in Ellsworth literally rose up in arms.[7] At one point, the local Catholic priest was tarred, feathered, and run out of town.[8]

The issue was finally settled by the Maine Supreme Judicial Court, which overrode all Catholic objections in a ruling that was nonetheless fairly typical for the time.[9] For the most part, however, the state government was not openly nativist. The U.S. nativist political party, known as the Know-Nothing party (since it was originally a secret society) achieved statewide recognition in Maine only in 1854, when Anson Morrill ran successfully for the governorship on a fusion ticket of Maine Law and Know-Nothing parties. In nearby Massachusetts, the government was overrun by Know-Nothing politicians.

Any fears of the natives that their identity might be endangered proved unfounded. In general, the Irish assimilated rapidly into the state. The expanding economy easily accommodated them, and they were employed in large numbers to construct canals and dams, and to work in the textile mills. Their experience with eviction in Ireland propelled many, even at great sacrifice, to become property owners. This, along with the fact that many served during the Civil War, brought the Irish in Maine social and political influence rather quickly. They began aggressively entering politics and filling the ranks of the Democratic party in Maine, as well as in other states where the party was more powerful. They also dominated the Catholic church hierarchy.

On account of immigration, as well as due to the dynamic economy, Maine's population grew more rapidly in the 1830–60 period than that of any other New England state. During this period, "Downeast" Washington County (the easternmost county in the United States) possessed a population larger than it would a century later.

TRANSITION, 1860–1900

After the Civil War, Maine experienced a more challenging form of separateness: economic and population decline. Major technological innovations rendered several key industries obsolete. The demand for wood was quickly surpassed by demands for iron, oil, and coal. Ships were operated by steam, not by sail. While the shipyards at Bath would be able to make the transition, many others in the state were eventually abandoned. In growing numbers, farmers were leaving the thin and rocky soil of New England for the rich lands opening up in the West, prompting Grange leaders, such as D. H. Thing of Mount Vernon, to plead with young men to stick with farming in Maine.[10]

At first, it was not apparent that the state was drifting into economic backwaters. If the bounty of the fisheries had begun to decline, the hotels in Portland, Rockland, and Bar Harbor were reaping the benefits of an emerging tourist industry. Even if shipbuilding had taken a serious blow, the post–Civil War boom in textiles seemed to make up for this. The new industrialization lured a mass migration of French Canadians from Canada's St. Lawrence valley, which was undergoing an agrarian depression in the 1860s.

From 1865 until the turn of the century, thousands of French Canadians migrated to New England. Besides New Hampshire, Maine would come to have the highest percentage of first- and second-generation Franco-Americans, accounting for nearly one-sixth of the state's population.[11] The distribution of the immigrants was uneven, with some towns receiving virtually none, and others, such as Lewiston, becoming over 80 percent Franco-American. In general, settlement of French Canadians was heaviest in the industrial centers, such as Auburn, Biddeford, Brunswick, Rumford, and Waterville, in addition to Lewiston. The Franco-Americans occupied the unskilled manufacturing positions which the Irish had held earlier, as well as new positions created by the expanding textile industry.

Perhaps because the Franco-Americans kept to themselves and lived in the few urban centers, nativist reactions were mild compared to the past. The state was more settled at the time, and seems to have expressed its prejudices in its laws, rather than in lawlessness. In 1893, the twenty-ninth amendment to the Maine constitution was perceived as nativist by Franco-Americans. This measure required that voters be able to read the constitution in English as well as write their names. Already enrolled voters were exempt.

Assimilation was slower for Franco-Americans, who stood out from the general population until the 1960s. This was partly because of the language barrier, but also because of the close proximity of Canada, allowing old ties to be maintained. Another force was the nationalistic campaign known as *la survivance*. While dependent on French newspapers and societies, *la survivance* was centered around the Catholic churches and their parochial schools, which, until the 1960s, actively preserved the cultural heritage through bilingual masses and curricula. The overall equation behind *la survivance* seems to have been a fusion of ethnic and religious norms, whereby a "loss of language meant a loss of faith, and a loss of faith meant a loss of identity."[12]

Perhaps another impediment to assimilation was that the political culture of the Franco-Americans differed from that of the Yankees and Irish. Coming from a highly conservative agricultural society in the St. Lawrence valley, with antecedents in the feudal society of France, the Franco-Americans possessed what may be called a traditionalistic political culture. This culture accepts a political oligarchy drawn from a self-perpetuating elite, which in the case of the French-Canadians was the Catholic clergy. The lack of experience in political action that characterized the French Canadians of this period was perpetuated when the Catholic Church and the British government came to a "working agreement" after 1759. In return for religious freedom, the Church prescribed submission to the British crown.[13]

Partly because of their political culture, and partly because many considered their stay in the United States temporary, the Franco-Americans never used their numerical power to its full potential beyond local politics. Franco-Americans did not even consistently vote for Franco-Americans, as in the case of the 1956 congressional primary, when Franco-Americans voted for

Yankee Frank M. Coffin over a Franco-American candidate.[14] The Irish dominance of the Catholic hierarchy in Maine early on instigated the only Franco-American statewide action. Starting in the last decades of the nineteenth century, they fought for control over their own parishes.

Under the Catholic law known as "Corporation Sole," the bishop of Portland, a position that tended to be held by someone Irish, exercised almost complete control over all Catholic parishes in the state. This circumstance was particularly troublesome to the Franco-Americans because the Irish leaders actively fought for the assimilation of all Catholics, which was in direct opposition to *la survivance*. In 1908, the Franco-American Le Comite Permanent de la Cause Nationale du Maine commissioned a private census of the state to prove their numerical superiority (and, hence, their right to greater influence in the diocese). A compromise in representation was eventually worked out through the creation of a bishop's advisory council.

Franco-American political power was felt more effectively and consistently in local government. In other states, such as Massachusetts, Franco-Americans sometimes avoided the Democratic party principally because it was associated with the Irish. Democrats there also seemed to oppose Franco-American conservatism. The weakness of the Democratic party in Maine, and the nativism among Maine Republicanism, helped impel the Franco-Americans to the Democratic party in that state. A similar process took place in Vermont.[15] Communities in Maine with large Franco-American populations soon revealed the power of those groups in local elections. In Waterville, Lewiston, Biddeford, Sanford, and other manufacturing communities, Franco-Americans began consistently serving as mayors, city councilors, aldermen, and selectmen in the early twentieth century.

Growing out of an urban environment, Franco-American local politics were sometimes characterized by an individualistic culture. In this culture, politics tends to be seen as a form of business in which some corruption is considered inevitable. Lewiston, in particular, came to possess a Democratic machine.[16] Political scandals in the 1930s led voters to adopt a new city charter, but the machine continued in power. Perhaps, despite apparent differences, the traditionalistic culture of the Franco-Americans prepared them for the individualistic culture. Both cultures, at any rate, tend to take for granted a political elite.

If it had not been for Maine's immigrants, particularly its Franco-Americans, the state's population might have declined sharply after 1860. As it was, from 1860 to 1870, the state's population did drop slightly (by 1,364), and between 1870 and 1900, the population increased from 627,000 to only

694,000, while the population of the rest of the country was doubling. Of Maine's 1900 population, some 93,000 persons (14 percent) were foreign born.[17]

ENTRENCHMENT, 1900–1960

With the onset of the twentieth century, Maine's separateness from an industrialized and urban society became increasingly more visible. For various reasons, native traits and attitudes seem to have been strengthened, even exaggerated, during this period, which in turn reinforced the state's aloofness. One factor was the cultural isolation produced by economic and population declines. In much the same way as occurred in Appalachia, Maine society began to seem inward looking and even autonomous from the national mainstream.

Another factor seems to have been that social traits are products of many different forces. Pride, independence, and a sense of belonging to "a place apart," which were fostered by the state's one-time prosperity, were also supported by the frontier lifestyle that is still retained to some extent. No doubt defensiveness also played a part in the retention of these traits. One historian has written that a central theme in Maine history has been an "ambivalence—toward Boston, toward cities, toward the west, and toward governments."[18] This ambivalence, in turn, has been viewed as contributing to "a sort of inferiority complex which manifests itself by bragging about itself in relation to others, [and] in attempting to find fault with others."[19]

The nativism that flared up for a last time during this period seems to support some of these ideas. The nineteenth century closed with a serious economic depression. At this time, the permanence of the Franco-American presence became unequivocal, and Yankee families who had not moved out of the mill towns earlier now took their cue. The rise of the pulp and paper industry (when pulp replaced rag) lured some new immigrants from southern and eastern Europe, who supplemented the steady inflow of Franco-Americans.

During the 1920s, Maine became a stronghold for the Ku Klux Klan, whose membership at its height (in 1924) was about 40,000 people, or slightly over 5 percent of the state's population.[20] The Klan's campaign to put Bibles back in schools, fill the Protestant churches, and replace corrupt politicians with "100 percent Americans," read much like a Know-Nothing platform from the 1840s. The Klan's supporters included rural farmers and prominent civic leaders, such as Owen Brewster, who would serve as governor and U.S. Senator. As in the 1840s, hostility was focused on Catholicism.

For the Franco-Americans, as well as the Irish, Italians, and Poles, Catholicism was not only a church but an important foundation of group identity.

Although surface appearances might suggest otherwise, the 1900–1960 period was a time when Maine's population became more homogeneous. The static economy, and the isolation it imposed on the state, restricted change and gave the population a chance to develop a distinctive character. In the interval from 1900 to 1940, the population grew by only about 150,000. While agriculture was generally successful during this time, it declined as a way of life for many people as family farms were consolidated into larger commercial units. The rise of the pulp and paper industry coincided with the decline of textiles, as the south became the center of that industry. It seems to be a pattern in Maine that one major industry regularly replaces another. In that way, the state avoids a crisis, but it also fails to make substantial progress. The phenomenon has contributed to the seeming timelessness that has sometimes characterized the state and, in particular, this period.

With such a static economy, coupled with the onset of the Great Depression, immigration into Maine during these years never occurred on the same scale that it did earlier. Although Maine had enough advantages to attract some immigrants, the mid-Atlantic states, southern New England, and the western states possessed far more resources, and new settlements tended to grow in those areas. The Italians, Poles, Greeks, and Albanians who came to Maine, together with other nationalities, were numerically too small to change the character of the state significantly. Maine continues to be a state whose population is divided between a mostly Anglo-Saxon/Scotch-Irish native stock and a large French-Canadian minority.

Even as the Franco-Americans kept to themselves, there was a slow process of integration into the dominant Yankee culture. The majority of the Franco-Americans were becoming bilingual. Studies also have shown that they minimized their cultural differences with the Yankees, believing that language was the primary basis of differentiation.[21] Both groups shared a strong work ethic and valued civic responsibility. Despite their affiliation with the Democratic party, Maine Franco-Americans were deeply conservative, especially on social issues. Each group also sought to preserve its society in the face of a materialistic, mainstream culture often perceived as antagonistic. Perhaps the most important factor binding the people of Maine was the sense of belonging to a place apart. Despite their demographic differences, citizens seemed united in perceiving a gulf between them and residents of other states. The state's sense of its separateness as a polity made its people Mainers in addition to being Yankees or Franco-Americans or Protestants or Catholics.

Toward the close of the 1900–1960 period, Maine's moderate style of politics, which continues to characterize the state, became more manifest. Governor John McKernan ascribed the moderation to the pragmatism of Maine people, although it undoubtedly grows from other causes, too, such as the cautiousness of a people who sometimes seem to have had the role of observers rather than participants in social, economic, and political trends in the United States.[22] Moderation has also been encouraged by social and political diversity.

Starting in the late 1950s, a two-party system of politics slowly evolved on a statewide basis. Many progressive policies, such as those concerning the environment, welfare, and education, began at about this time. With Republicans and Democrats waging more competitive battles, issues were discussed more publicly. The governor and legislature had to seek compromises more often. Moderation became the practical expression of the state's moralistic political culture, which expects the consensus of the people to set the tenor of government.

DEVELOPMENT, 1960–1990

Maine's separateness has been challenged since the 1950s. Rapid development attests to the fact that Maine is no longer an outpost. Instead, people seek it out almost as they did in the very early days of statehood. Motorists traveling north on Interstate 95, shortly after they cross the bridge over the Piscataquis River, which separates Maine from New Hampshire, encounter a sign reading, "Maine: The Way Life Should Be." In the past two decades, the idea of Maine as a place where one can enjoy a slower and perhaps more traditional lifestyle than is possible in the metropolitan centers of the Northeast has attracted new residents. The changes of this period, propelled by a generally dynamic state economy, have done more than increase population statistics and alter the appearance of the land. The cultural unity of the state, including its moralistic orientation, has begun to be challenged by new, and in some cases opposing, forces.

For the Franco-Americans, Maine's modernization has encouraged greater assimilation. After nearly a century of *la survivance*, ethnicity broke down in less than a decade. This change was partly based on economic development. Service industries grew so rapidly that by the early 1970s, they were among the most important sources of employment. They included government and professional services as well as wholesale and retail trades. In cities such as Lewiston, many of the employees in the service industry were Franco-Americans who were forced to seek new employment when the textile mills shut down in the 1950s. This occupational change has been seen as contributing to the rapid assimilation of the Franco-Americans.[23] As opposed to factory work, the service industry requires constant interaction with English-speaking clients, as well as encouraging a strong ethos of upward mobility.

Other factors also contributed to Franco-American assimilation. After the Second World War, the Franco-Americans developed a large middle class of their own. Under new economic conditions, many families left the tenement areas in the mill towns for residential districts, breaking up the ethnic communities.[24] The assimilation of Franco-Americans was unusual not only for its swiftness, but because it occurred in all generations of the ethnic group at the same time (most cases of minority assimilation take place in the younger generation).[25]

Since their ethnic identity was based heavily on language, Franco-Americans were prone to rapid assimilation as soon as French ceased to be their primary language.[26] New employment opportunities, a growth in the number of mixed marriages—associated with a growing middle class—and the decline of the parochial school system (which was part of a national trend during the 1960s) stimulated assimilation. In 1971, Lewiston elected a non-French mayor for the first time in forty years.

At the same time that the Franco-Americans were disappearing as a distinctive ethnic group, Maine's American Indians were consciously and politically differentiating themselves from the general population. As in the case of the Franco-Americans, however, this cultural change was in response to national and even international trends emphasizing native heritages. Long in decline, the number of Maine Indians, estimated at 36,000 in 1615, had shrunk to 1,400 by 1980. Despite the decline, the descendent tribes of the Abenakis and Etchemins had a powerful voice in the form of litigation.

During the 1970s, Maine's two remaining Indian tribes—the Passamaquoddies and the Penobscots—filed suit against the state for the restitution of 12.5 million acres, which they alleged the state had taken from them illegally. Around these proceedings, Indian tribal consciousness could coalesce in a new and assertive way. In the 1970 gubernatorial election year, the Passamaquoddies gained publicity for their claims by their persistence in obtaining an opinion about their claims from each of the candidates prior to election and by bargaining their political support. Early in the same year, a group of Indians in full tribal regalia went to Augusta and demanded the payment of livestock, produce, textiles, and silver as guaranteed in an old treaty assumed by Maine when it became a state.

The land dispute was particularly dramatized when members of the Passamaquoddy tribe blocked off a road crossing their territory and charged tolls, and when a Passamaquoddy woman demanded that the city of Old Town vacate land that she claimed rightfully belonged to her tribe. The most effective spotlight on their claims, however, was the Maine Municipal Bond Bank's withdrawal of a $27 million bond because of uncertainty in property titles in over half the state. Eventually, the federal government agreed to pay the two tribes over $80 million.

The 1970–80 decade was also important demographically. Maine's population, increasing by almost 131,000, well surpassed the one million mark (1,124,660).[27] Part of the unexpected growth could be accounted for in what sociologists and demographers called a new migratory trend, the reversed or urban-to-rural migration. As part of that process, in the mid-1970s an estimated 36,000 people began moving into the state each year.[28]

This trend, which was again nationwide, saw cities lose some of their population to neighboring rural or semi-rural areas. Studies showed that the prime motivation for migration to rural areas was a quality-of-life factor that included such rural characteristics as natural scenery, a low crime rate, a low cost of living, and a supposedly simpler style of life.[29] With its vast tracts of forest and hundreds of abandoned farms, Maine was an attractive place for reversed migration, even while the state was experiencing traditional migration, especially to the Portland region in the south. To the new Maine in-migrants, the state was once again a frontier with a "marvelous destiny." Its geographic separateness, preserved by the stagnant economy of the 1900–1960 years, was sought by back-to-nature artisans, suburbanites, and retirees—all of whom were anxious to "get away" from a more urban lifestyle.

Reversed migration created some concern in Maine, as in other states, such as Vermont. Some Maine residents worried that the features of their small communities might be changed. Evidence, however, often pointed to the contrary. Newcomers became active in preserving rural life because it had been one of their incentives to relocate. Even when Maine in-migrants were not rural because their income was derived from nearby urban centers, they often sought the outward forms of a rural lifestyle. Many reported living on farms, although few were farmers. Rural art forms, such as bluegrass festivals, contra dancing, and agricultural fairs, were enthusiastically sought out, or even revived in places, by in-migrants.

One area of conflict between natives and in-migrants has been school policy. The in-migrants sometimes advocate innovative, alternative schooling in contrast to the natives' preference for more traditional education. Another area of conflict concerns modernization and commercialization. Natives have tried to cultivate changes for economic reasons, while in-migrants have more often taken a conservationist attitude. In a different policy sector, natives and in-migrants joined forces around the state to fight the federal government's efforts in 1986 to designate Maine a site for a nuclear waste dump. On the other hand, the two groups tend to conflict over state policies on nuclear power. They were on opposing sides in several state referendums in the 1980s seeking to close Maine Yankee, the state's nuclear power facility at Wiscasset, and to prohibit construction of future nuclear facilities.

While Maine was experiencing reversed migration, it also underwent a fair amount of rural-to-urban and urban-to-suburban change. Southern coastal counties like York and Cumberland grew by approximately 50 percent and 45 percent, respectively, between 1970 and 1990. Development was also significant along the central corridor of the state along Interstate 95, especially around such cities as Bangor and Augusta. Many of the in-migrants to Maine's urban centers are part of the outward spread of population from the greater Boston area, and they reflect an urban lifestyle. As such, they strengthen the individualistic political culture over the state's moralistic tradition.

Although a majority of Maine people do not share the individualistic culture, this may change as development in areas associated with the culture increases at a greater rate than growth in other areas. Right now, the most direct challenge faced by Maine's participatory culture is the professionalization of government. Demands for complex legislation have helped to precipitate the transformation of the citizen's legislature. The expanding role of the state government and its fairly liberal tendencies have been responsible for the recent appearance of a strong state bureaucracy. A 1989 survey reported that many Mainers feel alienated from their government.[30] However, this kind of reaction seems to confirm the durability of the moralistic culture because citizens still expect to be active participants in their political system.

In terms of the future, the question may be raised: How long can Maine can consider itself "a place apart"? In 1986, the *Boston Globe* reported that "Portland's glitter is eyed enviously"[31] by other parts of Maine, an attitude that would suggest Maine citizens are rapidly taking on, or trying to take on, the cultural tendencies of more urban states. Certain events in the past two decades provide strong evidence that Maine's separateness is disappearing. The state became increasingly dependent on federal assistance during that period, even with the Reagan cutbacks. Even earlier, the construction of Interstate 95 and the arrival in the state of television in the 1950s did much to open Maine to national influences. In the 1960s, that process was furthered when Dow Air Force Base in Bangor was transformed into an international airport. In 1988, the Maine Turnpike Authority decided, despite resistance, to widen Interstate 95 in the southern counties of York and Cumberland. In years past, it was said that Maine's biggest export was its young people, but that pattern is changing. Today, Maine people who are looking for employment, or who want a more urban lifestyle, might be satisfied by settling in the Portland area.

Yet other evidence indicates that Maine citizens are not willing to be considered as simply part of the national mainstream. State loyalty or patriotism remains high; some Maine residents—like the citizens of New Hampshire—worry that their state is becoming a satellite of Massachusetts. Perhaps the Maine lifestyle will become something to acquire and perpetuate self-consciously. The in-migrants of the 1970s and 1980s, in seeking a rural lifestyle, showed something of that desire. Already, some citizens are careful not to lose their Maine accents, even as they become highly educated. The accent signifies membership and deep roots, rare in a society becoming increasingly mobile. As time passes, however, Maine will have to recognize that its separateness is more a state of mind than a physical fact.

CONCLUSION

While Maine has a history of social diversity, it has a population that is still remarkably homogeneous in certain ways. Perhaps the most important factor uniting Maine residents is their sense of belonging to "a place apart." The state's geographic location and its economic history have instilled a tradition of separateness among its citizens. The frontier-like natural environment, much of it still largely untouched, encourages people to identify with the physical beauty of their state, particularly as development escalates elsewhere in New England.

Maine shares a moralistic political culture with the other northern New England states, but Maine has some noticeable differences. Its tendency toward moderation, its history as a frontier, and its sense of separateness make Maine's political culture distinct from that of Vermont and New Hampshire. Many of the forces that have contributed to Maine's uniqueness have also nurtured its participatory politics. The expansive geography and harsh climate have demanded both the independence of the individual and the closeness of the community. The stagnant economy of the 1900–1960 years post-poned a confrontation between the moralistic culture and the individualistic culture associated with an urban society.

In the past, the moralistic culture was sometimes severely compromised. Nativism demonstrated one such compromise. Currently, certain moderniz-ing factors also threaten the cultural unity of the state. The presence of a powerful, rather recently noticed, state bureaucracy challenges the partici-patory, community-oriented culture in important ways. Moreover, the dem-ographic predominance of the small town is declining in the face of gradual urbanization and increased population mobility.

CHAPTER THREE

Maine's Traditional Politics and Its Transformation

In 1954 a revolution took place in Maine politics. The Republican party, which had run the state almost without interruption for one hundred years, was defeated in a gubernatorial election by a young Democratic legislator of immigrant (Polish) parents, Edmund S. Muskie. In a landslide victory, Muskie became governor, ending Maine's one-party, Republican rule. Today Maine is known as "one of the nation's most intensely competitive states in partisan politics."[1] Many factors have contributed to the transformation of Maine's traditional political system in recent decades, factors that include the political culture of the state, the nature of federal party patronage, and the strategies used by the Democratic and Republican parties.

REPUBLICAN HEGEMONY

Except for Vermont, Maine was probably the most thoroughly Republican state in the nation until the mid-1950s. The two states, in fact, proved their loyalty to the G.O.P. in 1936 when they became what one writer has called a "lonely two-state coalition," after they voted for Alfred Landon for president over Franklin D. Roosevelt.[2] Today, with Maine's two-party politics well established, it is difficult to envision how monolithic the Republican party was until the early 1950s. During the previous one hundred years, it seemed like a part of the landscape.

The daily papers normally represented only varying shades of Republican ideology. When young people came to register to vote in primaries, they might be shown only the Republican candidate lists. If they insisted on seeing the lists of Democratic candidates, they might even be asked if their fathers knew what they were doing.[3] There is a story sometimes attributed to

Maine, sometimes to Vermont, in which an election warden is counting out the votes and is shocked when he suddenly comes upon one Democratic vote. A short while later, he finds a second Democratic vote, at which time he promptly tears up both of the votes, saying, "They are illegal. The Democrat, whoever he is, voted twice!"

Part of the Republican party's strength in Maine came from the circumstances of the party's formation. The Maine Republican party was formed in July 1854, soon after the formation of the national Republican party, and just one hundred years before Edmund Muskie won the governorship. As in other states, Maine Republicans were made up of a fusion of many different forces: antislavery and independent Democrats, Whigs, Prohibitionists, and Know-Nothings. What brought together these diverse parties was their opposition to the spread of slavery. This opposition was encapsulated in the condemnation of the Kansas-Nebraska Act.

That measure, passed by the Congress in 1854, repealed the Missouri Compromise (1820) by permitting slavery in the territories of Kansas and Nebraska, where it had been prohibited prior to 1854. Maine, which gained its statehood under the Missouri Compromise, had many citizens who had a personal interest in repudiating the Kansas-Nebraska Act. When the Civil War broke out, Maine's contribution was steep. The number of men from Maine who enlisted in the Union forces, for example, represented over 10 percent of the state's total population.[4] The Republican party's influence was greatly extended, and by the same token, the Democratic party was discredited because it had taken a proslavery, compromise stance in its nomination of James Buchanan for president in 1856. Years after the Civil War, state Republican leaders like William Pierce Frye and James Gillespie Blaine fanned the memories by rhetorically waving the "bloody shirt of the rebellion" and repeating the campaign cry, "vote as you shot." For many years a Democrat in Maine was something of a synonym for a renegade. Through its origins, the Republican party in Maine became a representative of the state's moralistic political culture, which envisions a government responsible for the direction of society. This was a period of great exuberance in Maine, when economic development triggered efforts to reform society. In the 1850s, the temperance movement in Maine was strong enough to enact a prohibition law that was enforced for approximately eighty years.

The Republican party's formidable strength in Maine was based on ideology as well as origins. By making prohibition a plank in its platform, the Republican party in Maine made the party even more compatible with Maine's moralistic political culture. The Republican stance that saw government controls as something to be suspected, if not restricted, dovetailed neatly with some of the other important cultural aspects of the state. The frontier character of Maine in its early days emphasized the independence of the individual, particularly on his or her own land. The Maine electorate was historically suspicious of a government removed from its people, which was one of the reasons Maine separated from Massachusetts in 1820. The suspicion of distant government controls was also a product of the state's participatory political culture. The Maine electorate seems to have considered its Republican representatives as "watchdogs" in Augusta and Washington.[5]

During the late nineteenth century, Maine voters could rest assured that their interests were represented in Washington. Because of its connections with the federal government during this period, Maine's Republican party enjoyed a prestige that lasted for many years. The administration of President Benjamin Harrison (1888–92) has been referred to as "the Maine administration."[6] With Thomas Brackett Reed as Speaker of the House, James G. Blaine as Secretary of State, Eugene Hale as majority leader of the Senate, Nelson Dingley as House Chairman of the Ways and Means Committee, and Melville Fuller as the Chief Justice of the U.S. Supreme Court, the nation seemed mostly in the hands of Maine politicians. This kind of illustriousness of Maine's G.O.P. had a precedent in the figure of Hannibal Hamlin. Hamlin, who made the famous declaration "I am leaving the Democratic party forever!" (after it adopted a proslavery, compromise platform), became Maine's first Republican governor before going on to become the Vice President of the United States under Abraham Lincoln.

The power of the Republican party in Maine was also increased by its connections with big business. In fact, Republicanism and corporate interests were often the same thing in Maine for two reasons: (1) the extractible nature of the state's resources virtually guaranteed the involvement of large corporations in state government, and (2) Maine was a one-party, Republican state. An alliance of lumber and paper, textile, and utility interests supported the Republican party wholeheartedly in return for weak environmental policies, defense from rate cutters or competitors, and favorable tax policies. Until the 1970s, a clear indication of Maine's control by the extractive corporations was the existence of many loopholes in the state's water pollution laws, rendering them virtually ineffectual.[7]

Along with the nature of the state's resources, demographics helped maintain Republican control. Between 1850 and 1950, the state's population grew only slightly, in part because of the departure of the state's youth in search of economic opportunities not available in Maine. This exodus acted to increase the median age of the population, which helped to create more widespread conservatism and, hence, Republican strength.[8] The state's legislative apportionment also reinforced conservative policies by favoring rural areas. What Democratic support existed was found largely among Franco-Americans and other minorities clustered in the state's industrial centers, such as Lewiston and Biddeford, which were slightly discriminated against in apportionment.

Even the state's custom of conducting state elections in September, instead of November like the rest of the nation, assisted the Republican party. National Democratic victories helped to carry Democratic candidates in many states, especially during election years.[9] In Maine, this could hardly occur because state elections were held prior to national elections. This factor does not seem to have been overlooked by the Republicans in Maine, who were able to prevent November elections until 1957. At that time, a constitutional amendment was adopted to make Maine's election dates conform with the rest of the nation.

Important as these elements of strength were for the Republican party, its approval by Maine voters was due more fundamentally to general voter satisfaction with the way in which it handled state affairs. Unlike one-party systems in some other states, the Maine Republican party governed in a generally responsible fashion. If the Republican politicians were not seen as particularly progressive or imaginative, neither were they known for incompetence or corruption. They kept the state on a sound fiscal course during a time when it had a static population and ranked among the lowest in the country in per capita income. The success of the party could be seen in its ability to hold the Democrats at bay, even though the Democratic party always had a solid corps of supporters.

The hopelessness of Maine Democrats was exhibited strikingly in 1948 by the fact that Republican candidates in half of the legislative districts faced no opposition whatsoever.[10] Indeed, after 1932, most of the state's most promising Democrats were siphoned off to Washington where they benefited from federal patronage. One example was Dr. Clinton Clauson (Waterville), who preferred to keep his position as federal collector of revenue for the state of Maine rather than run for governor, although he was mentioned prominently as a candidate several times after 1946.[11]

REPUBLICAN FACTIONALISM

Since the party was supported by so many formidable forces, one may wonder how the Republican hold on Maine was ever dislodged. Ironically, the party's overwhelming strength in both Washington and Augusta was probably the biggest cause of its downfall. Internal cohesion tends to break down in parties that have had years to entrench themselves as the dominant party. Contests for power do not revolve around what party will rule; instead, they revolve around which faction of the dominant party will rule. This became the case in Maine.[12]

Consistent with the state's participatory culture, Maine's Republican party was not a very tight-knit organization. Republican primaries (which were tantamount to general elections) did not reveal a contest between "organization" and "anti-organization" forces as was true in some other one-party states. Instead, the primaries tended to show a multifactional pattern with numerous candidates. The outcomes usually depended on personality considerations, which is still the case today. When President Roosevelt came into office in 1933, federal Republican patronage stopped, and many topline Maine Republicans returned to their state. During the 1930s and 1940s, there were probably too many candidates available for elective and appointive office, and younger party members began to resent the secondary position in which they found themselves.[13]

As factionalism spread, several heated contests occurred. Governor Frederick Payne beat longtime U.S. Senator Owen Brewster in a hard-fought 1952 primary in which Brewster was seeking re-nomination. Four years earlier, Margaret Chase Smith had beaten Horace Hildreth and Sumner Sewall, both former governors, to win the Republican nomination for the U.S. Senate. When one Robert L. Jones challenged Smith in the 1954 Republican primary, he implied at one point that Smith supporters had tried to bribe him to leave the race. The charges were never proved, and Smith won the primary overwhelmingly, but such internecine conflict began to discredit the party.

Republican factionalism was encouraged by certain outside forces. Nationally, the Republican party was ideologically divided during the years immediately following World War II. Republicans had once favored free enterprise at home and isolationism in foreign policy. After the Second World War, when the United States emerged as a world power with broadened responsibilities, Republicans began to question their beliefs. For a time, this led to splits in the national party as different factions attempted to define a new ideology—a process that naturally affected the party in Maine.

Republican factionalism and disenchantment grew during the governorship of Burton Cross (1953–55), especially during his unsuccessful reelection campaign in 1954. Cross, a florist by trade and something of a government reformer, made himself unpopular to both his constituents and party colleagues. By cutting the state budget, and trying to reform the state's Highway Commission and Liquor Commission, both of which had become corrupt, Cross made many political enemies. A lack of diplomacy hurt him with various groups of voters. His denunciation of the potato price-support program helped to get him into trouble with the Aroostook County potato farmers. A remark to the inhabitants of poverty-stricken Washington County that they should "lift up their own bootstraps" did more than enrage the inhabitants. The statement was eventually syndicated by the Soviet news agency Tass as an example of capitalism's disregard for the downtrodden.[14]

Normally in Maine, a Republican governor was routinely supported for reelection by his party. Cross's 1954 campaign for reelection, however, produced the dismal spectacle of members of his party abandoning him. Prominent Republican Neil Bishop led the formation of "Republicans for Muskie" clubs in the state. Obed Millet, a Republican legislator and agricultural leader, helped to put together "Farmers for Muskie" clubs.[15] The collapse of the automatic, statewide Republican majority in Maine dates from the dramatic 1954 election, when Democrat Edmund S. Muskie upset Governor Cross.

DEMOCRATIC GROWTH

While the Republican party was splintering, a group of young Maine politicians was assembling a new and dynamic Democratic organization. When Dwight D. Eisenhower became president in 1952, Democratic federal patronage stopped, and many Democrats, like Frank M. Coffin, returned to state affairs. Coffin, a Harvard Law School graduate and member of a family that had worked for the Maine Democratic party for generations, was responsible for some successful strategies when he became chair of the Democratic Platform Committee in 1954. His approach stressed an "open" style of politics, new at the time, enlisting the support of schoolteachers, farmers, and textile workers. Citizen sentiment on a large variety of issues was sought through questionnaires circulated throughout the state. The result was widespread enthusiasm.

In Edmund Muskie, the Democratic party had the charismatic leader that the Republican party lacked. His personal charm and candidness, as well as his message of economic growth through industrial development, earned him popular support early in the 1954 campaign. His relative youth became a political asset. He performed particularly well on television (which had come to the state only the year before). The Democrats' use of television in 1954 was also part of the party's "hands-on," accessible style of politics, which successfully tapped into the state's participatory tradition. A child of immigrant parents, Muskie represented the growing diversification of the state's population. Although Maine was not yet seeing the more diverse in-migration, which would occur during the 1970s, new groups in the electorate were becoming influential. Largely because of the Second World War, Maine's Democratic Franco-Americans developed a large middle class of their own, a factor that contributed to their assimilation and greater political involvement. These factors contributed to the breakdown of the century-long Republican consensus not only in Maine, but also in Vermont, which nearly elected a Democratic governor in 1954, and which would elect its first statewide Democratic official in 1958.

Muskie's campaign and personality helped overcome the rural electorate's idea of a Democrat as a "big city hack." Don Nicoll, who was an adviser to Muskie when he was a U.S. Senator, once explained how Muskie felt very much at home with Maine's Yankees: "He has their reticence, a low-key quality, a kind of flinty insistence on facts . . . [a] deliberate approach to life. . . . Essentially, it's an unhurried rural quality."[16] Muskie also looked the part with his lanky frame and heavy, imposing jaw. As the underdog, Muskie also came to personify the independence and individualism cherished in Maine. In the 1950s, Maine had fallen behind the economic development seen in other states, and nurtured its independence from the national mainstream, perhaps defensively. Muskie enjoyed popular support partly because his own campaign against the Republicans symbolized the odds that Maine was up against in a rapidly industrializing and wealthy society, and the need for competence and new ideas in government if progress were to be made.

The campaign had a kind of breathless exhilaration. Even though the Democratic party could barely scrape together $15,000 for the entire gubernatorial campaign, Muskie covered the state. Pushing across the countryside, he would stop in a town for ten or fifteen minutes, shake hands with citizens, and then head out for the next town. At night he would stay in the homes of party members. His campaign, rustic as it was, resulted in great success. He received huge margins in the Democratic mill towns, and he cut into the Republican strength in the countryside. The results were 135,673 for Muskie and 113,298 for Cross. Interestingly, when Vermont's Phillip Hoff became the first Democrat to win the governorship in that state in 1962, he revealed many of the same character traits as Muskie, such as youth, charisma, and role as an underdog.

The transformation of the state's political system could, in one sense, have been anticipated by the splintering of the Republican party, and by the dissatisfaction with the party by groups that had once helped form the Republican coalition, such as working-class persons and ethnic minorities. The economic and cultural changes of the mid-twentieth century had brought about a more complex political environment in Maine, one that now gave rise to competing political parties, at least in statewide races. In another sense, though, the transformation of the state's political system was sudden and, at least in the beginning of the campaign, unexpected. During his 1968 campaign for Vice President, Muskie recounted for a Texas crowd his feelings on the election night of 1954:

> I never had an experience like that. If I win elections from now until the year 2000—this election, if we win it, won't be nearly the exhilarating experience of that one. We won against hopeless odds. We won with almost no resources. We had to literally walk that state from one end to the other. We had to talk to Republicans who had never seen a live Democrat in their lives. We had to learn the political skills none of us had ever developed. We had to do it against . . . a political organization which had had a century to entrench itself. . . .[17]

BIPARTISAN POLITICS

The rise of the Democratic party in Maine is important mostly because it initiated the bipartisan politics in existence today. Bipartisan politics, and the political moderation it has encouraged, have become the practical realization of the state's participatory political culture. This is not to say that the years of one-party Republican rule deviated from that culture. The state's population was less diverse and more static in the period of one-party politics, and thus found itself adequately represented by only one party. Also, the loosely organized Republican party, which emphasized the personalities and personal organizations of candidates, was in keeping with the participatory culture of the state. Although campaign strategies and federal party patronage have importantly influenced party development in Maine, changes in the state's economy and population have been equally influential.

As governor, Muskie implemented several important programs with the cooperation of the Republican majorities in the legislature. He created the Department of Industry and Commerce, which was very popular, especially after it enticed several new industries to the state.[18] His appointments, carefully cleared by the Republican-controlled Executive Council, minimized partisanship. As a party builder, Muskie has been compared with Hubert H. Humphrey in Minnesota, George McGovern in South Dakota, G. Mennen Williams in Michigan, and William Proxmire and Gaylord Nelson in Wisconsin.[19] In 1956, Muskie was reelected with a plurality that was approximately double his 1954 margin. At the same time, Frank Coffin won the first of two terms in the U.S. House of Representatives. Two years later, Muskie became Maine's first Democratic U.S. Senator in over forty years, and Clinton Clausen, who was finally persuaded to run, was elected governor.

During the 1960s and early 1970s, a system of bipartisan politics was established. After Governor Clausen died suddenly in office in December 1959, Republican John Reed was elevated to the governorship from the position of president of the state senate. Although Reed was elected in 1960 and reelected in 1962, his margin in the latter year over Democratic candidate Maynard C. Dolloff was small. In 1966, Reed was defeated by Democrat Kenneth M. Curtis, a popular Maine secretary of state who would serve as the state's chief executive for two terms. Although, at age thirty-six, Curtis was the youngest governor in the nation at the time of his election, he was successful in instituting innovative and important changes, such as the introduction of a governor's cabinet. The former plethora of boards and commissions that had made the state bureaucracy faceless and sometimes unaccountable was restructured into a handful of departments directly accountable to the governor. Governor Curtis also succeeded in winning passage, with Republican cooperation, of a state income tax in 1969.

Two-party politics in Maine has evolved mostly in a context of moderation. Intense partisan combat is fairly rare. Politics had always been loosely run and moderate in the sense of pragmatic. However, conflicting concerns were balanced and compromises were sought more frequently than during the Republican past. Ideologically conservative Republicans have not won statewide elections since the early 1950s, when Senator Owen Brewster, once a member of the Ku Klux Klan, and Robert L. Jones, a supporter of Senator Joseph McCarthy, were defeated in Republican primaries. Senator Margaret Chase Smith, who won reelection in 1954, is perhaps best remembered for her "declaration of conscience" speech before the Senate in which she eloquently denounced McCarthyism. Environmental legislation, which had been virtually nonexistent, got under way with Muskie and was continued by his successors, Republicans and Democrats alike. By the mid-1970s, Maine was in the forefront of some environmental policies, such as wastewater treatment.

William S. Cohen, who won a seat in the U.S. House in 1972 (and the Senate in 1978), has cast consistently moderate-to-liberal votes. Other Republican leaders in the state, including Harrison Richardson and Kenneth MacLeod, have been considered progressive.[20] During the 1960s, Richardson was a House majority leader and MacLeod was Senate president. Both men worked closely with Governor Curtis in the enactment of Maine's income tax in 1969. Likewise, the cautiousness and moderation that characterized Muskie's political style was perpetuated by the Democrats who succeeded him. During the 1972 Democratic state convention, liberal members of the party were unable to gather enough support to expand the platform to include equal rights for homosexuals and amnesty for Vietnam War draft resisters.

The moderation and lack of ideological emphasis gave Maine's government a strong continuity during a period of two-party competition. Although liberal preferences in the state grew faster than conservative ones, the overall effect was still an increase in moderation, especially in light of the fact that the state had been very conservative in the past. New organizations appeared to balance the old. Labor unions are one example. Their rise has been closely associated with the growth of the Democratic party. Another group, environmentalists, became instrumental in Maine politics in the 1960s and have grown in strength. The number of registered Democrats more than doubled in the 1954–74 years, moving from 99,386 to 212,175.[21] On the other hand, the number of registered Republicans declined, from 262,367 to 227,828, although they still held a slight majority of the registered electorate on the eve of James Longley's unexpected gubernatorial victory in 1974.

CONCLUSION

The century of almost uninterrupted Republican rule in Maine was replaced by a competitive, two-party system of politics in a relatively short period of time. Examined closely, the breakdown of the G.O.P. was largely an outgrowth of its position as the undisputed party. Multifactionalism is encouraged in one-party politics. In Maine, this was especially the case because the Republican party was never a tight-knit organization. During the 1932–52 period, when the U.S. presidency was filled by Democrats, federal Republican patronage stopped, and many of Maine's topline Republicans returned to the state, which already possessed a surplus of candidates. Conversely, Maine's Democratic party was strengthened when federal Democratic patronage stopped in 1952. The party, which needed to build itself from the bottom up, depended heavily on the expertise and leadership of such individuals as Frank Coffin and Clinton Clausen, as well as Edmund Muskie.

Maine's two-party politics evolved in a way that involved strong competition but loosely organized party structures. Campaigns tend to center around issues and the personalities of the candidates, rather than strong ideology. In general, power has been centered in the hands of moderate Democrats and liberal Republicans. These and other factors show that the transformation of Maine's traditional political system has encouraged political stability. In general, the transformation of Maine politics in the 1950s and 1960s reflected the overall development of the state during that period. Maine's economic and demographic diversification was translated into a broadening of its political system and its policy priorities.

CHAPTER FOUR

Contemporary Maine Politics

By 1974, Maine politics had evolved into a two-party system, similar to the systems of the other northeastern states since the end of World War II. Our concerns in this chapter are with the structure of the parties at the present time, and the place of interest groups in state politics.

THE PARTY BALANCE

The largest political grouping in Maine in 1990 was composed of independent (technically, "unenrolled") voters (see table 1).[1] They comprised some 37 percent of the electorate, with Democrats having 33 percent, and Republicans claiming the allegiance of 30 percent of the registered voters. The growth of independents was particularly noticeable during the 1970s and early 1980s, when their numbers approximately doubled. Although the increase in independents has slowed somewhat since the mid-1980s, their presence has had a major impact on Maine politics.

Unlike parties in some states, Democrats and Republicans in Maine have generally revealed little differences in per capita income. Maine parties show less division along class lines than they do according to cultural and ethnic factors. A survey in the 1970s determined that Republicans were disproportionately found among college-educated voters, among older voters, and among residents of smaller communities.[2] Democrats showed lower levels of formal education and more urban residential patterns, and they were the largest political group among voters between the ages of thirty-five and fifty-four. Independent voters tended to be fairly young, and to have lived in the state for shorter periods of time than Democrats and Republicans. Consistent with the state's moralistic political culture, voter turnout in

Table 1: Political Party Registration in Selected Years

Year	Democrats	Republicans	Independents (Unenrolled)
1976	224,753	226,280	175,417
1980	242,209	218,556	223,664
1984	252,296	219,397	272,999
1990	272,089	246,277	306,292

Source: State of Maine, Office of Secretary of State.

all groups has been relatively high. In the 1990 congressional elections, for instance, Maine's level of turnout among registered voters (55 percent) was the highest of any state.

THE ELECTORAL BATTLE

Independent voters have had an impact on gubernatorial elections. The national spotlight fell on Maine in the 1974 election when independent James Longley won a stunning gubernatorial victory. He campaigned on a platform calling for sharply reduced state government spending. Although the Longley success has not been repeated, his victory seemed to make subsequent gubernatorial races attractive to independent candidates of various political persuasions.

The Longley victory occurred because of a fortuitous combination of several factors.[3] These included the candidate's residence and the political climate at the time of the election. A wealthy insurance executive whom Governor Kenneth Curtis had named to head a group of businesspeople who were to study ways to bring about reductions in government expenditures, Longley became a political activist when state officials appeared to ignore his group's recommendations. In the 1974 elections, which took place in the aftermath of the Watergate scandals, citizen politicians were unusually popular. In his campaign for governor, Longley was able to put together a large vote from his home city of Lewiston, Maine's second largest city and normally a heavily Democratic city, with substantial statewide support from usually Republican voters, who were not swayed by the Republican gubernatorial nominee's uncommonly inept campaign. Longley won the three-man race by just under 40 percent of the vote.

Following the very conservative (and controversial) Longley administration, like-minded conservative candidates mounted statewide campaigns as independents in three of the next four gubernatorial elections: Buddy Franklin (a Bangor minister) in 1978, John Menario (a Portland developer) in 1986, and Andrew Adam (a self-styled libertarian) in 1990. Adam's candidacy was largely ignored by the major party candidates; he obtained only 9 percent of the vote in a hard-fought race in which Governor John McKernan narrowly won reelection over former governor Joseph Brennan. In contrast, Franklin and Menario each mounted strong independent campaigns in their years, and were widely covered by the media. They obtained 25 percent and 15 of the vote, respectively. In 1986, a second independent candidate, Sherry Huber, a former state legislator running on a platform stressing cultural liberalism and environmental issues, entered the race and also won 15 percent of the vote. (When Governor Brennan successfully sought reelection in 1982, he faced no independent challenge.) The independent candidates, particularly ones in 1978 and 1986, forced the major party candidates to address ideological issues more than they probably otherwise would have done. However, the presence of independents also seemed to shunt highly issue-oriented voters away from the parties. As a result, the parties were able to take fairly moderate positions on most issues. Such a pattern was especially noticeable in 1986, when independents Huber and Menario garnered most of the strongly liberal and the strongly conservative votes in a four-person race.

The long-run results of the dramatic Longley victory thus seem to be twofold. It has encouraged the entry of independents into gubernatorial races, particularly when an incumbent is not running. The Longley win has not, however, perpetuated the combative and ideologically charged atmosphere that Longley himself brought to state government. Paradoxically, the presence of independents in races for the governorship has fostered a greater degree of centrism or moderation in the two parties.

As far as elections to the U.S. Congress are concerned, Maine has had a bipartisan delegation since 1960 (when the state's seats in the U.S. House dropped from three to two). Independent candidates have played little role here, where the important aspect of races for House seats since the early 1970s has been the power of incumbency. In 1974, Democratic incumbent Peter Kyros was upset by Republican David Emery. Since then, incumbent representatives have generally not faced serious challenges. At the same time, in races in which no incumbent has been running, the elections have tended to be close. David Emery was reelected with increasingly large margins in 1976, 1978, and 1980. In 1982, he gave up the seat to run unsuccessfully against George Mitchell for the U.S. Senate. His place was taken by Republican John McKernan, who won a narrow race in 1982, but who widened his margin in 1984. In 1986, when McKernan sought the governorship, outgoing Democratic Governor Joseph Brennan entered the First District race, in the southern part of the state, and won by a fairly close margin over Republican Rollin Ives. In 1990, when Brennan challenged McKernan in the gubernatorial race, the seat was won by Democrat Tom Andrews, a Portland legislator who defeated David Emery, seeking to regain the position, by a lopsided margin.

The Second District, which covers the northern two-thirds of the state, has been in Republican hands since 1972. In that year, Democratic Congressman William Hathaway relinquished his seat to wage a successful campaign against veteran senator Margaret Chase Smith. Hathaway's place was taken by William Cohen, who defeated Elmer Violette, the Democratic floor leader in the state senate, by about 17,000 votes. Cohen faced only token opposition in subsequent races. He moved to the U.S. Senate in 1978, defeating Hathaway, who was trying for a second term. Cohen's successor, Olympia Snowe, a Republican state senator, was elected in a hard-fought contest over Mark Gartley, a Vietnam War veteran. Snowe's portion of the vote in 1978 was only 51 percent. It rose to over 70 percent in her 1980 reelection and remained close to that level through the 1988 election. In 1990, on the other hand, Snowe narrowly won reelection over state legislator Pat McGowan in an election year that was hard on incumbents generally in the state.

Maine's U.S. Senate seats have not provided incumbents with as much electoral safety as members of the House have enjoyed. William Hathaway won election to the Senate in 1972 by defeating Senator Smith, who had represented Maine in that chamber since 1948. Hathaway, in turn, was soundly beaten in 1978 by Congressman Cohen, who attacked Hathaway as being a doctrinaire liberal and insufficiently strong on defense issues. During much of 1981 and 1982, it appeared that Senator George Mitchell, who had been appointed to the Senate in 1980 after President Jimmy Carter named Senator Muskie as U.S. secretary of state, might encounter the same fate. However, because his opponent, Congressman David Emery, was seen as very ideologically conservative, Mitchell won in a landslide. U.S. Senate races tend to highlight the candidates' positions on particular issues more than House races. In recent elections, the stress on issues has seemed to put one candidate at a significant disadvantage—since 1972 no U.S. Senate candidate has won with less than 58 percent of the vote.

Turning to the legislature, the Democratic and Republican parties have been competitive since the early 1970s. Democrats have enjoyed solid, though not overwhelming, control of both houses since 1983. The rise of Democratic strength in legislative races has taken place broadly across the state, although the core of the party's strength is in urban areas. In 1986–88, every county had some Democratic representation in the house of representatives. Republicans also compete on a statewide basis; in 1986–88, they had legislators in every county delegation in the house save one (Piscataquis County). In the 1988–90 and 1990–92 sessions, all sixteen of Maine's counties had bipartisan House delegations.

The Democratic advantage in the legislature is due, to a considerable degree, to the great strength the party enjoys in Maine's cities. After the 1988 elections, for example, Democrats held thirty-three of the thirty-eight House seats located in or mostly in the nine largest communities (those with populations of approximately 20,000 or higher). Lewiston and Portland are traditionally Democratic, but for the 1988–90 legislature, the once Republican cities of Auburn, South Portland, and Augusta also elected solid Democratic delegations. The success of the Democratic party is likely to persist, in part because incumbency has become a major factor in winning elections. Taking the 1986, 1988, and 1990 elections together, over 80 percent of incumbent legislators sought reelection, and some 91 percent of those candidates were successful.

MAINE POLITICAL PARTIES IN NATIONAL CONTEXT

How do the Maine political parties compare ideologically with their national counterparts? For the most part, Democrats in Maine seem to be similar in their policy ideas to the Democratic parties in other northern states. They generally favor expanded government spending for education and social services, and greater reliance on progressive taxes to finance programs. Democratic primaries have generally not found candidates pitted against each other on sharply differing issue positions. Instead, the outcome of primary contests has usually depended on the candidates' personal skills.

In contrast, Maine Republicans have had difficulty adjusting to the policies of their national party. Their problem has been the growth of conservatism in the national party that has proved hard for many middle-of-the-road Maine Republicans to accept. The state delegation strongly opposed the selection of Barry Goldwater at the 1964 national Republican convention. Nonetheless, in subsequent years, leadership of the state party fell to activists who were more conservative than the rank and file. Although the party generally nominated moderates in congressional races, conservative candidates won the party's gubernatorial primaries in 1970, 1974, 1978, and 1982. (The results occurred in some instances because moderate votes were divided among several candidates.) In the general elections, Republican nominees lost, usually by large margins, to Democratic candidates (except in 1974, when both parties' nominees lost to independent James Longley).

More recently, moderates have scored some victories. John McKernan won the Republican primary for governor in 1986 by a two-to-one margin over a conservative state legislator. Edward O'Meara, a member of Senator William Cohen's staff, won his party's congressional nomination in the First District against conservative Linda Bean-Jones in June 1988. Another moderate success took place in the 1988 state party convention. The party refused to accept an amendment, endorsed mostly by conservative delegates, to add a pro-life amendment to the party platform. (The national Republican platform did contain such a plank.) Commenting on what he saw as the difference between state Republicans and national Republicans while he attended the 1988 national convention, Governor McKernan observed: "Maine people are pragmatic. There's not a lot of ideologues on either side. They're more interested in bread and butter issues."[4] In the 1990 primaries, McKernan won renomination as Republican candidate for governor without opposition.

ORGANIZATION AND MONEY

The organization of Maine's political parties involves a structure of party committees that is fairly typical among the states. The basic level is the town committee, which is selected by a town or municipal caucus, composed of all the members of the party in the community. The caucuses assemble every two years, usually in February or March, when they have traditionally selected delegates to the state conventions that meet during April or May, and elected their town committees for the next two years. Traditionally, the delegate-selection role meant that the town caucuses could influence the kind of delegation that the state convention put together, every four years, to attend the national presidential nominating conventions. That function sometimes caused a flurry of excitement at the time of the town caucuses, as presidential candidates invaded the state to speak with party activists in as many communities as they could. However, attendance by local party members at the caucuses was so poor in 1988 (about 5 percent of registered party members participated) that the legislature later that year approved a measure that authorized the parties to hold presidential nominating primaries if they choose. However, neither party exercised the option in 1992.

In addition to town committees, both parties maintain county committees. The strength of the individual municipal and county committees varies widely. If a committee has strong leadership, it can be instrumental in a candidate's success in winning election to the legislature or to county office. In many cases, however, the committees are not active, and candidates are left on their own. Party organizations tend to be weak, especially in the smaller towns and sparsely populated counties.

Each party has a state committee and holds a state party convention every two years in the spring. The principal tasks are the writing of the party platform and the naming of delegates to the national party conventions (every four years). State conventions are usually rather elaborate, two-day affairs held in a civic auditorium in Portland, Lewiston, Augusta, Bangor, or Presque Isle, with over a thousand delegates in attendance. Candidates running for the Democratic or Republican nomination (in the party primaries held in June) for the U.S. House or Senate, or for governor typically provide hospitality suites and campaign intensively for support among the delegates. Because Maine politics is highly personalized, though, the parties' state conventions, like the state and county committees they oversee, are of less significance in winning and holding office than the candidates' own organizations.

A large change in Maine politics has been the soaring costs of political campaigns. Recent gubernatorial elections are illustrative. In 1982, Democrat Joseph Brennan and his Republican challenger, Charles Cragin, each spent slightly over $500,000 (total) in their respective primary and general election campaigns. In his 1986 race, John McKernan reported spending approximately $1.2 million. His opponent, Democrat James Tierney, expended about $1.1 million. Sherry Huber, one of the independent candidates in that year, also reported spending in excess of $1 million (mostly from her own sources). The four gubernatorial candidates in 1986 expended, in total, about $4 million.[5] In 1990, McKernan listed a spending total of $1.6 million, while his opponent, Joseph Brennan, expended $1.5 million. Despite some public dismay about campaign costs, Mainers defeated, in a 1989 referendum, a measure that would have provided public funding for gubernatorial candidates.

Campaigns conducted by state legislators are also becoming costly. In years past, many candidates could win an election, especially to the house of representatives, with an outlay of a few hundred dollars. In 1990, however, it was estimated that the typical candidate for a house seat spent between $4,000 and $5,000, and that a senate candidate expended between $20,000 and $35,000.[6] Increased costs are driven in part by candidate efforts to reach voters by mail. For instance, a direct mailing to all voters in a state senatorial district cost between $2,000 and $3,000 in 1990. Most legislative candidates have so far found the extensive use of television impractical. Legislative districts are so much smaller in geographic size than the state's two primary television markets (based in Portland and Bangor) that costs are high in relation to the possible gain in votes. On the other hand, the purchase of television time now composes a major portion of the campaign budgets of congressional and gubernatorial candidates.

Ample campaign funds do not, of course, guarantee that a candidate will win. In the 1988 Republican primary in the First Congressional District, Edward O'Meara defeated Linda Bean-Jones, whose family founded the well-known L. L. Bean sporting goods store in Freeport, Maine. Bean-Jones spent approximately $500,000 on her campaign, amounting to about $35 for each vote she received. As campaign spending increases, potential candidates must increasingly weigh the matter of campaign costs.

The problem that finance presents to candidates and potential candidates has helped make party organization more relevant in campaigns. Candidates for the legislature now depend on various party sources for significant portions of their funds. In recent years, party leadership committees in the Maine house and senate have aided candidates. In 1986, for instance, the Democratic leadership committee in the house provided about $85,000 to Democrats running for house seats. House Republican leaders in the same year funneled some $65,000 to their candidates.[7] The Republican State Committee and the Democratic State Committee occasionally aid legislative candidates, but their assistance is targeted mostly to their gubernatorial and congressional aspirants. Money for campaigns is raised from such sources as political action committees (PACs) and lobbyists and, to a much smaller extent, from a checkoff system through which Maine taxpayers may contribute a dollar when filing their state tax returns.

The most dramatic change in the 1980s was the rise of the legislative leadership committees.[8] Apart from their financial tasks, the committees figured importantly in the recruitment of legislative candidates. In 1984, nearly one-third of the 151 house districts had no Republican candidates, but by 1986 the party recruited candidates for all but ten seats. The reason for the gain could be traced to the efforts of politicians, such as the house Republican leader, Thomas Murphy of Kennebunk. Murphy worked with town committees across the state to locate and persuade local Republicans to become candidates. It is not uncommon for a legislative leader to visit every contested district in the state to help his or her party teammates with their campaigns. These activities unquestionably have provided a degree of cohesiveness and direction for the legislative parties. The process has taken place even as independent voters in Maine have become the largest single voting bloc. It bodes well for the continued health of the two parties.

Like other rural states whose economies have depended heavily on extractive industries, Maine has a history of powerful interest groups. When Duane Lockard wrote *New England State Politics* in 1959, he identified pulp and paper companies, utilities, and manufacturing concerns as the "big three" economic interests, and argued that they did more than influence Maine politics. As he phrased it, "'control' is probably a more accurate term."[9] The interests were based, of course, on the state's abundant resources of timber and water power. Executives of the companies that exploited the natural resources worked closely with the leaders of the dominant Republican party in formulating public policy.

The "big three" economic interests tended to focus most of their attention on the legislature. Their influence with legislators in the 1940s and 1950s was enhanced by the importance they had as employers of members of the legislature during and after their legislative service (as well as being employers of legislators' constituents). Further, the nearly total absence of legislative staff meant that lobbyists often served as unofficial aides to legislators and to the legislative committees.

It is useful to compare the current pattern of influence with the one of thirty years ago. In 1987, Douglas Hodgkin of Bates College surveyed members of the legislature to determine which interest groups seemed most influential.[10] The seven groups that legislators mentioned as most effective were (in the order of a "power score" calculated by Hodgkin): environmentalists, the Maine Teachers Association, labor unions, paper companies, the Maine Municipal Association, utility companies, and state executive departments.

Some major political changes that have occurred in Maine in the past three decades are revealed in the presence on the list of several new organizations. Labor unions are one example. Their rise has been closely associated with the growth of the Democratic party. Another group, environmentalists, became instrumental in Maine politics during the 1960s and has remained strong. The paper companies are still a force to be reckoned with because of their great significance in the state's economy. In fact, they account for about 10 percent of the lobbyists working during legislative sessions. However, pulp and paper interests, on numerous occasions since the 1960s, have been defeated by coalitions of environmental groups. Although utilities remain influential, the manufacturing groups that constituted the third segment of the "big three" in the 1950s, made up of textile and shoe companies for the most part, are no longer seen as powerful. Many of these companies have left the state.

The rise of a broad diversity of interest groups is a fundamental change in Maine politics since World War II. For such a major development, it took place with surprising little political combat. The primary reason seems to be that the business organizations that had been so powerful in the immediate postwar years were "simply no longer interested in paying the price to influence Maine's political landscape."[11] The changes that we have already described—the growth in political activity of minority groups, the arrival in the state of new migrants, the emergence of a competitive Democratic party, the rise of career politicians in the legislature—all contributed to making the process of influencing the formation of public policy more complex. Christian Potholm of Bowdoin College writes that, at present, Maine businesses "will not actively recruit citizen legislators . . . ," and "will not cooperate . . . in meaningful ways to alter the makeup of the Legislature. They are not interested in the struggle or the hassle."[12] Their retreat has left the field open to a variety of new, and generally more progressive, groups.

Maine interest groups are, then, a good deal more diverse than in the past. Moreover, alterations in their power and influence constitute only one of the important changes that have occurred in Maine politics. Related shifts have taken place in the way in which interest organizations work with the political parties, and also with each other. Additionally, the state now has a substantial number of idea-oriented or issue-oriented groups to compete with the more established economic groups. We look at these developments in turn.

In 1984, state Senator John Baldacci, a Bangor Democrat and cochair of the legislature's Public Utilities Committee, initiated a widely publicized investigation of the opinion-polling activities of utility companies. Baldacci and some other Democrats believed that the utilities were aiding Republican candidates by quietly sharing polling data with them.[13] To the substantial embarrassment of Baldacci's group, its investigation revealed that utilities had actually provided polling data to Democratic Governor Joseph Brennan during Brennan's reelection campaign in 1982. The companies sometime later supplied the same information to Brennan's Republican opponent, Charles Cragin. In the 1950s, Baldacci's suspicions that the utilities were helping only the Republicans might well have been correct. By the 1980s, even very conservative business organizations had accepted the reality of Maine's two-party politics and, accordingly, tried to maintain friendly relations with both parties.

Although Maine is a small state, the number of organizations registered with the secretary of state, for the purpose of influencing legislation, exceeds 350. Because of their growing number, groups often join hands to form broad coalitions to support or fight measures that impinge on their shared goals.[14] For several years, a struggle took place over workers' compensation. High benefit rates, and repeated industry threats to leave the state, have fostered various legislative hearings and one special legislative session. Business desires to keep the costs of the program manageable from a business perspective have been addressed through a Worker Compensation Reform Committee that includes approximately thirty business organizations and associations, including the Maine Restaurant Association, the Maine Grocers Association, and the Maine Hospital Association. Interest groups no longer seem to "go it alone" as much as in the more freewheeling days of the 1950s.

In addition to economic umbrella organizations, think tanks and similar organizations have emerged as important actors in the world of interest groups.[15] One example is the Hannibal Hamlin Institute for Economic Policy Studies. The institute takes a free-market stance on economic issues and seeks to limit the reach of state government. A different group is Mainewatch, which is mostly interested in resource protection and which is considered generally supportive of government initiatives, especially where they protect the environment. Mainewatch was headed in the late 1980s by Sherry Huber, who ran unsuccessfully for governor as an independent in 1986. Each of these organizations has an executive director and a budget of over $100,000. Think tanks are beginning to thrive because many policy issues are highly complex and require considerable research. The Hamlin Institute fought hard against a proposal to levy a sales tax on services, which was advanced by a commission named by Governor McKernan to examine possible new sources of revenue. For its part, Mainewatch resisted unsuccessfully a 1988 decision by the Maine Turnpike Authority to widen the Maine Turnpike in the southern counties of York and Cumberland.

One of the most important of the idea groups is Maine's Women's Lobby, founded in 1978.[16] During the 1987 legislative session, the organization claimed that it was instrumental in helping to secure passage of twenty-five of the twenty-eight bills on which it took a position. Its key issues have involved child care, teen pregnancy, and increases in the Aid-to-Dependent-Children programs. The Women's Lobby generally takes a liberal stance on political issues. Contrasting examples of conservative organizations that contribute viewpoints to the legislative process are the Maine Impact Coalition, which was founded by Linda Bean-Jones, and the Maine Christian Civic League. The league was once interested in the cause of prohibition only, but more recently it has staked out positions on a variety of issues, such as pornography and gay rights. On abortion, it takes a strong pro-life stance.

LOBBYISTS AT WORK

During the 1989 legislative session, the secretary of state's office reported that 372 primary lobbyists and about 200 associate lobbyists were registered to represent interest groups in the legislative process. The power and influence of individual lobbyists and their organizations varied tremendously, of course. A longstanding practice in Maine is that the most influential groups tend to use law firms to represent them. The law firms most heavily involved in state politics usually have as partners or associates several political figures, sometimes recently retired from office.

Currently, the firm of Preti, Flaherty, Beliveau, and Pachios may be the most prominent.[17] The firm was the first of several Portland-based law firms engaged in lobbying to establish a regular office in Augusta, a recognition of the growing impact of state government on their clients. In the 1989 legislative session, Preti, Flaherty, Beliveau, and Pachios reportedly represented thirty-seven organizations and collected fees of approximately $300,000.[18] Its clients have ranged from Bar Harbor Airways, Inc., and the International Paper Company to the Maine Fishermen's Alliance and Maine Schools of Cosmetology. The firm's political coloration is Democratic. Peter Flaherty was a member of Joseph Brennan's executive staff. Severin M. Beliveau attempted to succeed Brennan, but failed to win the Democratic nomination in 1986.

In the past decade, Beliveau has been perhaps the state's most effective and best-known lobbyist. He has held numerous political and governmental positions—member of the Democratic National Committee, state Democratic chair, state legislator, and member of the University of Maine System's Board of Trustees. He comes from a prominent legal family: his father served on the Maine Supreme Judicial Court, and his grandfather and uncles were trial judges. Some state legislators find Beliveau unsurpassed as a political facilitator. One state senator described him in this way: "Severin is charming, witty, personal, and very bright. He is in a class by himself. He doesn't exactly lean on you, or play hardball, but instead uses common sense, constituent pressure, and very subtle threats to get you to at least consider his point of view.''[19]

The rise of the Preti, Flaherty, Beliveau, and Pachios firm has to some extent come at the expense of Verrill and Dana, still a very influential (and Republican-leaning) law firm located in Portland. Its ties to the Maine Republican party go well back into the nineteenth century. One of its early partners was Thomas Brackett Reed, Speaker of the U.S. House of Representatives in the 1890s. Before his election to the governorship, John McKernan was a partner in Verrill and Dana. Still other partners have included Charles Cragin, the unsuccessful Republican candidate for governor in 1982, Howard Dana, who managed President Ronald Reagan's 1980 campaign in the state, and Loyall Sewall, who chaired the Republican State Committee in the mid-1980s. In 1989, Verrill and Dana provided legislative representation for twenty-four clients and amassed nearly $200,000 in fees.

Not all lobbyists are attorneys working in prestigious law firms. Some are former state employees who remain in Augusta to work with the private sector. David Flanagan, once Governor Brennan's legal counsel, joined Central Maine Power (CMP) as a lobbyist after leaving state government. CMP has used, in addition, several former legislators on its lobbying team. Jadine O'Brien, state personnel director under Governor Brennan, found employment as lobbyist for Blue Cross and Blue Shield after she left office. Acknowledging that she knew little about the insurance industry, she stated that the arrangement was nonetheless a good one: "They thought they could teach me the basics, and I brought them a knowledge of state government. It was a perfect match.''[20] Flanagan's and O'Brien's career paths are not unusual. Former executive branch employees are strong candidates for lobbyist positions, as are former legislators. As policymaking grows more complex, key decisions often take place in the executive departments that implement statutes. Individuals who can establish access with appropriate administrative units, by virtue of their career experience, are thus valued by interest groups.

Maine has some fairly strong lobby-registration laws, which the legislature recently tightened further. Until 1988, lobbyists were required to report only that portion of the salary they received for actual lobbying in the statehouse; and only lobbyists who worked more than eight hours per month had to disclose financial information. Under new requirements that went into force in that year, all lobbyists must disclose financial information, and the total amount of compensation received by the lobbyist or lobbying firm must be recorded with the state. Another important rule adopted in 1988 was a one-year prohibition on state, local, and county officials appearing before their former agencies to discuss issues that were pending at the time of their departure. A year-long study by the legislature's State and Local Government Committee led to the new regulation. As one legislator said a bit puckishly: "Every now and then a citizens' legislature gets control and when they do, they give them [the lobbyists] a jab."[21]

POPULAR LAWMAKING

A final topic in this survey of contemporary politics involves the initiative and the referendum. Maine's participatory culture and the growth in the complexity of state policies have combined to bring about increasing use of these devices for popular lawmaking. Under the Maine Constitution, a statewide referendum must take place to approve bond issues and constitutional amendments, after the measures are first proposed by the legislature. These proposals have traditionally enjoyed a high rate of success. Voters have approved about 90 percent of the amendments and bond proposals that have appeared as ballot questions in the past several decades.[22] In contrast, referendums that have taken place in response to an initiative have tended to be more controversial. An initiative gets under way in Maine when the number of voters equivalent to 10 percent of the total vote in the last gubernatorial election signs petitions seeking either to repeal a law already enacted, or to establish a new law. Under the constitution, an initiated measure must first be considered by the legislature. If the legislature fails to accept the proposal as it is set out in the initiative, a referendum is called.

Between 1911 (when the initiative and referendum were first used) and 1970, only six initiated statutes were considered. In the comparatively short period between 1971 and 1991, however, a total of twenty-two such measures were voted upon. Twelve won approval. Generally, initiatives designed to repeal laws already on the books have not fared well. Rejections have included efforts to end the hunting season on moose (1983), to terminate the forced deposit on bottles initiated to encourage their return (1979), and to abolish the Maine income tax (1971). In 1991, however, voters overturned a decision of the Maine Turnpike Authority authorizing the widening of the Maine Turnpike, and established a new transportation policy that gives preference to nonconstruction alternatives to meet transportation needs in the future.

Still, most successful initiatives have set policy in areas where the state government had not spoken. Examples include the establishing of flat-rate telephone service for local calls (1986), maintaining the continued operation of the state's nuclear reactor, Maine Yankee, at Wiscasset (1987), indexing the state's income tax to allow the schedules to shift according to rates of inflation (1982), establishing a public preserve in the Bigelow Mountain area (1977), banning slot machines (1980), and permitting large stores to sell merchandise on Sundays (1990).

In certain instances, the legislature probably turned an initiated measure over to a referendum (without acting on it) primarily because of the question's importance to Maine voters, not because the legislature opposed the policy idea. Some legislators worry that issues are being "put out to referendum" too easily. However, groups unable to line up support in the legislature for their ideas can be expected to try to use the initiative/referendum process if they think they might have a better chance of winning popular support. The Natural Resources Council of Maine was a major supporter of the 1991 transportation referendum. In 1986, the Maine Christian Civic League unsuccessfully sponsored an antipornography initiative that was bitterly contested and involved several other interest groups. The fairly frequent appearance of referendum questions on Maine ballots is likely to continue.

CONCLUSION

Politics in Maine exemplifies a very loosely organized two-party system in which the key factor in a political campaign is the personality of the candidate. With voters divided about evenly among Republicans, Democrats, and independents, neither party has a permanent hold on the legislature, the governorship, or the congressional delegation. Each party has enjoyed its greatest successes where it has been able to nominate more attractive candidates. Democrats have been able to identify more closely with the rise of the career legislator than have Republicans, and the party has enjoyed majority control of the legislature for the past decade. The congressional delegation has been about evenly divided between the parties, with the Republicans having the more senior members. Congressional Republicans have been, since the mid-1970s, more liberal—and better attuned to Maine's political environment—than have many of the Republicans seeking seats in the state legislature.

In organizational terms, Maine parties have almost switched places with each other since the "traditional system" of the 1950s. At that time, the dominant Republicans were strong in the towns and counties, while the small organization that the Democrats maintained was focused on the state government, centering around such charismatic figures as Edmund Muskie.

At the present time, neither party has a particularly dependable organization, but the Democrats are better organized in local areas, especially in the larger towns. Republicans must count heavily on nominating attractive statewide candidates to win, and their organizational efforts have largely centered on state politics.

For much of its history, Maine had unusually powerful interest groups that exploited its natural resources of wood and water, and took advantage of its amateurish state government to win favorable policies. With the great expansion of interests in Augusta in the past two decades, the power of the traditional economic interests has diminished. Nonetheless, interest groups and lobbyists remain key players in state government. As state policymaking becomes ever more complex, interest groups are drawn into the process to supply information and expertise. In addition to influencing the legislative process, groups are involved in the executive branch, where they try to affect the implementation of laws, and in the electoral arena, where they occasionally take a hand in initiatives and referenda.

CHAPTER FIVE

The Constitutional Tradition

Like all state constitutions, Maine's charter provides the fundamental structures and guidelines from which all state policymaking must proceed. The
various branches of the state government are supposed to act in accordance
with the provisions of the Maine Constitution and the U.S. Constitution. If
the legislature fails to follow these provisions, the laws that it makes can be
thrown out by the courts as unconstitutional. The state charter also furnishes
a window through which one can glimpse the political and social growth
of the state. To begin an examination of the Maine Constitution, a look at
the differences between state constitutions and the U.S. Constitution is
useful.

State charters resemble the federal Constitution in some respects, but
they perform a very different function. Their primary purpose is to limit the
exercise of power. This trait arises from the fact that the states inherited all
the power of the British government after the Revolution. Because of fears
of unrestrained power, citizens quickly circumscribed state power with constitutional provisions. The U.S. Constitution, on the other hand, grants
power to the national government, which otherwise would have no legitimate basis of existence.

State constitutions are also characterized by their accessibility to the people. Compared to the federal Constitution, state charters are much easier to
amend. The Maine Constitution is amended whenever the legislature, by a
two-thirds vote of both houses, proposes a constitutional amendment that the
voters then ratify in an election. This ratification process contrasts with the
more onerous procedure whereby the approval of thirty-eight states (three-
quarters of the states) is required to approve a federal constitutional amendment.

HISTORY OF THE CONSTITUTION OF MAINE

As part of the process of securing statehood, citizens of the District of Maine convened a constitutional convention in Portland in October 1819.[1] The convention was composed of nearly three hundred delegates, who were drawn from every incorporated town in the district. The delegates represented a wide range of occupations: some were shipbuilders and traders; others were farmers and fishermen; still others were lawyers and politicians. The primary question the convention had to resolve was whether to write a new constitution for Maine, or to build the state's charter from the Massachusetts Constitution, under which the district was then governed.

Some delegates, such as William King, the state's first governor, wanted to strike out independently. However, the majority seemed to share the view of William Pitt Preble, delegate from Saco, that the Massachusetts document should be relied on because the convention lacked "sufficient time . . . [for] such an ambitious undertaking" as drafting a very different charter.[2] The Massachusetts Constitution of 1780 would become by the twentieth century the oldest charter in the United States. Written by John Adams, it is considered a pioneering statement of political thought. Unlike other early state constitutions, which established weak governments, the Massachusetts document "subordinate[d] the individual to society." Its political theory "taught . . . that a republican political system . . . must enjoy a wide latitude of action in the pursuit of the public good."[3]

The Maine Constitution was ratified in December 1819. As of 1991, it had acquired 159 amendments. About one-quarter of that number have been added within the last fifteen years, reflecting the great expansion in the functions of the state government during this recent period. In Maine, the amendments are periodically codified into the text of the charter with the intention of keeping it comprehensible to the people. Thus, the charter reads as a single text, with no list of amendments at the end of the document, as is the case with the U.S. Constitution. The process of codification has been conducted by the Chief Justice of the Maine Supreme Judicial Court every ten years since 1875.

CONTENTS OF THE CONSTITUTION OF MAINE

In this section, we sketch first the contents of the contemporary constitution. Later we focus on the specific changes produced by amendments adopted since the 1820s.

The first article of Maine's Constitution, most recently codified in 1983, contains twenty-four sections known as the "Declaration of Rights." Of the ten articles, this has received the least alteration since 1819. Citizens are guaranteed, among other things, free speech and freedom from "unreasonable searches and seizures." They are promised that in all criminal prosecutions, they have the right to a "speedy, public and impartial trial," and they cannot be compelled to give evidence against themselves. The rights set forth in Maine's charter and in other early state constitutions formed the basis for the Bill of Rights of the U.S. Constitution, which was adopted in 1791.

Maine's Declaration of Rights also incorporates language from the Declaration of Independence. Power is inherent in the people, in whose authority "all free governments are founded." The people have the right to institute, alter, or reform their government "when their safety and happiness require it." The Maine Constitution was, in some respects, more democratic than that of Massachusetts. It protected freedom of worship as well as speech, and it made no distinction between Protestants and members of other religious groups. The 1780 Massachusetts Constitution made it a duty to worship the "Supreme Being," required church attendance, and prescribed a certain amount of tax discrimination against Catholics and Jews.

Article II addresses the qualifications for electors. Universal suffrage is provided for all citizens eighteen years or older, except persons under guardianship for mental illness and persons in the military service stationed in the state. In addition, students residing at any "seminary of learning" are not entitled to vote in local elections in the place where the school is situated.

Articles III, IV, V, and VI outline the structure of the state government. Article III establishes the principal of separation of powers, while Article IV concerns the structure of the Maine legislature. Apportionment is to be conducted by a joint commission. In the event that an apportionment plan is not produced within 130 days after the legislature has convened, the Supreme Judicial Court is required to make the apportionment. This court is also empowered to hear any challenge of inequitable apportionment.

Article IV also outlines the regular legislative sessions, stating that the legislature can convene "at such other times" on the call of the president of the senate and the Speaker of the house. The legislature is given "full power" to establish all laws for the defense and benefit of the state's citizens. While Article IV grants sole power of impeachment to the house of representatives, the senate is given sole power to try all impeachments. The number of representatives is fixed at 151; the number of senators varies from 31 to 35.

Article V is concerned with the executive branch. The governor is the only official elected statewide; the term is set at four years (in 1819, it was a one-year term). The governor is required to have been a citizen of the United States for at least fifteen years, and a resident of Maine for at least five years. In addition, any person filling the governorship cannot hold any other office under the jurisdiction of the United States, Maine, "or any other power."

Article V states that the governor is the chief law enforcer of the state. The governor may, on "extraordinary occasions," convene the legislature. Except for judges of probate and justices of the peace, the governor is empowered to nominate all judicial officers. The last parts of Article V outline some of the duties of the secretary of state and the treasurer. The secretary is required to keep all records of official proceedings of the governor, as well as those of the legislature. The treasurer is empowered to appropriate funds for the payment of the state's debts if the legislature fails to do so.

Article VI delegates judicial authority to a Supreme Judicial Court and to "such other courts as the Legislature shall . . . establish." Except for the positions of justice of the peace and member of the Judicial Council, no justice is allowed to hold office under the jurisdiction of the United States or any other state. The rest of Article VI outlines the tenure of judicial officers and the election (by the people) of judges and registers of probate.

Article VII deals with the organization of the state militia. The governor is given the power to appoint all commissioned officers as well as the adjutant general, while the legislature is required to establish the necessary qualifications to hold a commission in the militia.

Article VIII is divided into two parts. The first part, which has received little alteration since 1819, establishes the role of the state in the education of its citizens. The second part grants home rule to the state's municipalities, allowing them to alter and amend their charters on all local matters "not prohibited by this Constitution or general law."

Articles IX and X outline a number of provisions that touch on all three branches of the state government, and also establish the financial restrictions and powers within which the government must work.

The basic structure of the Maine Constitution stresses broad popular participation and a state government equipped with fairly extensive powers. This was apparent in the state's original constitution, where suffrage and civil rights were broader than they were in Massachusetts, and where the governorship was considerably more powerful than it was in most states at the time (Maine's governor had veto power as well as appointive power). The state legislature began as the primary branch of government, and it has since maintained its independence. Such continuity in Maine's constitution is part of the moderation that characterizes the state's politics. This moderation, in turn, is reflected in the careful balance of power between the people and their government.

Over the years, the Maine Constitution has had to be amended to make it relevant to changing circumstances. Although the number of amendments (159) is much larger than the number of federal constitutional amendments, it is not so by state standards. Maine's fundamental charter ranks among the third of the states with the shortest constitutions, a grouping that also includes all the other New England states. State constitutions tend to differ regionally. As a New England state, Maine has what Daniel J. Elazar has termed a "commonwealth constitution."[4] This type of charter is usually brief and concerned mostly with setting forth the essentials of government. States in other parts of the country have tended to develop longer documents. In those jurisdictions, the constitution becomes a bargain or contract among contending political forces. As the forces change, the entire constitution is sometimes discarded and replaced by a new charter. Louisiana, for instance, has operated under eleven constitutions since it entered the Union in 1812. In contrast, Maine has tended to show long-run agreement on political questions, at least about matters it wants to settle on a constitutional basis. That habit seems to be a characteristic of its moralistic, broadly participatory political culture.

For the most part, amendments have not generated significant political controversy. They have tended mostly to be statements about government and public policy that are widely shared by Maine citizens at the time of amendment adoption. Amendments must be proposed by a two-thirds vote of each house of the legislature, and must be approved by a majority vote in a popular referendum. Nearly 90 percent of the proposed amendments have been adopted. Yet the amendments are not insignificant. They have enabled the Maine Constitution to remain relevant to a governmental process vastly different, in many respects, from the one it was originally designed to direct. The constitutional areas especially affected have been state institutions, state-local relations, the suffrage, and public policy.

State Institutions and the Maine Constitution

Created as the most powerful branch of government by the original constitution, the legislature has retained its strength through certain amendments. Paradoxically, even the amendments that restrict the legislature conserve the institution's original power. This has happened because the adoption of restrictive measures often offsets powers accumulated by the legislature.

The bulk of the amendments extending legislative power have been budgetary in nature. They have been concerned especially with the issuance of bonds and the level of permissible state debt. Most of them constitute an exception to the sixth amendment of 1848, one of the most restrictive of all measures placed on the legislature. This amendment forbade the loaning of state credit and limited the state debt to $300,000. The original document had not set a debt limit.

The sixth amendment was adopted with the sole intention of circumscribing the powers of the legislature. This amendment was the result of serious financial difficulties in which the state found itself during the 1840s. During this time, Maine had overextended its credit in order to meet the costs of government and the sudden onset of the Northeastern Boundary Dispute.[5] The sixth amendment was written more as a guideline and a pledge than as a realistic expectation. As such, exceptions to it (in the form of bond issues) have been rather numerous over the years. This is not to belittle the restriction set out in the sixth amendment, which is both literal and symbolic.

Beginning in the 1950s, a series of amendments has placed some procedural restrictions on the financial powers of the legislature. Among these, there has been the seventy-fifth amendment (1951), which requires that a statement of the state's outstanding debts must accompany all proposals to the voters for the issuance of new state bonds. The 151st amendment (1984) has placed a time limit on the life of authorized bonds. In one sense, these amendments help to bring the tenor of the constitution closer to what it had been in 1848, when the sixth amendment had just been ratified, and to distance it from the tone of the document in the 1940s before the restrictions were imposed.

Other amendments have also affected the legislature. Among those that extend its power are the seventeenth amendment (1876), which promises that the legislature shall never "surrender" its power of taxation, and the nineteenth amendment (1876), which allows the legislature to call a constitutional convention in order to amend the constitution (though this has never been exercised). More recently, the 115th amendment (1970) enables the legislature to convene itself into special sessions, a power formerly lodged with the governor alone.

Among the amendments particularly restrictive to the legislature, are the sixth, already mentioned, and the fourteenth (1876), which promises that acts of incorporation will be established under general laws and not under special legislation. The 127th amendment (1975) limits legislative amendment and repeal of laws initiated or approved by the people.

Maine's executive branch has not been immune to alteration either. During the nineteenth century, there was a protracted battle over executive power. Initially, as mentioned, the governor had extensive appointive powers, which included the naming of judicial, civilian, and military personnel. In 1856, several of these offices were made subject to popular election (ninth amendment, 1856). These included judges and registers of probate, municipal judges, and county sheriffs.

Beginning in the 1870s, state politicians began to rethink some of their earlier actions against executive power. This was partly because there were many officials responsible to a governor who had no direct influence over their selection. In Maine, this new thinking resulted in the repeal of portions of the ninth amendment. Under the sixteenth amendment (1876), the appointment of judges of municipal and police courts reverted to the governor, and the governor's power to appoint the adjutant and quartermaster generals was restored under the twenty-eighth amendment (1893).

The governor has gained some significant powers during the twentieth century. The thirty-eighth amendment (1917) allows the governor to remove county sheriffs in certain instances, and the seventy-eighth amendment (1955) expands the governor's pardon powers. In 1957, under the eighty-fourth amendment, the governor's term was extended from two years to four. In 1975, the Executive Council was abolished by the 129th amendment.

The Executive Council, consisting of seven members elected by the legislature, had been created by the 1819 constitution. Although the council was meant to "advise the Governor in the executive part of government," it provided one of the most significant restrictions to early gubernatorial power in Maine. The Executive Council was a vestige of Revolutionary suspicion of centralized power, and Maine "inherited" its council from the Massachusetts Constitution.

If the council did not already hamstring a governor, it could become an obstacle when the governor's party was not in control of the legislature. Frequent efforts were made to remove the council—by constitutional commissions in 1875 and 1962, by Governor Edmund Muskie, and by the Democratic party for decades. When those attempts succeeded in abolishing the council under the 129th amendment (1975), Maine's governorship was finally concentrated into the hands of the chief executive.

While many states have incorporated into their constitutions specifications concerning the structure of their executive branch, Maine's document says relatively little on the matter. Most of the broad changes in the state executive, particularly its growth from a handful of employees in the 1820s to the approximately 12,000 employees in its current workforce, have been accomplished through statutory revision.

The state courts have received the least amount of constitutional revision. With the growth of judicial business, the legislature has been able to establish new courts and new levels of courts without resorting to amendments. The only court officially sanctioned by the constitution is the Supreme Judicial Court. The major changes that have occurred in that court through constitutional amendment have concerned judicial tenure. Originally, justices were allowed to serve until age seventy. This was altered by the third amendment (1840), which established seven-year terms and removed the age limit. The 132nd amendment (1976) allows justices to serve for six months after the expiration of their term, or until their successor is named, whichever occurs first.

State-Local Relations and the Maine Constitution

Like local governments in all states, Maine's towns and cities are, in constitutional theory, "creatures of the state." The state may direct their actions as it desires, and its powers include the authority to create, modify, and abolish local governmental jurisdictions. The original constitution was silent on the topic, but several amendments have significantly developed this relationship.

One of these was the twenty-second amendment, which, in 1878, barred municipalities from creating debts exceeding 5 percent of their property valuations. The legislature had earlier allowed localities to sell a limited amount of bonds for the purpose of constructing railroads. Pressures on the legislature for further relaxation of the credit limitations on individual communities were so intense that the amendment was adopted to regulate the situation across the state. The municipal debt limit was later raised to 10 percent, where it remains today.

In general, amendments to the constitution concerning the state's localities have provided them with additional powers. The most important came in 1969 with the 111th amendment, which granted home rule to the state's municipalities. Under the provisions of home rule, local residents were given the power to alter or amend their charters on all local matters not prohibited by constitutional or general law. Previously, all changes in municipal charters had to be approved by the legislature. Thus, the structure and functions of local government could more readily reflect the overall philosophy of government in any particular community.

Suffrage and the Maine Constitution

Another important dimension of the Maine Constitution is suffrage. At the time of the 1819 constitution, the states had sole power to determine who could vote. Gradually, the federal government began to circumscribe state power in this area, through amendments to the federal Constitution, such as those granting suffrage to blacks, women, and persons eighteen years of age or older.

The seventh amendment (1848) marked the beginning of a long struggle to alter the manner of electing state officials. The original constitution required winning candidates for the house, the senate, and the governorship to obtain a clear majority of all votes cast in the particular election. In the absence of a majority, reballoting was necessary in the case of the house. The senate decided elections where no candidate for the senate had received a majority. In the case of the governorship, the entire legislature was called on to settle the contest.

When splinter parties evolved in the 1830s and 1840s, the majority system of elections broke down. In the 1846 house elections in Maine, some 40 percent of the districts had no majority winners and required additional contests. The solution to the problem was plurality elections, in which the candidate with the highest number of votes (whether or not a majority of all votes cast) is declared the winner. The seventh amendment (1848) established this procedure for the house of representatives, but voters rejected the plan for other offices.

In 1868 and 1872, elections for certain senate seats had to be decided by the senate itself because of the absence of a majority winner. In 1875, the thirteenth amendment was enacted to establish the plurality rule for senatorial elections. The governor, though, was still being chosen by the required majority vote. In three successive gubernatorial elections, beginning in 1878, no candidate obtained a majority of the votes. In one of these elections, the legislature chose a candidate who had not even obtained a plurality. In 1880, voters finally approved the twenty-fourth amendment, establishing plurality elections for governor.

Continuing the tradition in Maine where a fairly considerable amount of power was invested in the hands of the people, amendments defining the right to vote have generally expanded the suffrage. In the constitution of 1819, electors were restricted to male citizens twenty-one years of age or older (excepting paupers and American Indians) who were residents of Maine at least three months preceding an election. All of these provisions have been modified. The passage of the seventy-seventh (1954) and one-hundredth (1965) amendments ended the official discrimination against Indians and paupers, though in practice the limiting provisions had often been overlooked. The voting age was lowered to twenty by the 113th amendment (1969), and then to eighteen by the 116th (1971). Residency requirements were removed under the 123rd amendment in 1974. In addition, a number of amendments have facilitated voting in various ways, such as authorizing the use of voting machines (59th amendment, 1935).

One of the most important suffrage amendments was the thirty-first. When this was passed, in 1909, Maine became the first eastern state to adopt the direct initiative and referendum.[6] The initiative allows the people to enact statutes without legislative consent. The referendum allows them to veto measures already enacted by the legislature, as well as to approve initiatives.

Since 1909, the initiative and referendum have been used fairly frequently, especially in more recent years. Partly because of this, there is a trend toward restricting the use of these measures. Among the amendments that restrict the thirty-first amendment is the seventy-second amendment (1951), stipulating that any measure adopted through referendum which fails to produce adequate revenues for its services will become inoperative. The 144th amendment (1981) specifies that no signature on a petition older than one year is valid. The purpose behind these restrictions, as well as several others, seems to be to prevent interest groups and small numbers of voters from manipulating the referendum and initiative processes for their own advantage.

In considering other amendments that have restricted suffrage, it should be noted that Maine failed to adopt a woman's suffrage bill prior to the Susan B. Anthony amendment, which became a part of the United States Constitution in 1919. The twenty-ninth amendment, enacted in 1893, required that voters be able to read the Maine Constitution in English, as well as write their names. Already enrolled voters were exempted. Enacted during the period of heavy in-migration of French Canadians, as well as other nationalities, the amendment was regarded as nativist and was strongly resented in French communities.[7]

Public Policy and the Maine Constitution

To a considerable extent, the amendments authorizing new bond issues out-line Maine's expanding public policy responsibilities. Among these amend-ments, which are numerous, are ones for soldiers' bonuses (forty-fifth, 1920), for fostering industrial development (eighty-second, 1957) and recre-ational development (102nd, 1965), for student loans (105th, 1967), for fish-eries and agricultural enterprises (108th, 1967), and for Indian housing (119th, 1972). Other amendments have addressed school financing and road building.

Maine's use of constitutional amendments to establish social policy in-vites attention to the twenty-sixth amendment, which, in 1885, "forever prohibited" the use of alcoholic beverages. Although this amendment had already been established as a statute (the "Maine Law") in the 1850s, it rested on an uncertain basis because of Democratic opposition. The inten-tion behind the twenty-sixth amendment was to provide a more secure basis for the law. Indeed, the twenty-sixth amendment was effective until it was repealed in 1934 under the fifty-fourth amendment.

Ensuring the thoroughness and protection of civil rights has been an im-portant aspect of Maine's amendment process. As already mentioned, suf-frage restrictions on Indians were removed in the 1950s. Another anti-discriminatory measure is the seventy-ninth amendment (1955), which re-moves the requirement that the governor be a natural-born citizen of the United States. Under the 158th amendment, adopted in 1988, all sexist lan-guage must be removed from the constitution.

Another example of Maine's constitutional social policy is the fourteenth amendment. Passed in 1875, this act promises that charters of incorporation will not be created under special legislation, but under general laws. The in-tention behind this amendment was to wipe out privilege, favoritism, and monopoly, which began to be associated with charters of incorporation given out by special legislation. In this sense, the fourteenth amendment was an important symbol, as well as a guarantee, of egalitarianism. In propo-sing the fourteenth amendment, Maine's legislature significantly de-limited the scope of its actions, but perhaps not as dramatically as one might at first suppose. The case of *Taylor* v. *Portsmouth, Kittery, & York Railroad* (91 Maine 193, 1893) established the rule of law that if the legis-lature should grant a special charter, which might have been formed under general laws, only the state itself (not private citizens) can inquire into such an act's validity.[8]

THE NATIONAL CONTEXT OF MAINE'S CONSTITUTION

Political scientists have sometimes analyzed the evolution of state constitutions according to certain time periods. One widely accepted analysis specifies three periods of state constitutional and institutional development.[9] The first period, lasting from approximately 1776 to 1870, was one of legislative supremacy and the extensive use of popular elections to fill public offices. Those practices reflected the great stress given to the value of representation in the states at that time. The second period, from 1870 to 1920, primarily witnessed an effort to limit the power of the legislature, which in many states had become irresponsible and corrupted by political machines. Political power in state government proceeded to be splintered among many independent boards and commissions. The third and most recent period (since 1920) has stressed coordination in state affairs, and hence has focused attention on the need for a strong governorship.

Maine's development has somewhat resembled that pattern. Starting with a strong legislature, the state experimented for a time with the popular election of certain officials during the 1850s, but abandoned that practice by the 1870s. The fourteenth amendment's requirement of general incorporation laws in 1875 circumscribed the legislature, with the intention of reestablishing a process that had been tainted. Maine has rarely used its constitution to arrange the details of its executive branch. Although a large number of boards and commissions were created in the late 1800s and early 1900s, they generally did not achieve constitutional status. When major executive reorganization took place in the 1970s, little constitutional change was thus required. However, the long-run impact of the state's constitutional growth in the twentieth century has clearly been one of enhancing the power of the governor and the legislature.

Perhaps the most important state constitutional issues in the next few years will involve civil rights. In several states, courts have interpreted those states' constitutions in a way that provides greater protection of the rights of individuals than the U.S. Supreme Court has granted under the U.S. Bill of Rights. This has not yet happened in Maine. However, in some recent cases, Maine Supreme Court justices have paid lip service to the idea that certain rights, such as free speech and the rights of criminal defendants, may enjoy greater protection in the provisions in the Maine Constitution than they do in the U.S. Constitution.[10] Should the U.S. Supreme Court retreat from enforcement of the federal Constitution's Bill of Rights, it is very likely that Maine courts would move to take up the slack, relying on Maine's Declaration of Rights.

CONCLUSION

The most salient feature of Maine's constitutional politics has been the generally successful reconciliation of two potentially clashing elements—the need for competent government and for a politically effective citizenry. Maine's borrowing from Massachusetts seemed to set the state on an effective course, since the Massachusetts Constitution of 1780 recognized the importance of both elements in a political society. The idea of balance can also be found in the long amending process. Many amendments pull and tug against each other. As an example, while the legislature has acquired powers to issue bonds (thereby eroding the sixth amendment), its powers have been restricted more recently. As another illustration, the very considerable powers given the people through the initiative and referendum have been recently clarified and more sharply regulated as the use of the devices has become more frequent. The result of such balancing has been that the constitutional structure set out in 1819 has largely been retained and made relevant to changing circumstances. Most particularly, the amendments to the Maine Constitution have both reflected, and helped to maintain, a spirit of moderation in the state's politics.

CHAPTER SIX

The State Legislature

Glancing through Maine newspapers during the last week of the 114th legislature's first session, which adjourned on July 1, 1989, one might be puzzled about what happened during the session. The house and senate seemed to have enacted many significant measures during the six-month session. A front-page story in the *Bangor Daily News,* headlined "Lawmakers finish busy '89 session," noted that the legislature had "overhauled the state income-tax code, stepped up efforts to relieve the burden of local property taxes and ordered state-subsidized insurance for thousands of poor people." The same session had also enacted "a far-reaching initiative designed to reduce the flow of rubbish into the state's rapidly filling landfills," plus measures to "require more young people to wear seat belts, limit driver's licenses for 15-year olds, tighten laws against drunken boating, stiffen penalties for drug pushers, and further limit the places where smokers may satisfy their habit."[1]

Despite that volume of business, however, other press reports were distinctly critical of the legislature. Shortly before it adjourned, a *Bangor Daily News* columnist wrote that "it's practically midsummer already and the Maine Legislature is still here, fiddling and diddling, daddling and doodling, around the State House. . . ." He opined that "the end of this Maine legislative session has to rank as one of the worst in recent memory in terms of confusion, procrastination and loose ends left hanging."[2] Complaints about the legislative process also occurred during the session. The *Maine Sunday Telegram*, referring to the rapid increase of legislative staff in recent years, observed that a big issue in the session was "whether [the legislature was] getting too big and too expensive."[3] The costs of operating the legislature were estimated to have increased by about 50 percent between 1987 and

1989 (to about $15 million). Aware of public concern about its costs, the legislature in 1989 authorized an extensive study of the legislative process to determine, among other things, the need for a full-time legislature.[4]

As these events suggest, the legislature currently has an uncertain role in state government and politics. Maine has long prided itself on having a "citizen legislature," although some citizens (such as retired persons) have been much better able to serve as legislators than others. Legislative turnover has traditionally been high. Legislative compensation (in 1992 a total of $17,625 for the two-year term, plus a per-diem allowance of approximately $60) has long been among the lowest in the states. Legislative service has mostly been considered a part-time enterprise. Pressing state issues were discussed at length in the house and senate, to be sure, but the legislature's decisions frequently depended heavily on outside sources of information. Since the mid-1970s, the legislature has expanded its staff to deal with its increased workload. Further, as more legislators begin to identify themselves as professionals and to seek continued reelection, the institution may be losing some of its "citizen" quality, even though the small size of legislative districts has long protected that quality. In a 1988 debate on legislative pay raises, a Portland legislator set out the problem in terms of alternative state models: "The big issue," he said, "is, do we want to be like New York or do we want to stay more like New Hampshire?"[5]

THE CONSTITUTION AND THE LEGISLATURE

In contrast to the current debate, the framers of the Maine Constitution were in agreement about the legislature's job. In 1820, it was regarded as the foremost institution of state government. Alone among the states, the legislature had the power to name the secretary of state, the treasurer, and the state auditor. In the 1850s, it gained the right to name the state attorney general. In 1970, a national study group asserted that the legislature's strongest feature was its formal independence from the executive branch.[6] Unlike the case in many states, such as New Hampshire, where the state constitution has historically restricted legislative salaries (they are limited to $100 per year in New Hampshire), the Maine Constitution places few limits on legislative power. The main restrictions have focused on financial procedures, such as the requirement of voter approval of bond issues, but these limitations have not proved to be onerous.

The principal legislative issue that plagued the framers of the Maine Constitution was apportionment.[7] That was understandable in the light of

Maine's scattered, and rapidly growing, population in the early 1800s, and its commitment to citizen participation in affairs of government. House seats were allocated to towns according to their populations, but with some limitations. No town was permitted more than seven representatives, and towns of less than 1,500 inhabitants were grouped to form separate districts, with the provision that the representative would rotate from year to year among the towns of the district. The framers could not agree on a fixed size for the house of representatives. Anticipating population growth, they specified only that the house would be between one hundred and two hundred members. The first house had 143 members. In 1841, after the house membership reached two hundred, a constitutional amendment reduced its size to 151 members, where it remains. With an average of 8,100 citizens per house district, Maine has fewer constituents per legislator than all states except Vermont and New Hampshire. The small size of these legislative districts tends to reinforce the citizen quality of Maine government, even in a time of professionalism and technology.

The framers allocated senate seats according to counties. In 1820, the three largest counties, York, Cumberland, and Lincoln, had four senators each, while the smallest counties, then the northernmost counties of Penobscot and Washington, had one each. The first senate had 21 members.

Historically, the legislative apportionment systems used in the Maine house and senate overrepresented rural areas, but did so only moderately. In fact, in studies in the 1950s, Maine ranked among the top third of the states of the Union in fairness of representation, and was one of only two New England states to fall in that category.[8] In contrast, until the early 1960s, Vermont allocated one seat in its house of representatives to every town regardless of size, which meant that as few as 12 percent of its voters could elect a majority of house members. After the U.S. Supreme Court declared that state legislative apportionments must be based on the principle of "one person, one vote," Maine joined all other states in revising its house and senate districts.[9]

An interesting change that has taken place since the mid-1960s relates to single-member districts. In 1966, the senate abandoned multimember districts, long defined by county boundaries, and established individual senatorial districts. The house switched (in 1975) from a mixed arrangement of single-member and multimember districts to a plan composed entirely of single-member districts. Earlier, nearly one-third of its members, mostly from urban centers, had been elected in multimember districts.

The two parties had to strike a bargain in the legislature to bring about single--member districts. Democrats liked the multimember districts because they believed that these districts provided the party with an advantage in legislative races in the larger cities. Because Democrats held a majority of the voters in most cities, they could win all of the legislative seats in those cities in an election. Republicans opposed multimember districts for the same reason, and sought to redistrict cities into separate single-member districts, some of which they could expect to win. For their part, Republicans were able to name all of the members of the Executive Council (the advisory body to the governor) in the early 1970s because they had a majority of the seats in the legislature. The Executive Council, empowered to confirm gubernatorial appointments, regularly hampered the administration of Democratic Governor Kenneth Curtis (1967–75) and the development of Democratic programs generally. Because abolition of the Executive Council required a constitutional amendment, both parties had to agree to the move. In return for Republican acceptance of removal of the Executive Council, Democrats agreed to single-member districts for all 151 house members.

THE LEGISLATORS

The changes in apportionment were accompanied by a greater diversity of people who won seats in the house and senate. Historically, despite Maine's participatory culture, the political and social bases of the legislature were fairly narrow. In the 1941 session, for instance, the two chambers had a combined total of 159 Republicans and only 23 Democrats. Approximately half of the members listed their occupations as farmers or owners of small businesses, and only four members were women.[10] It is useful to examine the ways in which the legislative membership has changed.

In the past decade, the legislature has had competitive political parties, with the Democrats in the majority in both chambers since 1983. Their margins have been substantial, but not overwhelming. In fact, only three times in the past twenty years have either the Republicans or the Democrats held as many as two-thirds of the seats in the senate, and no party has enjoyed that proportion of seats in the house during that period. The figure of two-thirds is important because the rules require that certain legislative measures be passed only with that size of majority. The fact that neither party has enjoyed an overpowering margin has generally fostered a bipartisan approach to legislative issues, where bargaining and compromise are crucial.

Another change is that legislators are becoming more experienced. Although the two-party system contributes to making elections more competitive than in the past, legislators seem to remain in office longer. Traditionally, turnover in each chamber approached 50 percent, and the working styles of legislators reflected their inexperience. In a survey in the early 1970s, many members reported that a major task they had to accomplish was learning the rules and practices of legislating.[11] In more recent sessions, that obligation has seemed to be less pressing. In the 113th legislature (1986–88), only about one-fifth of the members of the legislature were newcomers. The typical representative was in a third term, and the typical senator was serving a second term. About one-quarter of the senators and one-third of the representatives had had at least eight years of experience in the legislature. The considerable costs of campaigning, which sometimes exceed the two-year legislative salary, and the heavy time commitments now demanded by legislative work, contribute to making legislative service more of a profession.

What are the principal occupations of Maine legislators? Mostly they are types of work that permit legislators to build the wide circle of friends and acquaintances so necessary in politics. Legislative occupations must also permit a legislator to maintain a flexible working schedule. In a recent session (the 113th), the most common house members were retired (29 percent) or self-employed in such jobs as real estate broker, restaurant owner, author, machine shop owner, fisherman, grocery store owner, consultant, and the like (29 percent).[12] In the senate, only two members were retired, but self-employed persons constituted nearly half of the membership.

In both chambers, teachers composed a significant portion of the membership. Including retired educators, they made up nearly one-fifth of the 113th legislature. Through statute, the legislature has encouraged Maine public school teachers to run for legislative office. A measure enacted in 1983 requires an employer to arrange a leave of absence for a teacher for as long as the teacher remains in the legislature.

In contrast to educators, there have been few attorneys in some recent sessions. In the 1986–88 session, just five house members and only one state senator were attorneys. Certain legislative standing committees, such as the Legal Affairs Committee and the Judiciary Committee, face a shortage of legally trained members. The modest legislative salary and the ability of lawyers to advertise their services (which reduces the importance of the visibility of legislative service as a form of advertising) have contributed to a decline of lawyer-legislators.

Maine legislators are quite representative of different age groups in the population. In the 113th session, while the median age was 50, the range of ages was broad; twelve house members were in their twenties, and another eleven were over seventy. Younger house members often attend the University of Maine Law School in Portland while they are holding office. A prominent example is the current governor, John R. McKernan, Jr., who represented Bangor for two terms (in the 1970s) while obtaining his law degree. Legislators differ sharply from their constituents in educational attainment. Nearly two-thirds of the members in the 113th session had completed college, compared to only 14 percent of Maine citizens in 1980 over the age of twenty-five.[13]

Maine's legislators usually arrive in Augusta with considerable political experience. In the light of the state's strong town-meeting tradition, and the distribution of its population among a large number of small towns and cities, it is not surprising that a high portion of legislators have local office-holding experience. About half of the senators and representatives in 1986–88 had occupied (or were continuing to occupy) such positions in local government as city councilor, school board member, or member of a town board. Another common type of political experience is that associated with nonprofit agencies, social service groups, and other organizations that are quasi-public. Approximately one-third of the members of the house and senate reported serving on boards of directors or in some similar capacity for such organizations as the Maine Humanities Council, the Maine Lung Association, an area Agency on Aging, and the Coalition for Maine's Children. These organizations have grown rapidly in the past two decades, and most of them are involved in state policymaking.

An important change has been an increase in the number of women legislators. Their rise has made the legislature far more descriptively representative of the state's total population than in the past. In 1991, one-third of the legislators were women.[14] In recent sessions, women have also held major positions in the legislative leadership. Elizabeth Mitchell (D., Vassalboro) was the house majority leader in the 1981 and 1983 sessions. In 1989, Representative Mary Clark Webster (R., Cape Elizabeth) was the house minority leader. Nancy Randall Clark (D., Freeport) was the senate majority leader in the 1987, 1989, and 1991 sessions. Barbara A. Gill (R., South Portland) was her party's assistant floor leader in the senate for the 1983 and 1985 sessions. Her position was filled by Senator Pamela Lee Cahill (R., Woolwich) in the 1989 and 1991 sessions. The first woman legislative leader was Democrat Lucia Cormier of Rumford, who was the house minority leader in 1959. (In 1960, Cormier unsuccessfully challenged Senator Margaret Chase Smith. That U.S. Senate race was the first in U.S. history in which both major parties nominated a woman.)

THE LEGISLATIVE PROCESS

The Maine legislature must accomplish a great deal of work in a short span of time. In the 1989 regular session, the house and senate considered 1,781 bills and passed 731 of them. Many of these measures were controversial and complex. The legislators must try to ensure that as much public participation as possible take place as the legislature prepares measures, even as it adheres to the time deadlines it has established. The first regular session, which takes place in odd-numbered years, must adjourn by the third Wednesday in June. The second regular session, which occurs in even-numbered years, must adjourn no later than the third Wednesday in April, and is limited by the Maine Constitution to certain types of legislation, such as "budgetary" matters and "emergency" bills.

To understand the workings of the legislature, it is useful to focus on three arenas of decision making—the presiding officers, the party caucuses, and the standing committees. The powers and activities of each have shifted during the past few years because of legislative efforts to cope with an increased workload while still remaining, for the most part, a citizens' assembly. The steps in the legislative process once a bill reaches the floor of the legislature are also examined.

The Presiding Officers

In part-time state legislatures, the role of the presiding officers is normally crucial. These officials usually have much more information concerning legislative issues and legislative politics than individual members. Their commitment of time to the process is also usually far greater than that of other members. Maine's legislature has traditionally had powerful presiding officers. One of them, Thomas Brackett Reed, Speaker of the house in the late 19th century, later became Speaker of the U.S. House of Representatives. The authority of the Speaker and the president of the senate includes the power of naming all members of the standing committees, presiding over the debates in their respective chambers, participating in overseeing the legislative staffs, sending members to national and regional conferences, and representing the legislature to the public. In addition, legislative leaders have played increasingly strong roles in the nomination and election of the individual members.

The increase in the power of the leadership in recent years has stemmed from several sources. One has been a change in the tenure of the presiding officers. Historically, and by custom, the president of the senate and Speaker of the house each served one two-year term. After David Kennedy served three terms as Speaker (1967–72) and Kenneth MacLeod also served three terms as president of the senate (1969–74), longer tenure became a norm. The current leading example is Democratic Speaker John Martin (D., Eagle Lake), who has held office since 1975.

A second source of legislative power has been the acquisition of staff. In 1990, the legislature employed approximately 185 staff members. Approximately half of these people were technical and professional personnel who worked on a nonpartisan basis (for instance, researchers who staffed the standing committees). The remaining staff members mainly consisted of partisan employees assigned to the majority and minority leaders in each chamber, and to such offices as the clerk of the house and the secretary of the senate, which are under the control of the majority party. Through their staffs, members of the legislative leadership are able to stay abreast of, and influence quickly, developments throughout the legislative process. The present pattern contrasts sharply with the scarcely half-dozen aides that served the entire legislature until the early 1970s.

The growth of power of the presiding officers is illustrated by John Martin, who in 1992 was the longest-serving Speaker among the fifty state legislatures. First elected to the house in 1964, Martin represents Eagle Lake, a French community in the impoverished northern portion of Aroostook County, which borders on the Canadian provinces of Quebec and New Brunswick. Statehouse observers believe that the Speaker closely reflects the political culture of his district.[15] Like the Liberal Party in neighboring Canada, Martin ideologically supports an activist government, and he has authored numerous measures to that end. A particular example was the establishment of the Land Use Regulation Commission (LURC), which provided the state with zoning authority over the extensive lands owned by the paper companies. Martin's leadership rests on an unrivaled knowledge of the legislative process. One Republican floor leader during the 1970s referred to him as the "most technically perfect parliamentarian I have ever seen."[16] Martin has not hesitated to use his official powers to secure policy aims on the floor and in the work of the standing committees. In one celebrated instance, the Speaker removed the chair of the Taxation Committee in midsession, when the legislator's handling of an important tax measure provoked his ire. The legislator, who had represented a Portland district for several terms, did not run for reelection.

In recent sessions, while the presiding officers are usually reelected routinely, lively contests have often occurred for the other positions. The organizational battles for a recent session (the 1986–88 session) illustrate the variety of contests that take place. For that session, Senator Nancy Clark (D., Freeport) moved up to the position of senate majority leader without official opposition (she had been assistant majority leader in the preceding session). However, Senator Dennis L. Dutremble (D., Biddeford) had to defeat Senator R. Donald Twitchell (D., Norway) for the assistant majority leader post. On the Republican side, Senator Thomas R. Perkins (R., Blue Hill) narrowly retained the position of minority floor leader over Senator Charlotte Z. Sewall (R., Medomak). Senator Barbara Gill (R., South Portland), the assistant floor leader in the 1984–86 session, was ousted by Senator Charles M. Webster (R., Farmington).

Other races occurred in the house. Majority floor leader Representative John Diamond (D., Bangor) defeated Representative Paul F. Jacques (D., Waterville) to retain his position. For the vacant position of assistant majority floor leader, Representative Dan A. Gwadosky (D., Fairfield) defeated Representative Joseph Mayo (D., Thomaston). In the Republican party, Representative Thomas Murphy (R., Kennebunk) was unopposed for re-election to the post of minority leader. Finally, Representative Eugene Paradis defeated two other house Republicans to win the vacant position of assistant minority leader.

A third source of power for the legislative leadership is the Legislative Council. Composed of the ten members of the leadership (five from each house), the council has several functions. One involves the selection of bills to be considered at the second regular session of the legislature. Under a 1975 amendment to the constitution, the business of the second session is limited to certain categories of issues, such as "budgetary matters" and "legislation of an emergency nature." The council decides at the beginning of the session which of the many measures that legislators wish to introduce will be accepted. The council has less authority over the filing of bills in the first regular session, but it can determine whether a measure that a legislator desires to introduce after cloture (a calendar date after which no new legislation is supposed to be introduced) can be granted an exception.

In the hectic closing days of a legislative session, the council supervises the scheduling of measures and plays a critical role in deciding which bills receive funding. Because of their leadership positions, council members at this time become more decisive on budget matters than the members of the Appropriations Committee. The council's power is enhanced by bipartisan tendencies in the legislature, which means that council members may come together in agreement on procedures, even if their decisions are resented by rank-and-file legislators. The parties often agree on major questions, at least in roll-call votes, and confine their public disagreements to selected issues. During the 1980s, Democrats and Republicans fought rather consistently over how much power labor unions should have in the workplace, and how much financial support the state should provide local schools. Party differences were harder to detect in such controversial areas as taxation, environmental protection, and social welfare, even though those issues often gave rise to angry and prolonged debates in house and senate sessions.

A final part of the council's authority is related to activities between legislative sessions. The council establishes the research agenda for the standing committees between sessions, specifying which projects will be funded. It also manages the non-partisan legislative staff, including committee staff members, and oversees the legislature's budget. The council's most important employee is the legislative director, who is in charge of the day-to-day operation of the legislative staff. Although very powerful, the Legislative Council is still subject to Maine's law governing public meetings, which means that the council's proceedings are normally open to the public (except when personnel matters are considered). In many other states, the work of the Legislative Council would be conducted by rules committees in the house and senate. Meetings of those units are generally secret.

The Party Caucuses

A second part of the legislative process is the party caucus. Each house has a Democratic and a Republican caucus, which is composed of all the party's members in that chamber. In the house, the parties caucus occasionally in the early months of a session, and more frequently in the closing weeks. In the senate, the parties usually caucus weekly. Caucuses have historically played a major role in the Maine legislative process. Their traditional function was to provide a forum in which party members and their leaders could discuss legislation and legislative strategy during the session. The caucus was a kind of dress rehearsal for the floor debates and formal action on the floor. For the part-time legislator, the caucus provided an efficient means of gaining and sharing information, and of learning about and helping to formulate party strategy.

More recently, the caucuses have been less decisive in the legislative process. The growing complexity of legislative issues has made it difficult for them to retain their central role as the place where information is exchanged. Instead, committees have taken over that function to a considerable extent.

The caucuses are still important for the airing of opinions and grievances, and they provide a basis for developing, on occasion, a party approach or position on an issue, especially when the governor's interests are involved. At the beginning of a session, they also have the official task of nominating a party candidate for presiding officer and of electing the party floor leader and the assistant floor leader. The details of legislation, however, are primarily a matter for the committees.

The Standing Committees

Maine is one of a handful of states that uses the efficient (and timesaving) device of joint standing committees to consider legislative bills. The units are always composed of three senators and ten representatives. Committee seats are distributed between the parties in a manner roughly proportional to the seats that each party holds in the legislative chamber. In recent, Democratic-controlled sessions, committees have generally had two Democratic senators and one Republican senator, and six Democratic house members and four Republican members. Until the mid-1970s, a senator was normally named the committee chair. Due in large part to the influence of Speaker John Martin, a system of house and senate cochairpersons evolved. The two legislators usually take turns in presiding over committee sessions, and share in directing the committee's work. Each committee has a clerk. Of late, the legislature has maintained about twenty standing committees covering the major areas of legislative policymaking. Appropriations, Taxation, State and Local Government, Education, Human Resources, and Transportation are among the most important units.

The presiding officers determine the membership and the chairs of the committees. In the senate, every member of the majority party, including first-year members usually chairs a committee. As a senator gains seniority, he or she moves from chairing a less busy committee to heading a more powerful unit. In the house, members normally serve two or three terms before chairing a committee. The floor leaders try to select as chairs people who will manage the units competently, are politically congenial with the leadership, and have shown themselves to be effective in floor debates.

The committees' importance in formulating legislation seemed to start in the 106th session (1973), when the legislature first employed professional researchers as committee aides. Until then, the committees worked without staff and depended heavily on lobbyists and other outsiders for technical information. Currently, the Office of Policy and Legal Analysis (OPLA) is composed of approximately twenty-three persons, most of whom have graduate degrees, and provides assistance, including bill-drafting assistance, for the committees. One or two members of the office are assigned to a major committee. A single staff member may serve two less active committees. Between sessions, the committees undertake research with the help of the OPLA. In the period between June 1987 and January 1988, some thirty-five studies were undertaken on such topics as "Health Care Costs," "Early Childhood Education," "Overcrowding in Mental Health Institutes," and "The Impact of Heavy Trucks on Maine Highways." Once the formal legislative session is convened, the committee has accumulated a depth of expertise on a topic that makes its recommendations valuable for other legislators.

The much increased complexity of legislation has been a major reason why the committees have risen in power. Historically, discussion of bills could take place in the caucus, after the committees had reported the measures to the floor. Currently, however, the technical aspects of bills are too complex for that process to work well. Instead of relying on caucus deliberations, committees usually try to put bills into as final a form as possible before reporting them to the floor. The critical stage is a committee's "work session," which follows the public hearing on a bill (but which is still open to the public). During the work session, the bill is discussed thoroughly, amendments are drafted, and votes of committee members taken. If the leadership has strong views on the legislation, they will be made known at this point. The work sessions can be onerous. Toward the end of the 1989 regular session, the Education Committee held approximately fifteen such meetings on a complex student-aid bill. The Education Committee had to work out a compromise among a variety of viewpoints, because the student-aid issue had attracted the interest of the leaders of both parties and the governor's office.

In reporting legislation, standing committees can recommend that the legislation "ought to pass," "ought to pass as amended," or "ought not to pass." (There are no written reports beyond this indication of the committee's preference.) On a controversial measure, a committee may make a majority and a minority report. Bills reported with a "unanimous ought not pass" require a two-thirds affirmative vote of the chambers before they can be considered (which almost never happens). All other bills are placed on a legislative calendar and, under the rules of procedure of the house and senate, must be considered fairly promptly by the chambers. To facilitate the handling of a bill on the floor, committees perform a certain amount of advance lobbying. When handling a complex measure, the house and senate chairpersons may assign each committee member a certain number of legislators (not on the committee) to contact before the committee releases its report. Observers have noted that the portion of unanimous committee reports has increased in recent sessions, a likely outgrowth of consensus-building efforts undertaken by the committees in their work sessions.

Floor Action

After a measure is reported from committee, it moves through several more stages.[17] Initially, a committee report has to be accepted. Once it is accepted, the bill is given a first reading. In the house, a bill that has been favorably reported from committee by a unanimous vote is placed on the Consent Calendar. After two legislative days, it is considered as passed to be engrossed (put into final form). Any member by an objection can remove a bill from the Consent Calendar, in which case it will have to follow the normal procedure of separate readings. The senate has no procedure comparable to the Consent Calendar.

Other committee reports may not be accepted as easily. Complex bills sometimes generate split reports, wherein committee members submit different versions of a bill. Rejection of a favorable report or acceptance of an unfavorable report can kill a bill at this stage. For most bills, particularly those that are controversial, the second reading is the most important stage. Debate and the consideration of amendments take place at this point. Amendments are generally offered to most complex bills. Proceedings may become protracted, and the legislation may be postponed to allow each side more time to prepare its case. The legislature keeps a complete record of its debates. Following debate and amendment, a bill is passed to be engrossed. This task is carried out by the Office of the Revisor of Statutes. A bill that has passed to be engrossed in one house must move through similar stages in the other chamber. Very occasionally, a conference committee composed of three members of each house appointed by its presiding officer may be convened to reconcile differences in the house and senate versions of a measure. Because Maine uses joint standing committees to prepare legislation, however, house and senate disagreements are less common than in some other states.

Once a bill is engrossed, it is ready for enactment. By long-standing practice, this is accomplished first in the house, then in the senate. Although the rules of both chambers are similar, the legislative process usually takes less time in the senate than in the house, partly on account of the senate's smaller size. The senate also seems to display somewhat fewer philosophical and ideological conflicts than the house. That difference may exist because senators represent broader, more diverse constituencies than house members.

The legislature is stronger today than in the past. It has the resources to bargain effectively with the governor in formulating public policy. New programs in Maine normally have the imprint of both branches when they are finally set into law. This is not to say that the legislature can often overcome a determined governor in a policy dispute. The political and institutional resources available to the governor generally enable the chief executive to set the tone and direction of state government. However, the governor and the legislature have usually found ways to compromise their differences. In that respect, they reflect the Democratic and Republican parties that elect them, which are both moderate and pragmatic. Even as it continues to be the crucial representative body in the state government for Maine citizens, the legislature has a growing role in policymaking.

Will the legislature slowly become a professional body? That issue is debated each session. The best answer is that the house and senate will probably have a substantial number of career legislators, but that the chambers will still adhere to the essentially citizen quality that is so much a part of their history. The requirement for a truly professional legislature would, among other things, virtually mandate much higher legislative salaries. That prospect is dim unless the size of the house of representatives is reduced. Efforts have occasionally been made in that direction, but they have never gained much support. There is little likelihood that change will occur in the near future.

The feelings of Maine people about their legislature are illustrated in a letter that Representative John Diamond (D., Bangor), house majority leader during much of the 1980s, received from a constituent. The writer was upset with Diamond's endorsement of a certain health measure that affected the Bangor area. After explaining his concerns about the legislation, the writer broadened his criticism of Diamond's politics. He summed up the legislator's eight-year career in the house by stating that his service in government had been a betrayal of the public trust and that he had done "nothing whatsoever for the people of Maine." Despite that hostility, the writer wrote a final message that suggests the close, neighborlike relations most Maine politicians have with their constituents: "P.S. My parents send their regards."[18]

The Governor and the Administration

The Maine governorship reflects a different dimension of the state's political culture than does the legislature. Whereas the mostly "citizen legislature" stresses participation, the governorship emphasizes leadership and coordination, such as the development of consistent policies throughout the state. The need for consistency is implied in the state's moralistic culture, in which a commonwealth or communitarian conception of politics is uppermost, and no group or section of the state can be ignored in decision making in Augusta. Governor McKernan made reconciling gaps in economic advantage in different parts of Maine a major part of his 1986 gubernatorial campaign and in his subsequent administration. The effort to establish such policies is complicated by the state's geography. With its population scattered over nearly five hundred communities, some of them remote and inaccessible, effective implementation of state programs is often difficult.

Maine's location in the extreme northeastern part of the country has led to other geographically related problems. For instance, United States and Canadian trade policies often differ, which sometimes leaves Maine industries, such as fishing, caught in economic warfare with their counterparts in eastern Canada. The governor must deal with federal agencies, with Canadian provincial premiers, and with other state chief executives in defending the state's borders and coastal interests.

As chapter 5 pointed out, the Maine Constitution has not seriously burdened the governor. While it has kept three senior administrators (attorney general, secretary of state, treasurer) away from his control, it has not been used to fix the structure of the executive branch. In 1971, Maine was able to move from an executive branch primarily dominated by boards and commissions to a very different cabinet system of governance without the necessity of a constitutional amendment.[1] Those changes that have been made in the governor's constitutional power in the past three decades have strengthened the chief executive's hand in virtually every case. New powers have included a four-year term (beginning with the gubernatorial election of 1962) and important budgetary and fiscal authority that was, until 1975, assigned to an executive council.

THE GOVERNOR IN HISTORY

A look at the individuals who have held the Maine governorship since 1820 shows something of the evolution of this aspect of Maine politics.[2] Especially relevant are the kinds of backgrounds that politicians elected to the governorship brought to the job and the careers that they followed after leaving office.

Maine's earliest governors all served one-year terms, and about half left after the conclusion of the one term.[3] The state thus had a fairly large number of governors in the early years of statehood; twenty-one men served as chief executive between 1820 and 1860. Most of them were born in Massachusetts, New Hampshire, or southern Maine. A majority had studied law, but the governors represented a variety of occupations. Enoch Lincoln, who was governor from 1827 to 1829 and who died in office, was a well-known poet. Nearly all of the governors had occupied some public office before becoming Maine's chief executive; especially popular were state legislative positions, which a third held when elected to the governorship. Another one-fifth of the governors were elected directly from the post of U.S. congressperson. After completing their term as governor, more than half of the former chief executives returned to legislative service, winning seats in the Maine house of representatives, the Maine senate, the U.S. House of Representatives, or the U.S. Senate. Three governors left office to become judges.

Maine's early governors were mostly public persons with long records of service. Their careers suggest that they were adept in dealing with both state and federal issues. Maine had come into the Union as part of the Missouri Compromise of 1820, and federal issues continued to intrude into state politics in subsequent decades. An example was the 1842 Webster-Ashburton Treaty with England, which settled Maine's northern border and averted a war between the United States and Canada. The substantial political experience of the early governors suggests that political skills were highly valued as Maine tried to manage its rapidly growing, relatively egalitarian, frontier society.

In the years after 1860, Maine shifted from a state in which political parties had been competitive to a one-party Republican stronghold. Of the twenty-seven governors between 1860 and 1940, all but four were Republicans. Most were born in Maine, but they continued to come mainly from small towns. Less than half of this group were lawyers. Other common occupations included newspaper editor, physician, and business executive. One governor (William Cobb) had been the president of the Bath Iron Works, the state's largest shipbuilding firm, before he entered politics. Another (Joshua Chamberlain) had been a college president and a military hero for the Northern army at the Battle of Gettysburg.

Like the earlier chief executives, however, most governors in this period continued to have state legislative experience; about one-quarter of them were serving in the legislature at the time of their election as governor. The presidency of the state senate evolved as a popular steppingstone to the governorship. However, in contrast to the pre–Civil War period, fewer than half of the chief executives remained in public life after leaving the governor's office. Of those who did, most held federal positions, especially in the U.S. Congress. Former governors figured in the cohort of Maine Republicans who served prominently in the federal government in the late 1800s and early 1900s. An example was Nelson Dingley (governor, 1874–76), who chaired the Ways and Means Committee in the U.S. House of Representatives in the 1890s. Dingley became associated with one of the nation's most important tariff measures, the Dingley Act of 1897.

Governors elected in the past half-century (1940–90) have revealed some new background characteristics. While law continues to be the most predominant occupation, chief executives have tended to come from the larger communities, such as Portland, Lewiston, Bangor, Rumford, Waterville, and Augusta. That pattern reflects the rise of the Democratic party, whose partisans traditionally have been concentrated in urban centers. Like earlier chief executives, however, a majority of governors in the most recent decades had legislative service as part of the career route to the state's top office. Four of them (all Republicans) were president of the senate at the time of their election. That steppingstone was no longer used when Democrats began winning gubernatorial elections in the 1950s. (Although the Democrats held a majority of seats in the state senate in the 1980s, their senate presidents have not yet shown an inclination to use the office to run for governor.) About half of the governors took a federal position after leaving office. Two (Frederick Payne and Edmund Muskie) moved to the U.S. Senate; one (Joseph Brennan) was elected to the U.S. House; two others (Kenneth Curtis and John Reed) initially took appointive positions in Washington and eventually became U.S. ambassadors (to Canada and Sri Lanka, respectively). Most of the others went into the private sector. One governor (Horace Hildreth, 1945–49) served as president of Bucknell University in Pennsylvania for many years after leaving office.

Thus, two career traits of Maine governors through history seem to be their holding legislative office before becoming the state's chief executive and their serving in federal office (either elective or appointive) after leaving the governorship. Because Maine has no statewide elective office other than the governorship, the legislature is a crucial place for a prospective governor to line up political support. Among the New England states, more governors in Maine have served in their state legislature at some point in their careers than have the chief executives of any other state.[4] The possession of both legislative and executive experience has undoubtedly aided governors in building successful federal careers after leaving office.

THE ROLES OF THE GOVERNOR

In performing the job of governor, the chief executive plays several, sometimes conflicting roles, including the functions of chief of state, legislative leader, chief of administration, party leader, and ombudsman. While these tasks have always been associated with the gubernatorial office, they have grown more complex with each succeeding gubernatorial administration. In 1990, the governor of Maine had an executive-office staff of approximately twenty people. These staff members assume some functions that the chief executive once handled virtually alone. Like members of the legislature, the governor struggles to maintain personal contact with Maine citizens even as he oversees a government now spending between $1 and $2 billion per year.

Chief of State

In the role of chief of state, the governor speaks for all of state government, even though he officially heads only one branch. An important responsibility is representing the state in national and international forums. The governor visits Congress to testify on legislation relevant to state interests, and also meets regularly with members of the state's congressional delegation. Overseas travel is likewise part of a governor's schedule, as the Maine economy is increasingly affected by international economic events. In March 1989, Governor McKernan completed a nine-day trade mission to Belgium and

Switzerland; on his return, he indicated that he had worked out an arrangement whereby a Swiss manufacturing plant was to locate in southern Maine
and the state would provide certain funds to train its workers. As chief of
state, the governor is a member of the National Governors' Association, the
New England Governors' Conference, and the New England Governors' and
Provincial Premiers' Conference, an organization that brings together U.S.
and Canadian officials to address border problems. Governors Brennan and
McKernan each chaired that organization during their years in office.

Maine's location lends particular significance to the governor's out-of-
state activities. But within the state, the role of chief of state is equally important. Maine's participatory political culture insists that the governor be
close to the people. The governor greets visiting dignitaries, serves as honor-
ary chair of various civic and charitable committees, attends all manner of
social and sporting events, gives college and high school commencement
addresses, cuts ribbons for new buildings and parks, and talks to many citizen groups. Governor McKernan has been televised and photographed in
various settings during his administration: riding a bus with Augusta school-
children on the first day of school, playing basketball in Bangor to raise
money for an antidrug program, and cooking hamburgers in Capital Park for
state government employees.

During his first two years in office, McKernan's staff estimated that he
spent between 30 and 40 percent of his working time outside of the state capital.[5] In an effort to carry out a theme in his 1986 election campaign of bringing the "two Maines" together, McKernan inaugurated a "capital for a day"
program. Under the program, he and several members of his cabinet periodically conduct the business of state government in a community other than
Augusta. On June 1, 1989, Madison, in central Maine, became the twenty-
seventh community to become the focus of state business. In his visit to
Madison, the governor and several cabinet officers toured the town's two
major industries (a paper mill and a woodworking plant), presented an award
to Madison High School for its drug-prevention program, talked with town
residents and the press along Main Street, and held a one-hour town meeting
at the junior high school in the evening.

Although the role of chief of state is often ceremonial, the governor must
be ready to act decisively in a public emergency. In a crisis, his responsibilities as chief of state transcend all other functions. During the first week
of April 1987, large areas of central Maine were flooded because of a sudden
thaw after an above-average winter snowfall. Governor McKernan spent
most of the week visiting in the affected counties, overseeing rescue efforts,

and working with the congressional delegation and various federal administrators to secure financial assistance for flood victims. As one of the governor's chief aides commented, "when a crisis like that comes, everything else
stops."

Legislative and Policy Leader

A second gubernatorial role is that of legislative and policy leader. Although
the Maine legislature tries to protect its independence, it has long depended
on the governor to provide leadership in policy formulation. The chief executive's program is usually the focal point for legislative debates. The program is announced in various ways: through the governor's state-of-the-state
message at the beginning of a legislative session in January, through occasional special messages, and, above all, through the executive budget that
the governor recommends to support state operations. In early January 1989,
McKernan proposed a $3.2 billion two-year budget for the state for 1990–91.
In the following weeks, discussion in both legislative parties and in the media centered almost entirely on the governor's spending requests, which included new projects in solid waste management, education, housing, and
property-tax relief.

Under the state constitution, the governor has some specific legislative
powers. One is the authority to call the legislature into special session. Between 1981 and 1987, the chief executive called the legislature into special
session thirteen times, mostly to consider emergency measures and items remaining from the regular sessions. Special sessions generally last only one
or two days and are focused on the subject matter in the governor's call. For
instance, in October 1987, McKernan called a special session to settle a crisis
in the Maine workers' compensation system triggered by the threat of most
major insurance firms to withdraw from the program. The governor and legislators agreed on reforms that were needed to prevent the collapse of the
system. It has remained a politically volatile issue. The governor also has a
major voice in determining, together with the Legislative Council, what
measures are to be considered in regular sessions of the legislature.

Another power is the executive veto. If a governor vetoes a bill, the legislature must pass the measure by a two-thirds majority in each chamber for it
to become law. Maine chief executives have customarily used their veto
power sparingly, but with great success. During his eight years in office
(1979–87), Governor Joseph Brennan vetoed thirty-three measures, of
which the legislature later passed only four over his objections. Although the
Republican party was in the minority in both chambers during Republican

Governor John McKernan's first term in office (1987–91), the legislature never overrode his veto. Even though the veto is important to the governor as a means to prevent a measure from becoming law, the threat of a veto can be even more potent in securing legislation desired by the governor. McKernan seems to be adept at that process, as suggested in a newspaper report summarizing the results of the 1989 legislative session:

> McKernan told Democrats he would veto the entire state budget if it did not include 85 new positions at the Augusta Mental Health Institute. He said he would veto any property-tax relief package if it did not contain the GOP-backed homestead exemption. . . . And he warned that he would only accept "sin" taxes to finance an omnibus health care package. He got his way in each case.[6]

When the legislature is in session, the governor devotes more time to legislative business than to any other responsibility. Most of this work involves informal negotiation. Meetings with legislators range from personal conferences in the governor's Capitol office, to working lunches at the Blaine House (the governor's official residence) across the street from the Capitol, to organized meetings with the legislative leaders of both parties. During his first term of office, Governor McKernan met regularly with the legislative leadership while the legislature was in session. Of course, governors do not always get their own way. Governor Brennan struggled unsuccessfully through much of his administration to win legislative approval of a measure to require citizens to use automobile seatbelts. Despite his best efforts, McKernan was unable to secure passage of a measure to lengthen the Maine school year by one week. Grass-roots resistance to both ideas was strong and vocal. Neither measure had a serious chance of success in the legislature despite the endorsement by the chief executive.

Among Maine governors in the past several decades, only independent James Longley (1975–79) was mostly unsuccessful in his legislative relations. Longley's combative approach to many issues angered legislators, and he never developed a dependable core of supporters. More than half of the more than one hundred vetoes he cast during his term were overridden. For other governors, the fact that they have had to deal with legislative chambers occasionally controlled by the opposing party has not posed a major obstacle. As an example, Edmund Muskie (1955–59) faced legislatures where the Republican party held about two-thirds of the seats. Muskie reportedly won passage of about 65 percent of the bills he supported, and about

90 percent of the most important bills, by working cooperatively with the Republican leadership.[7]

Today, the outcomes are similar, although the process is more involved because legislation is generally more complex. Governor McKernan's initial legislative staff included three aides, each of whom specialized in the activities of approximately one-third of the administrative departments. The clusters included natural resources, human services, and economic development. Departments would forward their requests to the group, which in turn helped the governor fit the proposals into his overall legislative program.

Chief Administrator

A third role the governor plays is that of chief administrator. Unlike the tasks of chief of state and legislative leader—which have long occupied a prominent place on the governor's schedule—the responsibility of overseeing the executive branch has only recently claimed a major part of the governor's time. It was not until 1971 that Maine provided its chief executive with significant appointive powers. Before that time, the governor lacked administrative authority over many state operations. Beginning with Kenneth Curtis (1967–75), each succeeding governor appears to have devoted increasing attention to program implementation.

The governor currently supervises a cabinet composed of seventeen departmental commissioners, who are appointed by the chief executive (with the consent of the senate) and serve at his pleasure. During the McKernan administration, the cabinet normally meets once a week. The governor's agenda, and issues affecting several departments, are usually given greatest prominence. Nevertheless, portions of each cabinet meeting are given over to reports from individual commissioners on activities within their units. The governor has desired to have all commissioners informed on as many issues as possible. He regards them as representing the entire administration in their public appearances around the state. McKernan also meets individually with several commissioners each week on matters affecting their departments.

Part of the governor's success as administrative chief depends on his relations with the state workforce. Maine has approximately 12,000 executive-branch employees, about two-thirds of whom work in the Augusta area. Both governors Brennan and McKernan tried to improve employee morale and performance. In 1986, under Brennan, the Department of Finance and Administration was divided, so that a separate cabinet department (Department of Administration) could focus specifically on management problems. Within that department a new bureau of employee health was established. When McKernan took office, he named Charles Morrison, the former city manager of Auburn, as the commissioner of the Department of Administration. Morrison helped establish a Maine Executive Institute in cooperation with the Department of Public Administration at the University of Maine to provide two weeks of seminars annually for state agency managers. Beginning in 1987, McKernan devoted approximately one day per month to visiting administrative departments and speaking with their employees. During 1989, the Department of Administration directed the implementation of the Maine Financial and Administrative Statewide Information System (MFASIS). The new technology is intended to place the state government's financial, personnel, and program data in computer-user form for state employees.

Political Party Leader

In addition to the three roles discussed, the governor also serves as head of his or her political party and as such is called upon to help recruit candidates for office, to assist in fund-raising efforts, and to oversee the development of party policy in the legislature. In his first two years in office, McKernan generally held weekly meetings with Republican leaders during legislative sessions, separate from the bipartisan leadership meetings. In 1988, he took part in a fund-raising effort with the Republican State Committee that brought about $160,000 into party coffers. He also campaigned extensively for Republican candidates for the Maine house and senate in that year. Nonetheless, the governor's role in guiding his or her political party is probably less important in Maine than it is in states with more robust party organizations. The governor has very few patronage jobs to dispense. Further, all governors must work with both parties to win approval of their legislative recommendations. Most significantly, candidates generally win office in Maine on the basis of their own personal and political organizations. The party structures alone are too weak to be relied on.

Ombudsman

The role of ombudsman for the state's citizens is another part of the governor's responsibilities. Historically, a portion of the gubernatorial workweek was given over to visits with private citizens. Citizens would present individual problems and requests to the chief executive, who would then follow through with the matter or assign it to an assistant. The governor would often interview people personally before nominating them to state offices and commissions. Modern-day governors are too involved with their administrative and legislative responsibilities to engage heavily in this type of work. In his first year in office, McKernan named about a thousand persons to state government posts; the majority of appointments involved part-time boards and commissions. For every board, files are maintained of suggested candidates, many of whom are recommended by the organizations that deal with the agency. In the McKernan administration, the names were screened by the staff assistant for appointments and the chief of staff; the governor only rarely interviewed a candidate for such a position. In fact, less than 10 percent of his working time in Augusta was assigned to one-on-one meetings with private individuals. The governor's involvement with citizens seemed, instead, to take place mostly outside of the statehouse, especially in towns and cities around the state which he visited as part of Maine's "capital for a day" program.

STATE ADMINISTRATION

Development of the Maine executive branch since 1820 has witnessed the gradual centralization, and structural integration, of many separate agencies under the authority of the governor. The primary reason for administrative change has been the growth in the complexity of executive activities. At the turn of the century, there existed "an administrative organization which totaled some 27 offices, commissions, and boards."[8] Soon afterwards came such new state units as the Industrial Accident Commission, the Highway Commission, and the Department of Charities and Corrections. By 1931, there were twenty single offices and forty-five boards and commissions. Under Governor William Tudor Gardiner (1930–32), some limited consolidations were accomplished, but the state continued to add functions. In 1955, when Edmund Muskie took office, there were more than one hundred separate agencies, many of which were headed by administrators whose terms exceeded that of the governor. Finally, in 1971, Maine adopted the cabinet form of state administration. Under this form, nearly all administrative activities are organized into cabinet departments, each headed by a commissioner who is named by the governor and serves at his or her pleasure.

The arrangement of administrative departments is always in some degree of flux. In 1989, for instance, the legislature abolished the Office of Energy Resources, which had been established in 1973 to deal with a gasoline shortage in the state caused by an Arab embargo on shipments of oil to the United

States. In the same session, legislators were asked to create a new, cabinet-level department for health and another department to deal with children's welfare. Neither proposal won legislative approval in that session, and the Department of Human Services presently operates the programs in health and welfare. In 1990, the legislature authorized creation of a Children's Department, but Governor McKernan vetoed the measure. In late 1991, anticipating a shortfall of approximately $120 million in state revenues by the end of June 1992, McKernan proposed reducing the size of the administrative structure through the privitization of certain functons, such as state mental health centers and liquor stores.

How do Maine people view their state's bureaucracy? Generally, they seem to have a love-hate relationship with it. In a 1988 survey, they agreed by an approximately two-to-one margin with the statement that "it's government's responsibility to assure such basics as housing and health care."9 A substantial majority also indicated that they felt they could influence the government; only a third agreed with the view that "people like me are unable to affect or change the policies of government." Mainers divided fairly evenly on the proposition that "the state bureaucracy is so strong that things will stay pretty much the same no matter whom we elect to office." People who agreed with the last statement were concentrated among older residents, lower-income persons, and longtime residents. The various administrative agencies have grown dramatically in influence in recent years, and will continue to be major players in the state's efforts to meet the challenges of an ever more complex society.

SOME MAJOR DEPARTMENTS

One of the largest departments in the executive branch in number of workers is the Department of Transportation (DOT).10 The department's evolution is fairly typical of the way state administration as a whole grew. It emerged from the State Highway Commission, which was created in 1913 to build roads after the invention of the automobile. The commission was a three-member body, whose chair had a seven-year term. It was made a part of DOT in 1971 along with units regulating ferries, railroads, and airports. The department has seven field offices, which are responsible for maintaining 30,000 miles of state road. It is heavily financed by the state gas tax of nineteen cents per gallon, which can be used only for road and bridge construction and maintenance. Additionally, about one-third of DOT's funds come from the federal government. Unlike some states, Maine's transportation policies are rarely affected by partisan changes in the governorship. For example, the present DOT commissioner, Dana Connors, has served in both the Brennan and McKernan administrations. Connors and his immediate predecessor, George Campbell, had each been successful city managers in the state before being named DOT commissioner.

Another critical agency is the Department of Human Services (DHS). The department began in 1885 with the six-member State Board of Health. In 1913 the legislature created a five-member Board of Charities and Corrections. The boards were merged into a Department of Health and Welfare in 1931, and eventually into the present department in 1975. The current structure tries to make the department accessible to citizens in all areas of the state. DHS has two deputy commissioners, six bureaus, and five regional offices, each of which has at least two field offices. Many of the activities of the department are carried out in conjunction with citizen advisory groups, such as the Maine Council on Alcohol and Drug Abuse Prevention and Treatment, the Advisory Committee for the Division of Deafness, and the Maine Human Services Council. Unlike DOT, DHS underwent a change in philosophy when the governorship shifted from Brennan to McKernan. During the Brennan administration, poverty was thought to be best alleviated by improving the underlying social and economic conditions of the poor. Under McKernan's DHS commissioner, Rollin Ives, education and skill training for the disadvantaged have been promoted as the principal mechanism to lift people out of poverty to a point where they can be self-sufficient.

The Department of Mental Health and Mental Retardation manages six public hospitals in the state. Its main problems in recent years have stemmed from hospital overcrowding and inadequate financial support. In June 1988, the federal government announced that it was cutting $125,000 per month in Medicare funds for the Augusta Mental Health Institute (AMHI), the department's largest facility, because of staff shortages and inadequate recordkeeping. In 1989, the governor, the legislature, and the courts all struggled to find ways to solve the problems of that facility.

The Department of Corrections operates the state prison at Thomaston, four other correctional facilities, and the division of probation and parole. Maine's prison population increased 68 percent between 1980 and 1988, largely in response to the legislature's enacting more severe penalties for various offenses. The department has recently emphasized such approaches as work-release programs and the use of halfway houses, which are intended to reduce the inmate population and to assist the convicted criminal in returning to society. One program, called "intensive supervision," permits the convicted person to remain at his or her home and to travel back and forth to work only. In 1989 the legislature sent out to referendum an approximately $50 million bond issue to construct new prison space, but voters rejected the proposal. They also defeated a smaller bond issue for the same purpose in 1991.

Some administrative departments have relatively small numbers of employees, but major responsibilities because of the way the legislature formulates their mission. A good example is the Department of Education (DE), which has only a few hundred employees even though the state commits the largest portion of the state budget to this department. Most funds are funneled to localities where the vast majority of education personnel are concentrated. The department began in 1846 with a Board of Education, composed of one member from each county. The board named the education commissioner until 1971, when that power shifted to the governor. DE provides technical assistance and regulations for Maine's local school districts and also operates the state's vocational education system. A major problem the McKernan administration has sought to address is the relatively low aspirations of Maine high school students.

Another part of the administrative structure is the Executive Department itself, which contains several agencies, including the Governor's Office and the State Planning Office, which works with the governor and, to a lesser extent, the legislature in setting long-range goals for the state. It provides staff support for the Commission on Maine's Future, an organization of legislators, administrators, and citizens that issues periodic reports on problems and trends affecting Maine. The Planning Office also works on problems that cut across department lines, such as coastal and water resources planning.

Another interesting agency is the Office of Public Advocate, which represents the interests of citizens before independent regulatory bodies, such as the Public Utilities Commission. The Office of Public Advocate argues citizen concerns that otherwise might not be heard in these regulatory proceedings. During the 1989 legislative session, the office became embroiled in some partisan politics. The staff of the office was reduced in the final appropriation bill as the governor and the legislature struggled to find funds for other programs. Some Democrats complained that the McKernan administration was not interested in protecting consumers in future rate-increase cases heard by the Public Utilities Commission.

LEGISLATIVELY FILLED OFFICES

The Maine legislature selects four administrative officials: the attorney general, secretary of state, state treasurer, and state auditor. The most powerful of these officials is the attorney general (AG), who is the state's chief law enforcement officer and the legal representative of the state. Although the AG speaks for the governor and the legislature in the state courts, he or she has the final authority to determine what cases to pursue. Additionally, no state agency can proceed to court without the AG's approval. The office is made up of approximately eighty lawyers, most of whom staff the several administrative departments. About twenty attorneys, for instance, are assigned to the Department of Human Services to work on cases ranging from child abuse to challenges to the licensing procedures for foster homes.

The attorney general has the sole responsibility in Maine for prosecuting homicides, and works with local district attorneys on other criminal cases. In recent years, the office of attorney general has proved attractive to gubernatorial aspirants. Governor Brennan broadened his political support through his handling of the Indian Land Claims cases while attorney general (1975–79). His AG successor, James Tierney, the 1986 Democratic nominee for governor, had pursued numerous cases on behalf of consumers and environmental groups.

The secretary of state maintains the state archives. It is the office that preserves the articles of incorporation for businesses incorporated in Maine. In addition, some of the more controversial aspects of state government are located here. The secretary of state is responsible for the management of all state elections, including ballot printing, tabulations, and maintaining the financial records of candidates. It also is responsible for the registration of motor vehicles and the issuance of motor vehicle licenses.

The state treasurer's main job is to manage the income accruing to the state from various taxes and federal grants, and to sell bonds. The office processes a total of about three million checks per year, exclusive of unemployment compensation payments.

The state auditor is responsible for conducting an annual audit of the accounts of all state agencies and for reporting its findings to the legislature. Maine law requires that localities also have their finances audited once each year, either by the state auditor or a private company. Currently, the state auditor examines the records of about one-fifth of Maine's municipalities (mainly smaller communities) and of approximately three-quarters of the county governments.

CONCLUSION

The governor is the central player in the state government. Notwithstanding the importance of legislative deliberations, the governor's place in the processes of both policy formulation and policy implementation is critical. In modern-day state government, the governor is the most visible state official, the figure most often in the news, and the person who commands the largest sources of information through overseeing the state bureaucracy. Maine's special location seems to add to the prominence of the governor, who deals with international as well as national issues. The governor's power is, however, predominantly the power to persuade. The level of conflict in state government is greatly affected by how the governor uses that power. The chief executive must work with a legislature that is better organized than ever before, a technically sophisticated bureaucracy, and a court system whose decisions affect more and more areas of public policy.

CHAPTER EIGHT

The Court System

Like the other two branches of the state government, Maine courts reflect the distinctive features of the state's politics. Unlike the legislative and the executive branches, however, judges in Maine (with the exception of probate judges) are not subject to popular election. Instead, Maine is one of several New England states that choose judges through gubernatorial selection. However, because the constitution has never provided much detail about how the courts are to work, the elected branches of state government and, broadly speaking, the electorate itself have been able to shape the court system. Since statehood in 1820, the courts have probably changed more fundamentally, in both structure and operation, than have the other two branches.

This chapter examines how the court system's structure, working style, and decisions relate to the state's politics. Mainers seem to have a great deal of pride in their courts. Maine judges, especially the members of its Supreme Judicial Court, are highly respected. Justice in the sense of fairness is taken seriously; courts are frequently visited by public school and college classes. Both trial and appellate court decisions are reported regularly in the press. Major public issues affecting Maine citizens usually find their way into the courts. The resulting decisions are important elements of public policy. Additionally, the courts must deal with the pressures created by the increase in litigation. With caseloads having doubled in the past decade, the courts have been forced to modernize rapidly and to modify some historical practices.

THE CONSTITUTION AND THE COURTS

An understanding of the courts begins with the state constitution. The system that the constitution put in place in 1819 included "one Supreme Judicial

Court and such other courts the Legislature may from time to time establish." The legislature has periodically revamped the court system and modified the jurisdictions of the various courts. The first supreme court consisted
of a chief justice and two associate justices, and had both original and appellate jurisdiction.[1] It sat with either two or three justices at least once a year in
each of the counties, which then numbered nine. The trial court, called the
Court of Common Pleas, had duplicate jurisdiction with the supreme court in
handling original cases. It was composed of a chief justice and two associate
justices who held jury trials throughout the state. In 1839, it was replaced by
a District Court made up of four justices who performed the same function in
different parts of the state. In 1852, the legislature abolished the District
Court and for a time assigned all jury trial responsibilities to the justices of
the supreme court. Individual justices of the Supreme Judicial Court would
sit as trial justices in the various counties, and when needed they would come
together for appellate work. To enable the court to perform both trial and appellate work, the legislature expanded the number of justices to seven in
1852 and to eight in 1855.

That arrangement lasted for about three-quarters of a century. In a few
large counties, rising caseloads slowly required separate trial judges. Thus,
in 1920, such justices were in place in four counties (Cumberland, Kennebec, Penobscot, and Androscoggin), but the members of the Supreme Judicial Court handled trials in the remaining twelve counties. Finally, in 1929,
the legislature created the present Superior Court, whereby one or more trial
justices serve in every county. Because of lessened trial responsibilities, the
number of supreme court justices was reduced to six. However, until the
early 1970s, about half of the working time of supreme court justices still
consisted of trial court work (usually called "single justice work"). Since
that time, increased appellate caseloads led to the virtual disappearance of
that activity. Single justice work, which lasted in Maine longer than in almost any other state, seemed to have a beneficial impact. One outside group,
the Institute for Judicial Administration in New York City, described the system in 1969 when it was fully in operation:

> [I]t allows the justices to maintain closer contact with the public and
> with the members of the practicing bar. This helps the public image
> of the judicial system and makes for cohesiveness within the legal
> profession, contributing to the maintenance of high professional
> standards. [It also] contributes to judicial realism.[2]

THE DISTRICT COURT

Like all states, Maine has courts to handle minor cases, such as traffic cases, hunting and fishing violations, and civil cases involving small amounts of money. These courts have limited jurisdiction. They are the courts with which most citizens come into contact; persons appearing before them generally do not have to be represented by an attorney. The courts hear a very large number of cases, most of which are disposed of fairly quickly. Their judges work without juries. Until 1961, Maine's courts of limited jurisdiction consisted of a confusing group of tribunals. They took the form of approximately seventy-five municipal and trial justice courts, each of which was created by a separate statute. The courts were staffed by part-time judges. Most judges were lawyers, but some had their primary occupation in business or agriculture and performed the role of judge with little or no legal training. As a result, the administration of justice in these courts was uneven and unpredictable.

The arrangement ended in 1961 with the creation of the Maine District Court. In 1989–90, the District Court had twenty-five full-time judges, organized into thirteen districts, who held court at thirty-three locations throughout the state. Every county is served by at least one District Court judge. About one-third of the judges serve at large, which means that they hold court where they are needed anywhere in the state; the remaining judges are assigned to specific locations.

The District Court handles an astonishingly large number of cases. In 1989–90 it disposed of 315,123 cases, a number sufficient to have involved one of every four Maine residents as a plaintiff or defendant.[3] Its caseload has increased by about 40 percent since 1980. Approximately half of the cases in 1989–90 were in the category of "civil violations and traffic infractions." These matters mostly involved such offenses as parking violations and hunting and fishing license violations, and they made up the majority of the 113,820 waivers in 1989–90 (dispositions where the defendant waives a court appearance in favor of paying a fine). Other major types of cases handled by the District Court were criminal traffic offenses, other criminal offenses, such as disorderly conduct and theft, where the penalty did not exceed one year in jail or a $1,000 fine, and civil cases involving money judgments, divorce, family abuse, and small claims. The caseloads are especially heavy in courts located in urban areas. For instance, the District Court in Portland accounted for 64,000 cases (one-fifth of the state caseload) in 1989–90. Appeals from decisions of the District Court go to the Superior Court, the next level in the judiciary.

THE SUPERIOR COURT

The Superior Court is the state's trial court of general jurisdiction. Unlike District Court judges, who are mostly assigned to one location, the sixteen Superior Court justices travel about the state holding terms of court in the state's various counties. The Superior Court shares jurisdiction with the District Court over minor criminal and civil cases; the Superior Court will normally be used if the defendant in a criminal case or the plaintiff in a civil case wishes to have a jury trial. The Superior Court has exclusive jurisdiction over serious criminal offenses (such as murder, arson, rape, aggravated assault, and burglary), civil cases where the monetary amount of damages sought exceeds $30,000, and injunctions.

In 1989–90, the Superior Court disposed of 19,837 cases, of which slightly less than one-third were civil cases and the remaining two-thirds were criminal matters. As far as civil cases were concerned, personal injury matters accounted for the greatest number of dispositions, followed by contract disputes and damage cases. Criminal cases came mainly from two sources. About one-half of that caseload consisted of transfers of minor criminal cases from the District Court because the defendant had requested a jury trial. Most of the remaining cases stemmed from indictments by grand juries. In these instances, a grand jury had concluded (based on information supplied by a district attorney) that sufficient evidence existed to indicate that a serious crime had been committed and to charge a defendant.

Although the Superior Court is the only court in Maine to use juries, the vast majority of cases that come before it are settled without a jury. In 1989–90, only 4 percent of the criminal cases and 3 percent of the civil cases were resolved with the assistance of a jury. Why are juries used so rarely? One reason is that people believe that judges are more objective and better able than juries to handle complex sets of facts, especially in civil trials. Another factor is the greater cost of jury trials. Further, many cases are concluded before a trial can get under way. About half of the civil cases in recent years have ended with the voluntary dismissal of charges by the plaintiff or a stipulation agreed to by all parties. In these instances, the judge brings the parties to the case together, but does not impose a verdict. As far as criminal cases are concerned, a guilty plea is typically entered in about half of them. In another one-quarter of the cases, the district attorney will dismiss the complaint at some point before the proceedings are concluded.

If only those cases in which the trials were *completed* are considered, then juries are employed somewhat more frequently than the overall figures of 4 percent and 3 percent would suggest. In recent years, several dramatic murder trials in the state have used juries and have called attention to their importance in the judicial process. In fact, Maine appears to be resisting a national trend toward the reduced use of juries to resolve civil disputes. In a 1985 ruling, the Maine Supreme Judicial Court held that, under the state constitution, the right to a jury trial exists on any claim in which an award of money is sought.[4]

A longstanding issue in the operation of the District and Superior courts was the problem of guaranteeing the constitutional right of jury trial in a criminal case without overburdening the Superior Court with large numbers of minor cases. At one time, defendants who lost their cases in the District Court would request jury trials (*de novo* trials) in the Superior Court. The practice resulted in a fair amount of plea bargaining between the prosecution and defense in order to save judicial time, and was widely criticized. In 1982, the legislature enacted a measure regulating the handling of criminal cases that may be heard in either the District Court or the Superior Court. The measure authorizes a defendant to waive the right to a jury trial and to be tried in District Court. If the defendant wants a jury trial, he or she must make an affirmative request for it within twenty-one days of a plea entered in District Court. Otherwise the right to a jury trial "shall be deemed waived."

Despite the heavy caseload of some Maine courts, per capita crime rates in the state are among the lowest in the country. In 1989, Maine ranked 43rd in crimes per 10,000 persons, 46th in murders per 100,000 persons, and 44th in violent crimes per 100,000 persons.[5] It ranked 45th among the states in the numbers of sentenced state and federal prisoners per 100,000 persons. The relatively low crime rates have helped enable Maine to operate its judicial system with a fairly small number of judges.

A TRIAL JUDGE AT WORK

What is involved in the work of a trial court judge? In a 1987 article in the *Maine Bar Journal*, Kermit V. Lipez, who was appointed to the Superior Court bench the preceding year, described some of his experiences.[6] He observed that new trial justices are normally assigned to locations outside of their home county for the first year, so that they have an opportunity of "making mistakes" away from the view of former colleagues. As a newcomer, Lipez found it helpful to write out certain of the statements and presentations he was to make orally in order to avoid mistakes. He prepared a bench book on such topics as the Rule 11 proceeding, which takes place when a defendant pleads guilty to a Class A, B, or C offense, and for the task of charging a jury. He also provided the attorneys with copies of his jury charge since the judge's charge to the jury is often the basis for an appeal.

An important task for any justice is maintaining decorum in the court-room, and the responsibility sometimes poses novel challenges. In one instance, Lipez discovered that the jury foreman had marked the special ver-dict form provided to the foreman before the jury had even deliberated, re-cording a unanimous verdict for the defendant. The foreman was excused, and an alternate juror was found to serve in his place. Lipez thinks that the judge's charge to the jury should not necessarily be limited to matters raised in the trial. He believes that juries make assumptions about factors not brought out in the trial (for instance, the amount of insurance held by a de-fendant in an automobile negligence case), and he thinks that a judge should sometimes speak to such concerns. In one instance, jurors asked him to cover in his charge to them several matters not raised in the trial. Supervising the courtroom also means that a judge becomes involved with members of the press. Lipez discovered that the court reporters in the different counties have different working relationships with judges. Some will try to remain in the judge's chambers when conferences are taking place with attorneys, in the event that a judge hands down a ruling. Others will depend on the judge to inform them of his or her rulings.

After his first year on the bench, Justice Lipez found that sentencing was the hardest part of the job. It involves "an unwieldy mix of statutory goals, personal beliefs, inadequate information, limited resources, [and] conflict-ing demands. . . ." He thinks there is a tendency to ignore the victim at the time of a sentencing hearing. Accordingly, the judge may need to speak to that matter. Another difficult problem for a judge is dealing with expert med-ical testimony. So many cases involve medical evidence that Lipez con-cluded that being a judge "is a bit like going to medical school." Finally, Lipez noticed that a depressingly large number of controversies in his court were caused by alcoholism and drug abuse.

THE SUPREME JUDICIAL COURT

As its title implies, the Supreme Judicial Court, the only tribunal mentioned in the state constitution, is the highest court in Maine. It accepts appeals from lower courts. Appeals from its decisions, if they involve a question of U.S. constitutional law, are directed to the U.S. Supreme Court. Before dis-cussing Maine's high court, two points need to be made about semantics.

The apparent redundancy in the title ("Judicial Court") exists because the term *court* was used in colonial Massachusetts, from which Maine borrowed its institutional arrangements, to refer to legislative bodies as well as to judicial agencies. (The Massachusetts legislature is officially still called the Great and General Court.) Second, in the state's legal community, the Maine Supreme Judicial Court is commonly called the "Law Court," a term that arose because, historically, so much of the work of supreme court justices was single-justice (trial) work. The reference of "Law Court" is to the collective work of supreme court justices as they perform their appellate function of reviewing lower court decisions.

The Supreme Judicial Court has seven members, presided over by a chief justice. Its main job is to hear appeals from civil and criminal decisions in the Superior and District courts and to decide questions of law arising from those cases. In 1989, the Law Court disposed of 452 cases, including 341 with written opinions. Approximately 60 percent of its caseload involved civil matters, and about 40 percent embraced criminal proceedings. The Law Court altered the result of the lower court in 16 percent of the cases it heard, which were about evenly divided between civil and criminal matters. The Law Court's impact was especially pronounced in state agency administrative proceedings, such as liquor license revocations. Of the twenty-five such cases handled with written opinions, the court modified the lower court decisions in eight instances.

The relatively small portion of cases heard by the Supreme Court that end in a reversal (16 percent) resembles the pattern found in other states which, like Maine, have but one appeals court. Supreme courts in these states must review all cases appealed from the various trial courts, whether or not the cases raise novel or important points of law. The top courts in the smaller states differ from the supreme courts in those states, mostly large urban states, that use intermediate appeals courts. In those jurisdictions, the lower appeals courts first screen the cases, leaving only the most difficult and controversial issues for the top court.

In addition to reviewing cases from lower courts, the Maine Supreme Judicial Court has certain specialized functions. One is the appellate review of sentences. Until 1965, the court could review only the legality of sentences imposed by trial judges, not their propriety. In that year, the Court established an Appellate Division, composed of three judges, which had the authority to add to or reduce a convicted individual's sentence. In the 1980–88 period, the Appellate Division ordered a total of twelve sentence modifications. In 1989, the division was replaced by a Sentence Review Panel, composed of three judges with the power solely to grant or deny leaves to appeal from sentences. If the panel grants an appeal, the full supreme court reviews the sentence and hands down its judgment. Although modifications of the work of trial judges are infrequent, the supreme court's concern with sentencing practices seems to have helped make those practices more uniform among Maine courts.

Another function of the court is to provide, on the formal request of the governor or either house of the legislature, an advisory opinion on "important questions of law" being considered by the other branch of government. The justices of the court write about one advisory opinion per year (they sign the opinion individually). Recent opinions have dealt with such issues as forestry taxation, legislative procedures relative to the overriding of the governor's veto, and state ownership of certain lands.

A third responsibility of the Supreme Judicial Court is to deal with occasional problems of judicial misconduct. In instances of alleged misconduct, the Committee on Judicial Responsibility and Disability, composed of lawyers, judges, and laypersons, first undertakes a study of the allegations of misconduct. It recommends a course of action to the court, which makes the final decision. As an example, in 1985, the court suspended for one month District Judge John Benoit, who at that time presided over the Farmington/ Skowhegan courts, fined him $1,000, and formally censured him. Benoit was found to have ordered the jailing of people in three cases in which imprisonment was not an allowable punishment under Maine law.[7]

Maine's Law Court is one of only two state supreme courts that has no building of its own (the other is Louisiana). The court most often convenes in the Superior Court building in Portland. In the late 1980s, the legislature authorized a study commission to make plans for the construction of a supreme court building in Augusta, which may take several years to realize. The fact that the Supreme Judicial Court is a "homeless" court affects certain of its working procedures. While the justices sit together to hear a case on appeal argued orally and discuss it in a conference, they perform the actual opinion-writing tasks in chambers in their home county court houses, circulating the opinions among themselves by mail or fax machine.

Compared to other state supreme courts, the Law Court has traditionally revealed a high degree of consensus. Fewer than 10 percent of the cases decided on appeal have registered a dissenting opinion. When a dissenting opinion is presented, it usually seems to reflect the personal views of the justice or justices writing it. A survey several years ago among the justices found no one who recalled an instance where a dissenting opinion later became a majority opinion.[8] The absence of dissent from Maine Supreme Judicial Court opinions undoubtedly has cultural roots. The court, like other state political institutions, seems inclined to follow a moderate course on most issues. Its justices generally see their role as "law-interpreters" rather than as "law-makers." Nonetheless, the growing number of policy questions presented to the justices in the past two or three years has seemed to impel the justices to become more expressive. The supreme court in 1991 allowed the use of television cameras in courtrooms by a vote of four to three. The court was also sharply divided in a major shoreland-zoning case, to be considered presently.

Judicial Backgrounds

What backgrounds do the justices of the Law Court bring to their work? One common trait is prior judicial experience, nearly always on the Superior Court bench.[9] Four of the seven justices in 1990 had earlier served as Superior Court justices for periods ranging from five to twelve years, including two who had served as chief justice of the Superior Court. The other three Law Court justices had been appointed from private practice. They included the chief justice, Vincent McKusick, appointed in 1977, and the first woman member of the Supreme Judicial Court, Caroline Glassman, appointed in 1982. The appointment of lawyers in private practice directly to the supreme court was more common before the formation of the Superior Court. In the years between 1900 and 1920, according to one study, less than one-quarter of Maine supreme court justices had had as many as five years of judicial experience on lower courts of any kind.[10]

Another important characteristic of supreme court justices is extensive political experience. The seven justices in 1990 had generally been active in their political parties before their elevation to the bench, holding such positions as Republican leader of the state senate, Democratic mayor of Lewiston, candidate for the Portland city council, chair of the Portland Young Republican Club, and Democratic candidate for Congress from the Second Congressional District. At first blush, the high level of partisan activity among Maine's top judges seems surprising since party organizations are not strong in the state. The substantial party activity is probably related to the need of prospective high-court justices to become known around the state. No statewide elective office other than the governorship exists. Thus, service in their political parties seems to afford ambitious attorneys a means of building the political support needed to win a major judicial appointment.

Six of the seven 1990 justices obtained their undergraduate degrees from

Maine colleges (two from Bates College, two from Bowdoin College, one from Ricker College, one from the University of Maine). All but one, however, received his or her law degree from an out-of-state law school. The median age of the justices in 1990 was sixty-two years.

The most important judicial appointment a governor makes is filling the chief justiceship. Recent governors have been inclined to nominate individuals with whom they are politically and ideologically compatible. In so doing, they have tended to disregard the principle of seniority. In 1971, Governor Kenneth Curtis promoted Armand Dufresne, Jr., then an associate justice, to the position of chief justice. The appointment provoked some controversy because another, more senior associate justice had received a higher rating from the Maine Bar Association. Observers believed that in naming Dufresne, Curtis wanted to recognize the state's French community, which had strongly supported him in his election campaigns. Governor James Longley followed a similar approach in 1977, when he nominated Vincent McKusick, a Portland attorney, as chief justice. McKusick was a highly regarded lawyer who had represented major business organizations. He seemed to fit Longley's preference to have a relatively conservative chief justice, and one who also had a strong interest in court administration.

Court Decisions

The court has handed down several important rulings in recent years. In *Davies* v. *City of Bath* (1976), the Law Court permitted Maine citizens for the first time to sue the state and its political subdivisions under certain circumstances.[11] This ruling overturned the longstanding practice by Maine courts of shielding those government divisions against suits by citizens on the basis of the doctrine of governmental immunity. In 1989, the court handed down a critical ruling on a different problem. In *Bell* v. *Town of Wells*, the court effectively closed what had long been regarded as a public beach in that town.[12] It maintained that landowners' deeds gave them ownership of Moody Beach from a seawall to the low-tide mark, and that the public's right of access extended only to such activities as fishing and boating. This case was important because most of Maine's coastline is privately owned, and because only about thirty-five miles of the coast, like Moody Beach, is sandy and usable for swimming. After the decision, the Town of Wells began action to purchase some of the properties so that townspeople and tourists would have access to the beach.

Other significant cases have involved the liability of private companies for certain acts. In a 1986 case of a shipyard worker who died from exposure to asbestos, the court held that manufacturers can be held responsible for injuries caused by their products even though the exposure took place before the state's strict liability law went into effect. It further ruled that widows of victims could collect damages under Maine's Wrongful Death Act. On the other hand, in 1988 the court dismissed a $1-million award to victims of a traffic accident caused by an employee of a company who had consumed liquor at the company's Christmas party, in light of the fact that the company had a policy against the consumption of alcoholic beverages on its property, and so the employee had purchased the liquor elsewhere. The court believed that to hold the company liable would be to "prescribe a paternalistic duty upon employers generally." In a 1991 case, however, the court held that a passenger who permits an intoxicated person to drive his or her car can be tried as an accomplice to the crime of operating under the influence.

Several supreme court decisions have involved medical problems. The court held in 1988 that a fetus is not a person, and therefore cannot be the subject of a wrongful death claim. Maine is in the minority of states adhering to that position. In another case, it held that a patient can recover damages for serious mental distress because of the negligence of a psychotherapist. The defendant had become emotionally involved with the companion of a patient whom she was treating. The court held that no underlying tort or civil wrong had to exist to lodge a claim of distress in the light of the patient's condition. In 1986, it held that women as well as men may be prosecuted for statutory rape. Finally, in a dramatic ruling in late 1987, the court held that life support systems could be removed from a comatose patient in a situation where the patient, in this case a young man with irreversible brain injury, had indicated before his accident that he would not wish to be kept alive in such a circumstance. The court in that case cited authorities ranging from John Stuart Mill's *On Liberty* to various legal and medical articles.

Judicial Review

As part of its work, the Maine Supreme Judicial Court performs the important task of judicial review, whereby it determines the consistency of Maine laws with the state and federal constitutions. If it finds that a law is contrary to either constitution, it will declare it void. To illustrate, the court has been aggressive in protecting the right of free speech, which is guaranteed in both the U.S. and Maine constitutions. In *State* v. *Events International, Inc.* (1987), the court declared void a provision in the Maine Charitable Solicitation Law that required solicitors for charitable organizations to report, in certain instances, the percentage of each dollar contributed that was actually received by the charity.[13] Earlier, in a 1983 case, the court had invalidated an order of the the Maine Labor Relations Board banning dissident faculty members at the University of Maine from distributing information concerning a collective bargaining agreement.[14]

In other policy areas, according to a 1988 analysis by Maine Deputy Attorney General Cabanne Howard, the Law Court has "readily sustained legislation against a wide variety of attacks."[15] This posture is exemplified in the court's handling of cases concerned with legislative delegations of power to executive agencies and regulatory boards, especially ones dealing with environmental concerns. Here the court appears to have shifted its views in the past two decades. Howard points out that the Maine Supreme Judicial Court gave a fairly restrictive interpretation of the Wetlands Act of 1970 shortly after its enactment. However, in more recent times, it has upheld regulatory legislation according to standards that are highly deferential to the executive and legislative branches. In 1985, for instance, the court held that a plaintiff seeking to overturn a law on substantive due process grounds must undertake the difficult burden of establishing a "complete absense of any state of facts that would support the need for the [legislation]."[16] Because it has moved toward greater acceptance of the work of the elected branches, it seems unlikely that in the near future the court will exercise the power of judicial review much beyond the area of civil rights.

SPECIAL COURTS

Maine uses special courts for certain types of cases. One example is the probate courts, which have had constitutional status since 1819. The probate court in each county handles estates and trusts, adoptions and name changes, and guardianship cases. Initially, the governor named the probate judges, but since 1855 these judges have been elected on a partisan ballot. The judges, who serve four-year terms, are part-time and work without a jury. Appeals of probate court decisions on matters of law go to the Supreme Judicial Court.

An administrative court was created in 1973 to consider cases concerned with the suspension and revocation of licenses issued by administrative agencies, as well as agency refusal to grant licenses. The court's two judges are appointed by the governor and work without a jury. The vast majority of the cases in this court arise from the Bureau of Liquor Enforcement. Appeals on questions of law from this court are first heard in the superior court.

A third specialized court is the small-claims court, which is really a special session of the District Court, and which is convened in each district on certain days of the month. Procedures are more informal than during regular sessions of the District Court, and individuals involved in small-claims disputes generally do not need attorneys. Small-claims proceedings must be limited to cases where the contested amount is less than $1,400.

COURT ADMINISTRATION

The Maine courts have become big business in recent years. With case filings now exceeding 300,000 per year, judicial administration has grown in importance. Historically, the principal tool available to the Supreme Judicial Court was power to review lower court decisions. The high court had little control over trial courts because, historically, these courts were locally financed and staffed by the counties and towns in which they were located. Beginning in 1961, with the creation of the District Court, the state began to take over the funding of trial courts. In their present status as fully financed state agencies, both the District Court and the Superior Court have gradually become subject to centralized management. In 1975, Maine established the Administrative Office of the Courts, directed by a state court administrator who is appointed by and reports to the chief justice of the Supreme Judicial Court. The office prescribes and maintains fiscal records, prepares the judicial budget, examines dockets to determine where delays may exist that require additional personnel, oversees clerical functions, and looks after court facilities and matters of court security.

The Superior and District courts each have their own chief judge and court administrator. Those officials are responsible for working with local developers, county commissioners, and municipal officials to ensure that adequate court facilities exist in each county. Additionally, the chief justice of the Supreme Judicial Court and the state court administrator meet with them bimonthly to address administrative and policy issues. In recent years, the courts have computerized many of their operations. Criminal and traffic case processing has been automated in all District Court locations, and communication networks have been established between the Administrative Office of the Courts and regional court locations and various other state offices.

The growth of centralized judicial administration has not taken place without political conflicts. The most difficult problems have surrounded the integration of the District Court into the Judicial Department. Before the creation of the District Court, judges of trial courts of limited jurisdiction enjoyed considerable latitude in handling caseloads. With the arrival of Chief Justice Armand Dufresne, Jr., court modernization and centralization became high priorities. In December 1976, Dufresne abruptly dismissed the chief judge and the deputy chief judge of the District Court from their leadership jobs because he believed that the two officials were dragging their feet in implementing changes that he and the state court administrator were attempting to bring about.[17] To improve coordination, the new chief judge created a Planning and Advisory Committee, composed of seven district judges. The group produced a Bench Book for use throughout the Maine District Court's various locations.

One task involved in judicial administration is developing ways whereby certain categories of disputes can be settled without resort to the courts. The Maine Court Mediation Service provides for the mediation of domestic relations cases, small claims, landlord-tenant disputes, and other civil cases. Since 1984, Maine law has required mediation in all domestic relations cases in which minor children are involved and in those cases in which a trial is requested. Approximately sixty mediators, distributed among seven regions in the state, work with the various District Court and Superior Court judges on a part-time basis. In 1989–90, the Mediation Service handled 5,596 cases, resolving about half of them without a trial.

The Judicial Department also operates a Court Appointed Special Advocate Program (CASA) under which trained volunteers look after the needs of abused and neglected children. The volunteers replaced state-paid attorneys who had earlier performed the work. The CASA volunteer, who receives considerable training, is a party to all administrative and judicial matters affecting the child. Between 1986 and 1990, nearly 1,500 children were involved in the program.

CONCLUSION

That Maine has been able to operate successfully with a relatively small judiciary (approximately fifty judges) may partly be attributed to its moralistic culture. The state manifests a substantial degree of consensus on political values. While the courts establish important rules of public policy, they only rarely encounter and attempt to settle strongly partisan or ideological conflicts. When such issues do arise, the tendency of the Supreme Judicial Court as the state's only appeals court is to write opinions that adhere closely to the facts of the case. Decisions of the courts are widely accepted. Unlike some other state courts, the Maine judiciary is not a battleground among competing political or legal viewpoints. As the dean of the University of Maine Law School commented in 1988, the reason seems to be simply that "there isn't much ideology in Maine politics."[18]

The consensus on values has also permitted the courts to evolve into one of the nation's most centralized and well-coordinated state judiciaries. In the past, the courts, like the legislature, operated intimately, in an almost neighborhoodlike fashion, with citizens. That process is no longer possible. The centralization that has taken place in the courts has produced some tensions. However, because public officials and citizens alike tend to share the same values, the centralization has not created a gulf between the courts and the citizens. The quality of justice remains high, and judicial administration is almost certainly more efficient than in the past. Yet the volume of court business continues to grow, and the judicial system will become more complex. In the future, the state will almost certainly need an intermediate appeals court, located between the Supreme Judicial Court and the trial courts, to keep the Law Court's job manageable.

CHAPTER NINE

Maine's Budget as Policy

In the study of state policymaking, the budget is not always appreciated for its central role. Perhaps this stems from the complexity and arcane language of the budget, and the sheer bulk of its figures, making it seem rather too intimidating to be helpful. However, in a 1980 study of Vermont and New Hampshire, Richard Winters called the state budget "the primary instrument of public policy."[1] Maine's budget is no exception, and can be treated as a window through which to witness the development of important state policies. Maine's budget can also be seen as an important influence on governmental and popular attitudes toward certain policies, and even toward public policies in general.

THE BUDGET PROCESS

As in any state, Maine's budget is affected by many different factors, including the actions of the political parties, interest groups, the governor, executive agencies, the legislature, the courts, the media, and, of course, the public. Other considerations involve the context in which budgets are drawn up, and center on such issues as available revenue, total debt, projections of federal assistance and unfunded mandates, statutory and constitutional limitations, and, very importantly, the previous budget. Each approved budget is the reconciliation of these and other elements.

Preparing the budget is the first step. This takes place in all state agencies and departments, which prepare budget requests, sometimes called *biennial budget requests* because they outline the state government's needs for the next two fiscal years. Maine is among a minority of states that prepare their budgets biennially.[2] The budget is approved during the Maine legislature's first session (in an odd-numbered year), and the budget is revised during the second session (the following even-numbered year).

The reason for Maine's biennial budget is that, until recently, the legislature met every other year. A biennial budget is often more demanding on the already complex process of projecting future sources of revenue and expenditure. However, Maine has been fairly successful in managing the problem. In the 1980s, Maine enjoyed revenue surpluses when some states were experiencing revenue shortfalls. In 1990, however, the state encountered a revenue shortfall of slightly over $210 million for the 1990–91 biennium. Still, the process has worked sufficiently well that attempts to change it to an annual process have not been successful.

One reason why Maine's legislature began meeting every year was to oversee the budget more effectively. This change, which was constitutionally mandated, occurred in 1975. Probably because the legislature knew that it would be meeting the following year, only half of the budget document was approved in 1975, in what was the closest thing to an annual budget that Maine has ever had. The result was not considered a success, mainly because the departments and agencies had prepared biennial budget requests.[3] Whatever the reasons, the failure of this attempt to draw up an annual budget must only have reinforced the legislature's somewhat conservative posture toward procedures.

Under Maine law, on or before the first of September in even-numbered years, all state departments and agencies requesting state funds must submit their requests to the Bureau of the Budget. Because up to ten months pass between the submission of these requests and their approval as part of the final budget document, adjustments often need to be made. These alterations reflect, among other things, inflation and other changes in the economy, new developments in program needs, and changes in federal funding. Such flexibility is not only an important component of any budget process, it is crucial to the biennial schedule.

The governor receives the budget requests through the Bureau of the Budget. Reviewing each agency's requests, the governor, working with the bureau, may make adjustments as deemed necessary. When this review is finished, all the budget requests, as well as the recommendations of the governor, are assembled into a budget document. This usually occurs during January or February in odd-numbered years. Until about a decade ago, the budget requests did not reflect all of the revenue expected to be available; instead, the legislature budgeted only for the expected general and highway revenues, as well as liquor and lottery revenues. After the legislature de-

cided that it needed more information on which to base its budgetary decisions, all funds were included in the budget requests.[4] Since the early 1980s,
these funds have included federal expenditure funds and federal block
grants, as well as certain dedicated state revenues.

The governor's budget estimates will occasionally change as new information becomes available, sometimes complicating the legislature's work.
In June 1989, Governor John McKernan, confronting a slowdown in the
state economy, lowered his tax collection estimates for the existing fiscal
year and for the upcoming biennium (1990–91) by over $100 million and
scaled down his original spending requests by over $60 million. The revision
came just two weeks before the legislature was scheduled to adjourn, at a
time when lawmakers were beginning to make final decisions on spending
requests.

The budget document is divided into two principal parts. Part I is composed of funding requests for existing programs, including personnel needs,
or what state officials call requests "to keep the store open." Part II is devoted to requests for new and expanded programs and staff. Like the biennial
schedule, this format has long been popular with the legislature, which has
resisted efforts to make major modifications. Governor James Longley tried
to persuade the legislature to combine the two parts, so that the "total picture" of the state budget would be more readily ascertainable, but his plan
met with little support.[5] The two-part arrangement assumes a distinction between existing costs and new costs that is not always realistic. For example,
the third year of a three-year salary contract beginning in 1992 between
Maine and state government employees would be a Part I item in the 1994–95
biennial budget, even though the revenues for that budget are not yet authorized.

Legislative approval is the second step of the budget process. The legislature receives the budget proposals from the governor in the form of several
bills. For the 1990–91 biennium, the budget was composed of fifteen bills.
The legislature refers the budget document to the Joint Standing Committee
on Appropriations and Financial Affairs. The Appropriations Committee
next holds public hearings on the requested funding for each department or
agency. When the hearings are completed, adjustments to the bills are made
by the Appropriations Committee, which then votes on the new drafts. The
legislature receives the committee's report on the bills for final approval during June of odd-numbered years, because the fiscal year begins the next
month.

The procedure outlined above pertains to bills included in Part I of the budget document. These bills require funding for existing programs. Bills that are included in Part II are usually treated differently. These measures, which ordinarily seek to initiate major changes in an existing program or to create a new program, are generally referred to a joint standing committee whose jurisdiction embraces the subject matter of the proposed measure. For instance, a bill to restructure land-use laws would most likely be handled by the Energy and National Resources Committee. These bills are often not passed until the last day of the session to ensure that all existing programs have been funded. Out of the revenue that remains, the legislature appropriates money to the new bills. The Legislative Council sets priorities among the measures, and the legislature almost always follows council recommendations.

The third step of the budget process involves the execution of the budget. Neither the agencies nor the departments can expend their approved funding without executive authorization. Such authorization is conducted on a quarterly allotment system. Each agency or department submits an annual work program that outlines the year's expenses. The program is approved by the Bureau of the Budget on a quarterly basis. Only then can the agency expend its funding. Any necessary adjustments in the funding are made within each of the quarterly authorizations. These adjustments, however, cannot change the total amount of funding, something that only the legislature can approve.

After the execution of the budget, the final step in the process is its audit. The state auditor carries out this function and issues an annual report on the finances of state government.

Maine has a statute (5 MRSA, sec. 1664) which requires that the budget summary show the "balanced relations" between the total anticipated revenues and the total proposed expenditures. It is useful now to analyze revenues and expenditures in some detail. By separating the revenue into its major sources, we can examine how these sources have affected policy decisions. Through tracing the major expenditures, we can see how these policies have changed historically, expressing the responsibilities of the state over a long period.

REVENUES

State revenues grew from $24,000 in 1820, the first year of statehood, to over $2.4 billion in fiscal year 1991. It would be a mistake, however, to think that the gap between these figures is due only to the distance in years. During the 1820–1990 period, the sources of the state's income changed signifi-

Table 2: Maine Revenues Compared with All-State Average Revenues as a Percentage of Total General Revenues, Fiscal Year 1989

	Maine	All States
Federal Grants	24.1	22.4
Sales Taxes	27.9	28.7
Income Taxes	24.1	23.3
Charges	6.6	8.0
Other	17.3	17.6

Source: U.S. Bureau of the Census, State Government Finances in 1989 (Washington, D.C.: U.S. Government Printing Office, 1990).

cantly. In the past, revenue changes were often in direct response to the state's increasing responsibilities, if not the imminent threat of bankruptcy. But change did not always end in solvency, or in funding for a new program. New sources of revenue created new policy expectations, which in turn made new demands on revenue. It has been Maine's expanding revenue base which has been responsible for the creation of a large state bureaucracy.

As table 2 illustrates, Maine is similar to other states in revenue policies, except in federal grants, which have constituted a larger portion of the Maine budget than they do of the budgets of most other states. One reason for this is that Maine has usually been in the bottom third of the states in per capita income. Like most other states in that category, Maine has customarily received above-average levels of federal funds because many federal grant-in-aid programs are based partly on need.

Federal grants-in-aid expanded during the 1960s and 1970s, and even as they leveled off during the Carter and Reagan administrations, they formed a larger portion of state revenues than in earlier decades. During the same period, Maine's government began to shift control from fairly conservative Republicans to more liberal Democrats, who pursued grants more actively. Maine's ranking among the states in per capita revenues from the federal government changed from the national position of thirty-second in 1965 to seventh in 1989. The acquisitive orientation toward federal aid programs was only partly a product of partisan change, however.

The rise of the Democratic party occurred during a period when the state began collecting new types of revenue. In 1951, the state established a general sales tax on all retail sales except those falling under specific exemptions, such as food. (Exemptions have become numerous, currently totaling over $600 million per year.) The legislature established a personal and corporate income tax in 1969. Under challenge, it was approved by the state's voters in a 1970 referendum, to the surprise of many state officials. Sales and income taxes supply revenue that can be described as "elastic" because both forms of taxation are highly sensitive to changes in the state economy. Examples of "inelastic" revenue sources are the "sin taxes" on cigarettes, alcohol, hotel rooms, and horse racing, which tend to remain fairly stable despite economic fluctuations.

Richard Winters has argued that the creation of elastic revenue sources in Vermont (notably the income tax in 1931) eventually led to an acquisitive orientation toward federal aid programs.[6] High revenues starting in the mid-1950s led to expanded program funding and bureaucratic growth. These factors helped influence Vermont officials to depend on a rapid growth of spending programs, which translated into reliance on federal aid starting in the 1960s. Although Maine is not generally considered quite as progressive as Vermont, it experienced a similar pattern.

Once established in 1951, the sales tax rose quickly to become the state government's primary source of tax revenue, producing 75 percent of Maine's own-source revenue in 1960. The income tax, however, would surpass the sales tax as a catalyst of state policy change. Since its passage, the income tax's portion of state tax revenue has grown impressively, largely because of the tremendous increase in wages over the last two decades. The rapid growth of the state administration and the creation of programs in environmental and social policy during the 1960s and 1970s came at a time of economic growth in the state. The highly elastic revenues of the income and sales taxes were responsive to changes in the economy, providing the state treasury with necessary funds.

The other side of the coin is that the state budget suffers during periods of recession. At the end of 1989, Maine, like many other states, witnessed a slowdown in its economy, and a consequent challenge to its budget commitments. Sales and income tax returns fell below earlier projections, as was the case in other New England states. In early 1990, Governor McKernan estimated that Maine faced a $210 million shortfall in state revenue over the remaining 1990–91 biennium. The McKernan administration sought alternatives other than new taxes to compensate for the unexpected shortfalls. Among the suggested new revenue sources were a second state lottery and a tax amnesty program offering inducements to delinquent taxpayers if they paid their back taxes during 1990. Democrats and some Republicans were critical of the proposals, and the state faces the prospect of an increase in some tax rates in the early 1990s.

Because state spending, as well as need, is a major criterion of federal aid programs, Maine's share of federal dollars continued to grow with its expenditures. In 1989, Maine ranked seventh in the nation in terms of per capita federal aid, while Vermont followed at eighth.[7] New Hampshire, which still does not have an income or a sales tax, ranked near the bottom of the states in terms of per capita general expenditures and per capita federal grants.[8] While Maine and Vermont both ranked near the middle of the states in terms of their per capita expenditures, Vermont was somewhat higher. This supports the idea that Maine occupies a middle position in terms of state governmental activism among the three northern New England states.

From 1969 to 1987, Maine's income tax rates were revised once, in 1978. In 1987, the legislature passed a measure to incorporate the changes made by the federal Tax Reform Act of 1986 into Maine's income tax law. The move was necessary because Maine income tax provisions are coupled to federal income tax requirements. As an example, most deductions that are permitted under federal rules are permissible under state law. When the federal government enacted the 1986 revisions, it reduced its tax rates and eliminated many deductions. Until the state reduced its own rates, Maine taxpayers paid an excess of dollars to the state government because they could not claim the deductions permitted in previous years. The governor and legislature grappled with the problem in 1987 and 1988, during which time most Maine taxpayers received rebates.

In 1989, legislators reshaped the state income tax code. The revisions were based on recommendations of a nonpartisan consulting firm from Washington, D.C., which had been commissioned to review the state's tax system. The reforms have resulted in tax decreases for about 90 percent of Maine's taxpayers.[9] With the unexpected revenue shortfalls of 1989 and 1990, Maine's revised income tax structure has again become controversial. Some legislators, like state Senator Paul Gauvreau (D., Lewiston), blamed shortages of revenue partly on the recent reforms. Their argument has been that the changes in the income tax made it less progressive.

A continuing feature of Maine's tax policy is change, created out of the need to develop new revenue sources and to modify old sources to meet changing circumstances. This can be illustrated by glancing at the state's original forms of revenue. Until the 1840s, Maine was against the principle of direct taxation, considering it, in the words of the state treasurer in 1836, the "most odious and the most expensive way of sustaining the government."[10] Revenues were instead based on the sales of public lands, which boomed in the 1830s. Then changes in the national and state economy and a border dispute with Canada caused the state to borrow so heavily that its credit was nearly ruined. By 1840, Maine had no choice but to levy a property tax, which would become one of the most important sources of state revenue.[11]

Maine's reliance on the property tax, like that of most other states, began to diminish around the turn of the century. Today, the property tax is the primary source of revenue for local government, as it is in the other New England states. Recently, Maine has experienced a growing controversy about the property tax. Because property taxes are assessed according to real estate values, but must be paid out of current income, they have been particularly onerous in those parts of the state where property values have skyrocketed within the last two decades.

In 1989, lawmakers in Augusta passed a property-tax relief package that was one of the most important parts of the 1990–91 budget. Over half of the state revenues ($1.5 billion) were earmarked to assist local governments and school units.[12] Under the current revenue-sharing program, the state annually returns approximately 5 percent of sales and income tax revenues to towns and cities; the allotment for each locality is determined by a formula that weighs the community's population and wealth as measured by property valuation. In the budget crisis of 1991–92, Governor McKernan and members of the legislature discussed the possibility of suspending or terminating the revenue-sharing program. Its future in the 1990s is thus uncertain.

Another way in which the state has tried to ease the burden of the property tax is through a circuit-breaker program. For local taxpayers whose property taxes exceed 4.5 percent of their gross household income, the state will pay one-half of the amount of the difference. The program is available to persons whose annual incomes are less than $60,000; the maximum permissible refund is $3,000. The annual cost to the state for this tax relief program is about $20 million. In addition, under the Elderly Household Tax and Rent Refund program, citizens sixty-two years of age or older are eligible for additional funds to pay their property taxes if their incomes fall below certain levels.

EXPENDITURES

The expenditures made by Maine's government since 1820 chart the emergence and decline of various policies in the state and the growth of government responsibility. In 1820, the state's expenditures ($38,000) were essentially devoted to setting up and sustaining the new institutions of government. The greatest outlays were spent on the legislature and on government administration, while education followed as the third greatest expenditure.[13] By the eve of the Civil War, state spending priorities had changed. Except for the redemption of the funded debt (brought on by the excessive borrowing of the 1830s), education experienced the greatest outlay of state funds, followed by government administration and, lastly, by the legislature.

The pattern of spending was fairly consistent until 1915, when outlays for highway construction and maintenance, triggered by the automotive revolution, mushroomed. The peak years of Maine's highway construction (1917–32) and the onset of the Great Depression left the state in debt, and most allotments to highways were sharply curtailed for the next few years.[14] By the end of the 1930s, however, allocations to highways increased to the extent that transportation became the primary recipient of state funds, which was customary in rural states of that period. By the 1960s, the picture changed again. Education's share of state funds began to surpass those earmarked for transportation. Although this change reflected a more liberal climate in Augusta at the time, education became a high priority of both political parties.

During Governor Edmund Muskie's administration, the passage of the Sinclair Act consolidated scores of tiny high schools, some with only three or four regular teachers, into larger units called School Administrative Districts (SADs) to provide more facilities to students. Enrollment in Maine's universities and colleges subsequently rose in the next decade. In 1973, however, Maine ranked thirty-second in the nation in terms of its teacher salaries, and despite share increases in spending, the state was still far below the national average in terms of the overall money it allocated to education.[15] With this in mind, Maine's outlays to education in 1989, which on a per capita basis are fairly close to national averages, are more significant than they may appear at first glance.

As table 3 indicates, Maine is relatively generous in providing welfare assistance, with the 1989 welfare expenditures accounting for a roughly one-fifth larger portion of the Maine state budget than the corresponding average welfare percentage for all the states.[16] Several factors help to explain this difference, including Maine's moralistic political culture, its traditionally low per capita income, and the federal government's policy of granting additional funds to states that commit expenditures to federally approved programs.

Maine's strong commitment to welfare, like that of nearby Vermont, represents a strong divergence from its conservative Republican past. In 1936, Maine and Vermont were the only two states that did not vote to reelect Franklin D. Roosevelt. As late as the 1950s, Maine's assistance to persons

Table 3: Maine Expenditures Compared with All-State Average Expenditures as a
Percentage of Total General Expenditures, Fiscal Year 1989

	Maine	All States
Education	34.9	36.9
Public Welfare	23.6	19.8
Transportation	8.9	9.1
Health, Hospitals	5.5	8.2
Government Administration	4.3	3.5
Natural Resources	2.8	1.9
Other	20.0	20.6

Source: U.S. Bureau of the Census, State Government Finances in 1989 (Washington, D.C.: U.S. Government Printing Office, 1990).

who were blind, disabled, aged, or dependent children was only two-thirds of the prevailing national level.[17] By the early 1970s, welfare's portion of Maine's per capita expenditures had grown, but was still only around 90 percent of the national level. The growth came about slowly, and sometimes over strong opposition, but the emergence of liberal majorities in the state legislature permitted the higher standards of assistance to prevail.[18]

As table 3 shows, Maine spends somewhat less on health and hospitals than do other states, perhaps because of its small population. Greater portions of state funds, however, are spent on the natural environment in Maine as compared with national averages. This difference is not surprising, considering the state's rural character, its unique geography, and the enormous reliance that industries have on the natural environment. In addition, the economic development of recent years has had a strong impact on the environment, demanding a corresponding commitment from the state government. For example, the leading expenditure covered under Maine's natural resources allocations today is for solid waste management. The 1990–91 budget funded the creation of a new Solid Waste Management Authority to help implement an integrated, statewide program of waste management.[19]

Interestingly, Maine spends a bit more on its state government, again as measured by the percentage of funds committed in the total state budget, than do other states. The legislature, for instance, has recently ranked among the ten most costly state legislatures on a per capita basis, even though it is a mostly citizen body.[20] The large size of the legislature and the extensive network of administrative field offices needed to cover the scattered, rural population contribute toward larger-than-average administration expenditures. Another reason is that the state is still modernizing its state administration, a process propelled by the widespread economic development of recent years. Further, the state's fairly liberal orientation to social and environmental policies contributes to a substantial state bureaucracy.

Of late, Maine's expenditures have been receiving considerable public attention. In some recent years, the state's spending grew more rapidly than that of most other states. Between 1982 and 1988, for example, the state's expenditures increased 91 percent, compared to the national average of 52 percent.[21] Maine's budgets were sharply curtailed during the administration of Governor James Longley in the late 1970s, but this was more or less an exception to a trend of rapid growth in spending. As we have seen, Maine's generous social policies and the scattered nature of its rural population help explain spending discrepancies between Maine and the nation, but there are other causes as well. The fact that the state had been lagging in important policy areas, such as education, created a demand for rapid modernization.

Also, as federal assistance leveled off during the Reagan administration, greater expenditures were required of all the states. Maine's stable economic and political environment helped it to withstand much of the federal budget changes during the early 1980s.[22] However, as we have noticed, Maine had already established a generous list of programs that depended heavily on federal grants-in-aid. In recent years, the state has had to pick up a greater share of funding for some of these programs to keep them in existence. According to Governor McKernan, these additional costs represented more than $20 million of the 1990–91 budget.[23]

In 1990–91, Maine confronted its worst budget crisis since the Great Depression. The condition of state finances was sharply but inconclusively debated in the 1990 gubernatorial race, in which McKernan narrowly defeated Joseph Brennan. In the weeks after the election, state officials discovered that the revenue gap amounted to over $500 million. To deal with the shortfall, the state reduced spending in several critical programs, including welfare programs, laid off some state employees, and forced many others to take leave without pay.

The most serious problem was the estimated $1.2 billion shortfall that the McKernan administration forecast for the 1991–92 bienniem. The legislature grappled with that problem in a session marked by much conflict and confrontation between the two parties. The inability of the legislature and the governor to agree on a new budget forced the state to shut down many services on July 1, 1991. A new budget was not finally agreed to until July 17. To close the gap between revenues and expenditures, extensive spending reductions were made in many state programs. As examples, funds provided to towns for general assistance to needy persons were cut by $2 million, and the permissible amount of money recipients of the Aid for Dependent Children program might earn without a reduction in their program benefits was lowered from $200 a month to $120. To increase revenues, new taxes were levied on a temporary basis: the sales tax was increased from 5 to 6 percent (to expire June 30, 1993); a surcharge of 5 percent was levied on the 1991 and 1992 state tax bills of married persons filing jointly whose taxable income was less than $75,000 (for incomes over $75,000, the surcharge was 15 percent); the gasoline tax was increased 2 cents per gallon; the meals tax moved from 5 to 7 percent; the sales tax was extended to snack foods; and new fees were placed on such activities as camping and lodging in state parks.

A serious issue involved in the budget crisis was the linkage of the budget to reform of the workmen's compensation system. Governor McKernan refused to sign the new budget until the legislature agreed to reduce costs in workmen's compensation. McKernan argued that, in the absence of such reforms, the added costs to businesses contained in the tax increases would drive many jobs out of Maine. After much debate, the legislature enacted reforms that lowered the costs of workmen's compensation by about 20 percent, which the governor accepted (he had earlier tried to bring about a reduction of 35 percent). Many Maine politicians believe that if the practice of linking the budget to other issues should continue, future legislative sessions will be marked by similiar political combat, and protracted conflict, and that much of the traditional budget process will no longer operate.

CONCLUSION

Several generalizations are relevant to Maine's budget. Continuity and innovation are both important in the state's budget process. Certain budget procedures are retained because they still work, in the opinion of state officials and the citizenry. The biennial schedule and the two-part format of the budget (which largely determine the manner of its approval) are procedures that the state has not been willing to change. Significant developments have occurred, such as the requirement that all funds in each biennium be accounted for. This change has expanded the scope of appropriation power in the legislature.

Maine's revenue patterns are both a cause and an effect of growth in programs and program spending. The creation of elastic revenue sources in the 1950s and 1960s allowed state officials to rely more heavily on increases in state spending, particularly as control of the government switched from Republicans to Democrats. The increased spending and the emphasis on expanding programs have put renewed pressure on revenue sources, such as federal grants-in-aid. In coping with changes in federal assistance, and overall state development, Maine's expenditures have begun to place the state among the "high spending" states. Consequently, revenue shortfalls in the 1990s have already had more critical effects in Maine than in many other states.

CHAPTER TEN

Contemporary Policy Concerns

This chapter examines some key tensions in Maine's public policy environment. These tensions reflect distinctive features of the state's politics as Maine is called upon to make trade-offs among conflicting demands on its resources. The focus is on the directions being taken by state government, and the trends likely to be present in the 1990s.

JOBS VERSUS THE ENVIRONMENT

A traditionally low-income state blessed by an unusually handsome physical setting, Maine has long been concerned with balancing environmental protection with job creation. State government involvement in environmental problems began when the legislature created a Sanitary Water Board in 1941. The state has long depended on its rivers as a source of power for its industries, especially the textile industry. A significant part of the state's population settled along the several rivers running between the northern wildlands and the seacoast. The abuse of the rivers by effluent discharges from factories called attention to the problem. Edmund Muskie in *Journeys* writes about his early impression of the problem:

> It was our river, the Androscoggin, that stirred public concern and indignation even before World War II. The Androscoggin begins its run to the ocean in the high, clear mountain streams and lakes in the northwestern corner of Maine. It flows into New Hampshire, then back into Maine, picking up pulp and paper wastes in Berlin, New Hampshire, Rumford and Livermore Falls, Maine. In those days . . . , the wastes were visible long before the river reached

Lewiston. There was a tremendous stench, and the paint on houses
began to peel.[1]

The pollution problem caused by the pulp and paper industry was acute.
By one measure (the biochemical oxygen demand of the wastes), three paper
mills can produce more effluents than all domestic and municipal sewer systems in the state.[2] Although Maine made a few efforts to enact pollution legislation in the 1940s, the efforts were largely unsuccessful. This was a period
in Maine politics which Duane Lockard has characterized as one dominated
by "pine, power and paper."[3] Lobbies for the paper companies were sufficiently powerful that antipollution legislation was often emasculated. One
measure enacted in the late 1940s set fairly rigorous limits on the amount of
permissible discharges into rivers, and then proceeded to exempt from its
provisions most rivers in the state.

The rise of environmental regulations began in the 1960s. Several political developments contributed to a changed climate for legislation.[4] One was
the rise of the Democratic party to a position competitive with the Republican party. In 1966, Kenneth Curtis, a liberal Democrat with proenvironmen-
tal policy interests, was elected governor. Another factor was the proposed
federally funded Dickey Lincoln dam. The project would have flooded thousands of acres of northern Maine for the construction of a hydroelectric
power plant, whose power output would have lowered electric power rates.
The huge scope of the enterprise helped to coalesce environmental interests
against the dam. (The project eventually failed for lack of funding.) By the
end of the decade, the *Maine Times,* a widely read environmentally oriented
weekly newspaper, had begun publication, and the Natural Resources Council of Maine, the largest environmental lobby in the state, had established an
office in Augusta.

Beginning in 1970, the major present-day environmental statutes were
put in place.[5] One involved site location of new facilities and projects. The
provisions required prior approval of the state Board of Environmental Protection (BEP) before the construction or operation of such developments as
subdivisions in excess of twenty acres, parking lots or paved areas exceeding
three acres, buildings with a ground area in excess of 60,000 square feet, and
large-scale milling and excavation activities. The BEP requires, for example, that a development will fit "harmoniously into the existing natural environment," and that the developer have the financial and technical ability to
meet state air and water pollution control standards. The BEP, which is part

of the Department of Environmental Protection (DEP), has authority to place terms and conditions on its grants and permits.

Two other major environmental statutes are the Solid Waste Management Act of 1973 and the Alteration of Coastal Wetlands Act of 1975. The Solid Waste Act authorizes BEP to adopt rules governing the location and construction of solid-waste facilities. Part of the law provides communities with a state subsidy equivalent to 50 percent of the cost of maintaining a facility, as long as it is in "substantial compliance" with state regulations. The measure is especially important in Maine because a large portion of the state's groundwater is close to the land surface and susceptible to pollution from waste sources. In the mid-1970s, the state tried to regulate over 450 dumps throughout the state; because of opposition, DEP had to prioritize dumps according to those most seriously damaging to the environment.

In 1989, the legislature created the Waste Management Agency to oversee efforts to deal with the waste problem.[6] Major attention was given to recycling, with the aim to reduce by 50 percent the amount of trash created by Maine residents by 1994. Many new mandates call for further recycling by Maine residents. The state's existing bottle law, which had required deposits on beer and soft-drink containers only, was expanded to cover virtually all nondairy beverages. Plastic cans and certain other types of containers are banned. Businesses employing more than fifteen people are required by 1993 to recycle all office paper. Buyers of refrigerators, tires, and other goods that are hard to dispose of will be charged special fees to finance trash-disposal programs.

The evolution of Maine's environmental policy from primarily technical regulations to programs involving a range of issues and choices is illustrated by the Rivers Protection Act of 1983. Earlier pollution-control efforts were focused almost entirely on protecting people from the effects of certain types of private activity on private property that threatened the public's health, welfare, and safety. Factories were limited, for instance, in the amount of effluents that they could discharge into the waters of nearby streams. In the 1983 Rivers Protection Act, the emphasis was shifted to provide the greatest benefit for the public in weighing proposed uses of rivers. As an example, the measure specifies that, for the 31,000 miles of Maine rivers on which hydroelectric projects may be built, the public gain from a project must outweigh anticipated environmental losses. The BEP is asked to consider such factors as the impact of a project on soil, water quality, wildlife, fisheries, historic resources, public access, and flooding, in addition to energy benefits. The thrust of recent solid-waste and river-quality legislation has been to stress the interdependence of environmental factors. This, in turn, has put more power in the hands of state agencies to balance environmental and economic needs.

For many years, a battle was fought in Maine under the rubric of "payrolls vs. pickerel." Advances in environmental regulation were considered a threat to jobs in the pulp and paper companies and in other industries. Although the concern is less acute than in the past, the issue still reappears. In 1986, political fireworks erupted in the legislature over the "Big A" dam. The Big A was a proposed hydroelectric project of the Great Northern Paper Company on a branch of the Penobscot River in central Maine, at the point of the Big Amberjackmockamus Falls. The politics of the project are suggestive of the continuing tensions between the goals of job creation and preservation of the state's environment.

The desire of Great Northern to build the Big A dam stemmed from the company's financial problems. The company argued that it needed the additional power source to cover the cost of upgrading its mills and to save approximately a thousand jobs. With the additional cheap power, Great Northern claimed it could even add several hundred jobs to its plant. Opponents maintained that the proposed dam would endanger popular salmon fishing and destroy a major area for commercial whitewater rafting. Because the location of the dam was in a part of Maine with no organized local government, Great Northern's application was initially reviewed by the Land Use Regulation Commission (LURC), an agency created in 1969 to handle zoning and development in the state's unorganized areas. LURC applied the standards of the Rivers Protection Act and concluded that the economic benefits outweighed the environmental losses. The vote was four to three. The company's struggle did not, however, end with LURC. Because federal water-quality standards were involved, the application also had to be approved by BEP. In the early 1970s, BEP had been assigned the responsibility of examining the compatibility of hydroelectric projects with federal standards. Great Northern lost this second round of the process. In early 1986, BEP found by a six-to-two margin that water quality would be adversely affected by construction of the Big A dam.

The battle next moved to the legislature. Supporters of Big A attempted to enact a measure overriding the BEP decision by directing the commissioner of the Department of Environmental Protection, BEP's parent organization, to stipulate that water-quality standards had been satisfied. House Speaker John Martin, a strong advocate of Great Northern's position, was so incensed by BEP's rejection of Big A that he suggested BEP members who voted against the project should resign for violating—in his opinion—state law as reflected in certain provisions of the Rivers Protection Act. He suggested that impeachment proceedings be started if they were unwilling to step down. After lengthy debate, the house approved the bill overturning the BEP decision by a vote of 85 to 45. The senate, however, stalled the measure. At that point, Great Northern abruptly withdrew its application, even though it had expended about $6 million in its preparation for the project, which was estimated to be valued at about $100 million. Although environmentalists had succeeded in overcoming legislative efforts to repeal the BEP decision, many business leaders believed that the uproar damaged the climate for economic development.

The close votes in the regulatory boards and in the house indicate that the jobs-versus-environment issue still is divisive. In the past decade, the issue has been somewhat recast because of the changed workforce and the altered nature of what are regarded as environmental issues. Environmental policy questions in Maine currently center on the impact of overall development in the state; they are less inclined to focus only on the effects of one industry's discharges into streams and rivers. Health issues are now at least as important as the maintenance of payrolls.

Contamination of the state's groundwater is of particular concern because about 60 percent of Mainers obtain their drinking water from underground sources. In the 1980s, the state passed several bond issues to correct various hazards threatening that water supply, such as decaying underground fuel tanks. In 1990, the legislature raised the gasoline tax by one cent per gallon to provide additional funds to clean up spills from rusted fuel tanks.

The shift in the way environmental issues are defined has helped focus attention on management. A study in the early 1980s found that about 20 percent of the developments in the state, supposedly regulated by state law, had actually been built before any regulatory review had taken place.[7] A review of the Department of Environmental Protection in 1987 recommended that the agency increase its staff by 15 percent, primarily because major new programs were not being implemented and other laws were not being enforced. The McKernan administration has taken steps to expand the department's budget to meet these criticisms. In 1989, the state seemed to toughen its stance on enforcement when it joined the federal government in levying a nearly $1 million fine on the International Paper Company, which was found to have violated both state and federal environmental laws. In 1991, in a similar case, the J. M. Huber Company agreed to pay $328,000 in fines to the state and federal governments because its waferboard plant in Easton had violated air-emission standards.

A final change in the context in which environmental policies are formulated involves labor. Maine's workforce has become more oriented toward service-sector jobs and less toward traditional manufacturing positions, which eases tensions between economic growth and environmental protection. The commissioner of the Department of Economic and Community Development claimed in 1988 that the days of "smokestack chasing" are over.[8] In the 1960s, Maine looked at the possibilities of large "one-shot" industries to improve the economies of impoverished areas in its northern and eastern counties, such as efforts to build an oil refinery at Eastport, on the Canadian border, and to develop sugar beets as a second crop for potato-growing Aroostook County. Although neither project materialized, the economies of both areas gradually improved, in part because of economic growth elsewhere in the state. Current growth is taking place mostly in small businesses and among service industries, many of which do not pose the environmental hazards of traditional manufacturing. Economic development has been a critical aspect of recent gubernatorial administrations, and its underlying concepts are considered next.

PROMOTING ECONOMIC GROWTH: FOR HOW MANY?

In his strategy for economic growth, Governor Joseph Brennan gave particular emphasis to education. During his administration (1979–87), state education assessment scores began to be published in all school districts. Brennan also stressed improving the highway system through bonds, emphasizing the importance of infrastructure for business development. As a liberal Democrat, Brennan encountered some problems with the business community. For example, tourism received little emphasis during his administration, partly because that industry generally fought Democratic efforts to increase the state's minimum wage. However, in general, Brennan was widely praised for keeping the state's attention on the task of enhancing economic opportunities.

Consistent with the state's bipartisan tendencies, much of the McKernan economic development policy emerged from the Brennan strategy. Early in his administration, McKernan named a forty-two-member task force to design an economic development policy; the group reported in the fall of 1987, and much of the suggested package of legislation was enacted in the second session of the 113th legislature in 1988.[9] The main themes of the McKernan program have been an effort to weave together various public policies for development, a pursuit of greater administrative integration in managing those policies, and the targeting of state activities on specific regions.

Perhaps the most interesting feature is the emphasis given to targeting. Maine's expansive geography and participatory culture have generally made it difficult for state officials to provide development benefits to some citizens and not to others. Except in welfare programs, where the provision of assistance to needy persons (based on income categories) is accepted, state assistance tends to be distributed very widely. When the State Planning Office took over the small-cities portion of the Community Development Block Grant program in 1981 from the U.S Department of Housing and Urban Development, it increased sharply the number of recipient towns and cities.[10] A tendency exists for all counties and towns to share in state-sponsored aid.

On the other hand, the rise of the "two Maines" idea in the mid-1980s alerted the state government to the possibility that regional differences might continue to grow. That possibility was of major concern to the McKernan administration. As the first Republican administration in twenty years, it did not wish to be identified primarily with the more affluent, southern region. Although many of its key staff members lived in the Portland suburbs, it faced a Democratic house and senate whose leadership came predominantly from the northern half of the state. The administration sought to diffuse the potentially politically explosive notion of "two Maines" in part by targeting development funds to a multiplicity of sites throughout the state.

One program has been the identification of four regions—namely, central Aroostook County, the Katahdin region in northern Penobscot County, the Quoddy region in Washington County, and all of Waldo County in central Maine—as "job opportunity zones" (JOZs). In these areas, the unemployment rate has been approximately double that of the state as a whole (which was 4.4 percent in 1987). A committee composed of several cabinet officers oversees the program. Each department attempts to target some funds from its program to the four regions. Businesses in the JOZs are eligible for grants (of about $1,000) for each "full-time quality job" they create. The targeting of funds has affected the selection of highways for repair and upgrading. Because insufficient funds were available to upgrade all 1,300 miles of the major state roads needing improvement, only 800 miles were selected. The principal criterion was whether a road was in a "corridor of regional significance," that is, an area where roads were most immediately involved in commercial development. Still another effort is to attract specific types of industries to regions of the state suitable for their products. For instance, in northern Maine the state government is seeking to recruit industries producing very lightweight products and materials, such as computer disks, whose transportation costs to distant markets are relatively low.

Governor McKernan's economic development program makes a strong effort to connect education and human service programs with job creation. The state has sought to strengthen its vocational-technical institutes, particularly to enable them to provide "customized" training for businesses in need of particular skills. In response to the economic development task force, new funds have been provided to the Department of Education for televising community college courses in areas of the state not served by an existing educational unit. An important program is ASPIRE (Additional Support for People in Retraining and Education), enacted in 1988. ASPIRE seeks to help long-term welfare clients to gain marketable skills. It provides stipends and such services as day care while an individual is learning a new skill.

A related program is the Maine Aspirations Compact, which was put into motion by an executive order in January 1988. The compact tries to elevate the goals of Maine high school students. A longstanding problem has been that, although a high portion of Maine students graduate from high school, a noticeably low portion enroll in postsecondary education. The compact, which followed several years of creative education legislation, including the development of performance and assessment criteria for local schools, envisions business employees working in schools with students and teachers to relate coursework to job needs. Still another program is STAR (Strategic Training for Accelerated Re-employment), which is designed to enable workers in declining industries (such as shoe manufacturing) to gain new skills.

The ASPIRE and STAR programs depend heavily on adequate social services. To expand day-care arrangements, the state has undertaken a voucher system for low-income parents who are in an employment program; the state also provides entrepreneurial assistance for persons or businesses interested in setting up a day-care business.

A final aspect of economic development orients Maine toward other states and other countries. The legislature has enacted measures to provide services for businesses entering international markets. Additionally, the state plans more aggressive recruiting of new businesses, such as those engaged in specialty metals, electronics, finance, telecommunications, information processing, and forest and marine products. The state government is paying more attention to how the Maine business climate compares with that of the other New England states.

A study of the state's business conditions, conducted by the Corporation for Enterprise Development in Washington, D.C., indicated that in 1988, Maine ranked among the top ten states in three of its categories, namely, economic performance, business vitality, and government policies.[11] Economic factors helping to account for the high ratings included wide structural diversity in the economy, a low rate of business failures, and a low unemployment rate. The government policies category included tax and fiscal policy, governance, education policy, and the level of investment in infrastructure. However, a category in which the state was weak (ranking forty-third) was its capacity for continued growth. Weaknesses here included low levels of research and development dollars expended on a per capita basis, highway deficiencies, a shortage of graduate students in science and engineering, and a low percentage of adults with a college education.

One of the difficulties in planning for economic development is Maine's sprawling geography and many inaccessible communities. People living in one part of the state may have little awareness of the separate conditions existing in a faraway section. To deal with that problem, members of the legislature have begun to travel around the state in groups. In February 1987, for instance, some seventy-six legislators spent two and a half days traveling approximately seven hundred miles on two buses through Maine's central and northern counties.[12] During the tour, senators and representatives visited about fifty enterprises, including a potato farm, a blueberry-processing plant, a paper mill, and a campus of the University of Maine system. The trips have become more frequent as economic development issues have become more salient for legislators.

As Maine policymakers seek to resolve economic issues, they always find that they are closely involved with environmental questions. Although the two types of issues overlap in every state, their relationship is of particular importance in Maine. When Maine people say that their state is special, they almost invariably make reference to its physical environment. Protection of the environment is a major concern. A poll taken in 1989 found that 81 percent of a sample of residents agreed with this statement: "The natural beauty of Maine should be preserved even if it means spending more public money or interfering with private investment decisions."[13] Responding to a somewhat different phrasing of the issue, only 22 percent of the sample agreed that "our first priority should be to get quality jobs, not to preserve natural conditions." State politicians of both parties adhere to the premise that growth must take place on Maine terms, which means that it must be consistent with environmental protection.

CAN GROWTH BE MANAGED?

The Maine economy expanded significantly in the 1980s. According to one observer, the state had enjoyed "an economic renaissance with growth rates that have not been seen in more than a century."[14] However, beneath the apparent affluence, there was also a concern that rapid growth had costs and consequences. For one, the benefits of the rapid economic growth were not being equally distributed. Bowdoin College economist David Vail cautioned political leaders not to equate "economic growth with economic well being." He warned about the "predatory real estate development that is pushing the working class people out of affordable housing, squeezing fishermen from the waterfront and pricing potential farmers out of tillable land."[15]

By 1988, it was clear that rapid unplanned development could no longer be regarded as only a southern Maine phenomenon. Other substate regions and communities were having to confront the issue. In the town of Waldoboro, 29 building permits were issued in 1986 and 135 in 1987. In rural Greenville in western Maine, 90 shoreland building permits were issued and over 800 acres were subdivided. About fifty Maine communities enacted moratoria on subdivisions.[16]

In a very short period, the issue of growth became a major problem. In a random telephone survey in 1988 of 630 Maine registered voters conducted by the Capital News Service, the respondents named growth control as the state's most important issue. Concern for growth and the environment was the top issue for more than one-third of the voters. Two years earlier, in the spring of 1986, growth registered a concern of only 7 percent of the citizenry.

Governor McKernan stated: "It is clear to me that growth is a major issue in this state from a number of perspectives. . . . We have tried to walk that fine line of creating jobs in parts of the state that don't have them, but at the same time, realizing we do not want jobs at the expense of what makes Maine unique."[17] In the Capital News Service Survey, concern for growth was relatively constant across the state's regions, with citizens in each county ranking it first or second. Oxford County, bordering New Hampshire, registered the least concern. There, growth ran a poor second to concerns for jobs and employment, which were mentioned by 71 percent of the respondents. At the other end of the continuum, over 90 percent of coastal Lincoln County respondents listed growth as a problem. Concern for growth also cut across partisan, ideological, educational, and age groupings. Only those over age sixty-five ranked growth below their first-mentioned concern.

The response to pressures for state action was a major initiative during the 1988 legislative session. The final version of the proposed growth-management legislation evolved from a series of compromises among the members of the legislature's Energy and Natural Resources Committee, environmentalists (such as the Natural Resources Council of Maine), municipal representatives (in particular, the Maine Municipal Association), and the governor. At first, Governor McKernan opposed a process of state approval or review of local growth-management plans. However, Representative Michael H. Michaud, a Democrat from East Millinocket and the committee's cochair, led a fight to bring about state review under a proposal that would authorize $9 million over a two-year period. The latter course had been recommended by a special legislative commission that worked over six months assessing the state's growth-management needs. There were intense and heated discussions by the key actors, reflecting their interests and constituencies. Most felt that something had to be done and done quickly to deal with the "growth crisis," after more than a year of substantial media attention and analysis.

The bill's final passage represented a political compromise. On the strength of its unanimous endorsement by the Energy and Natural Resources Committee, the bill passed without floor debate. During the public hearings, many Maine people testified that uncontrolled growth was affecting land values, increasing property taxes, clogging inadequate highways, burdening sewer systems, and depleting communities of valuable open spaces; thereby, they demanded solutions beyond the reach of most volunteer citizen planners in local communities.

The 1988 legislative prescription was entitled "An Act to Promote Orderly Economic Growth and Natural Resource Conservation." It provides $3.5 million a year for planning assistance. About $1 million became available to assist towns directly. Another $600,000 was earmarked for regional planning councils, while the remaining $1.8 million went to create a new sixteen-employee state office and to increase the field enforcement of the Department of Environmental Protection.

Over the next ten years, this law required all towns and cities to write and implement a comprehensive plan that outlines how the residents want their community to look in the future. These plans will specify those areas of the community that are to be developed, as well as those that are to be protected and to remain rural. Thus, all 474 organized communities in Maine were to develop comprehensive plans and land-use ordinances to help cope with the extensive developmental pressures that the state has been experiencing and to guide their collective growth patterns.

Implementation of the law was within the domain of the Department of Economic and Community Development. The new job of deputy commissioner for comprehensive planning went to a former Maine Municipal Association lobbyist. This office was responsible for deciding which towns had the most development pressure. These "higher risk" communities had to submit their comprehensive plans to the state by January 1, 1991. Each Maine municipality was to submit a comprehensive plan to the state for review to be phased in during three time periods: January 1991, 1993, and 1996. These deadlines were based on population growth from 1980–87. Within a year of writing their plans, communities were required to enact their zoning ordinances.

Before its abrupt abolition in December 1991, because of the state budget crisis, the Office of Comprehensive Planning paid towns 75 percent of the cost of designing their comprehensive plans. It also worked with the towns and staffs of existing regional planning commissions to assure that each local plan met the state goals, such as promoting economic growth, encouraging affordable housing, and protecting natural resources.[18] It appears that while these state goals were explained in law, bureaucratic discretion nonetheless tended to give rise to varying interpretations of the law.

As a result of legislative compromise, the state government did not have strict approval authority over these local plans. However, if the plans were not certified as meeting state goals by the Office of Comprehensive Planning, communities risked being stripped of their power to approve development projects. Moreover, towns that failed to comply with the law could also forfeit certain types of state financial aid (for instance, state support for the legal defense of a local ordinance). In the future, state agencies that make grant awards to local governments for specific purposes may want to verify that a town's plan reflects the same general intent as the grant program. As part of the state's increased involvement in local planning, state certification will be required of municipal code enforcement officers by 1993.

Many communities have not actively engaged in basic planning and land-use protection. Private developers have been able to abuse the public interest more easily when a community lacks planning tools, such as comprehensive plans, zoning, site plan review and subdivision ordinances, and building codes. Estimates are that only about half of the state's localities had adopted

comprehensive plans by early 1988 when the new legislation was formulated. Even communities that enjoyed professional management, with town
and city managers, needed support for updating and enforcing their plans.
Because of the reduction of federal funding, many Maine localities in the
1980s did not take planning as seriously as their responsibilities to deal with
more immediate "crises," such as the closing of the town dump and the generation of additional revenue to replace lost federal dollars. Existing comprehensive plans and ordinances were often flawed, and, consequently,
communities lacked the ability to contain and effectively manage growth.

Within two years of the 1988 legislation, the state's economy began to fal-
ter, which caused successive budgetary shortfalls. Some business groups,
citizens, and developers argued that Maine's growth spurt was over and that
growth management was a moot issue. To help soften the blow of the revenue shortages in 1991–92, Governor McKernan successfully proposed elim-
inating the growth-management mandate and radically reducing the size of
the agency charged with its implementation.

A strong desire for enhancing local autonomy and citizen participation
still exists in the state. These goals have been protected by the town-meeting
tradition and Maine's fairly recent (1969) home-rule amendment to the state
constitution. Maine's shoreland zoning law and other environmental measures, developed and refined in the late 1960s and 1970s, seemed for a while
to help alleviate growth problems. However, as the state lost some of its traditional isolation, these remedies, while helpful to certain communities,
proved to be inadequate. The desire for local control and autonomy by town
residents has been challenged by growth and by a public perception that
more statewide action is necessary to manage growth. The result has been a
more vigorous, albeit short-lived, state government response.

HUMAN SERVICES IN A LOW-INCOME STATE

A fourth tension revealed in the state's policies deals with welfare and the
economy. Economically, Maine is presently something of a paradox. It wel-
comes millions of vacationers and tourists each year to enjoy its jagged
coastline and some of the handsomest scenery in the eastern United States—
well-kept village greens, white church steeples, picturesque fishing boats,
and spectacular views of the hundreds of islands that lie just off the coast.
The only national park in the eastern half of the United States (Acadia National Park) is located on Mount Desert Island, near Bar Harbor. Often un-
noticed by tourists, especially visitors whose travels in Maine are largely

confined to coastal U.S. Route 1, are contrasting interior regions afflicted with poverty. Some of these areas are among the most impoverished in New England, if not the United States.

Waldo County, in central Maine, was ranked last in 1987 among the fifty-seven counties in New England in per capita income. Unemployment in the state's easternmost county, Washington County, which has much seasonal employment, sometimes reaches 25 percent. Maine's rural underclass is known well beyond the state's borders. It has been depicted in Carolyn Chute's best-selling novel, *The Beans of Egypt, Maine*.[19] It is heard in the folk humor of Tim Sample, Marshall Dodge, and other Maine humorists. Its poverty and isolation are a worrisome, persistent problem for a state that adheres to a commonwealth idea of politics.

Historically, Maine has been one of the nation's poorest states. In the 1970s, when energy prices soared, the combination of Maine's low per capita income and high fuel bills made the state, arguably, the poorest in the country. On the other hand, in the 1980s, Maine enjoyed the economic boom that embraced all of New England. Its unemployment rate remained consistently lower than the national average, and its rising per capita income caused the state to rank twenty-eighth in the Union in 1988. That high position was remarkable in the light of Maine's history, but by the end of the 1980s the economy was seriously slackening. In early 1991, the state unemployment stood at 8.9 percent, about two percentage points above the national average, and its per capita income placed the state in thirty-eighth position among the states.

An important element in Maine's welfare policies relates to the differences between its poor and the poor in the rest of the country. Nearly all of the poor in Maine are white. In 1980, only 9.4 percent of the U.S. white population fell below the poverty line, but in Maine nearly all of the 13 percent of the population who were poor were white.[20] Maine's poor are concentrated in the most urban and the most rural settings in the state. The state lacks large ghetto-like concentrations of poor, but every city has its "pocket of poverty." Nonetheless, the highest concentrations of poor persons are in rural areas. In the 1980 census, over 20 percent of the population of Waldo and Washington counties fell below the poverty line. Another factor that shapes Maine's welfare policies is that, among persons who are not technically regarded as poor, a significant portion are paid at or very close to the minimum wage. In 1984, it was estimated that as many as 70,000 workers, or about 15 percent of the state's workforce, were in this category. These figures are swelled by seasonal employees, who are concentrated in the tourist and fishing industries, and by employees in the traditionally low-wage shoe shops and textile mills.

In recent decades, Maine has attempted to construct fairly generous social policies, even in the face of unfavorable economic conditions. Particularly since it came under Democratic control in the early 1980s, the legislature seems to have taken a distinctly liberal approach to welfare. In 1985–86, Maine ranked second among the states (behind New York) in state and local spending for welfare as a percentage of personal income, and third (behind Massachusetts and Rhode Island) in welfare spending as a percentage of total general expenditures. Pro-welfare attitudes are partly a product of the close relations between legislators and their constituents, partly a consequence of the state's isolation, and partly an outgrowth of the moralistic culture. Living predominantly in small towns, most legislators are very familiar with problems of poverty in their communities, and are conversant with ways to try to remedy them. Additionally, they tend to define social welfare issues in personal terms ("we try to take care of our own"), on the premise that the poor, especially the poor in rural Maine, will have little other recourse if the state government does not try to help.

Maine's efforts to provide services for low-income citizens are illustrated in recent battles over the state's minimum hourly wage. The state's minimum wage has for several years been among the highest in the country. The issue has tended to pit governors concerned about economic development against legislators, especially Democratic legislators, from low-income constituencies. In 1984, after a bitter legislative fight, the state raised the minimum wage from $3.35 per hour to $3.65 per hour, phased in over a three-year period. Reacting to the controversy, Governor Brennan commissioned a study of the impact of the wage requirement on the state's economy before he finally decided to sign the measure. By 1987, Maine had the highest minimum wage of any state.

One reason that the minimum wage is a lively issue in the Maine legislature is that there are always some legislators in the affected occupations. In 1983, certain Democrats, with support from the Maine AFL-CIO, attempted to increase the state minimum wage, but their proposal was defeated. The issue was brought back to the legislature in 1984, partly through the efforts of Representative Edith Beaulieu of Portland. Beaulieu, who cochaired the Labor Committee, was a cleaning person who lived in a part of Portland where, she said, "the majority [of people] are minimum wage workers."[21]

The growth spurt in the Maine economy in the late 1980s led the legislature to try to raise the minimum rate again in 1987. However, Governor

McKernan vetoed a proposed rise of 30 cents an hour over three years. In 1988, the state finally enacted a measure increasing the minimum hourly wage to $3.75 in 1989 and to $3.85 in 1990, but with the provision that the minimum wage not exceed the minimum hourly wage of the other five New England states. This came about only after the failure of a proposal to increase the minimum wage by 40 cents over a three-year period.

A related issue is workers' compensation. For several years, workers' benefits have been significantly higher in Maine than in other states. A principal reason has been the state's high accident rate, due in large part to the unusual risks borne by workers in the pulp and paper industry. Under a revised system approved in a special legislative session in 1987, benefits were reduced at the suggestion of a coalition of business groups. However, costs continued to escalate until a major revision was undertaken in the program in the 1991 session as part of an overall compromise on the state budget. The new system requires workers who are able to work to search statewide for a job, not just in the local area; regulates lawyers' fees in cases where lump sum payments are made; and provides for a state office of medical coordination, which will attempt to lower costs by establishing standard treatment methods for various on-the-job injuries.[22]

Several other welfare issues reveal ongoing tensions between citizen needs and available state funds. Some of these problems are aggravated by Maine's geography. The state in 1983 set up the Maine Health Care Finance Commission (MHCFC) to establish means for controlling the rising costs of hospital care. Maine has little competition between hospitals, and most hospital employees earn low wages. The MHCFC was charged with setting a limit on each hospital's annual revenues for services provided based on the anticipated number of patients. Partly as a result of MHCFC's work, hospital costs increased more slowly in Maine than they did nationally. However, some hospitals delayed the purchase of sophisticated medical equipment. Angry at the MHCFC's cost limits, the Maine Hospital Association sought to have the agency abolished. An attempt to initiate a public referendum on the issue, however, fell short of the necessary number of signatures. In 1989, the state redesigned the MHCFC to make it more responsive to providers in cases where cost increases are beyond their control. The legislature also appropriated some $14 million for low-income persons who cannot afford health insurance, and provided about $7 million to hospitals to offset debts created through uncompensated care. The state budget crisis in 1991–92 made the future of the MHCFC and the health insurance program uncertain.

Finally, the state has enacted certain pioneering social legislation for

older citizens and for children.[23] Maine was the first state to prohibit mandatory retirements for public employees. It also was first to enact legislation to
assist persons with winter fuel costs, a program particularly beneficial to elderly persons. Many of its programs for older citizens are administered
through five area agencies on aging. The agencies are governed by boards of
directors made up of elderly persons. As part of its effort to deal with the
problem of child abuse, in 1989 Maine became the first state to create the position of Child Welfare Services Ombudsman.[24] This official investigates
and tries to resolve disputes concerning the child welfare system, mostly involving the Department of Human Services. The ombudsman, autonomous
from other state agencies, reports once a year to the governor and to the legislature.

EDUCATION AND ASPIRATIONS

A fifth issue speaks to a psychological and educational problem among
many of Maine's young people: low aspirations regarding their own education and self-development. The issue has been identified with increasing
concern by influential academics in Maine, such as Richard Barringer, a former faculty member at the John F. Kennedy School at Harvard University
and a cabinet officer in the administrations of governors James Longley and
Joseph Brennan, and Robert Cobb, longtime Dean of the College of Education at the University of Maine.

Since it first emerged as a major public issue in the mid-1980s, the state's
"aspirations movement" has become a diverse group of education theorists
and practitioners, feminists, business leaders, alternative school advocates,
and promoters of programs for the gifted and talented. A widely attended
conference in 1987, "Aspirations of Maine Youth," signaled the "coming-
out party" of this coalition of activists. They hoped to broaden their political
base by attracting the attention of Maine's public and private sectors, as well
as the general public.

Familiar themes propagated by Maine's education leadership about the
dangerous trends in high school dropouts, low college attendance rates, and
the involvement of youth in such activities as drugs and sex had been reported for over a decade. However, the education establishment's plan for
involving others in the community—business, social institutions, and parents, as a statewide action group—did represent a novel departure from previous strategies. This collaborative effort translated what had been seen
mainly as a cultural problem—low self-esteem and the lack of educational
advancement among Mainers—into a crucial economic issue. As Henry

Bourgeois, president of the Maine Development Foundation, commented: "The single most important fact in business decisions in the 21st century will be quality of the work force." Select members of Maine's business community had become very concerned that there would not be enough workers trained in high technology available in the future.[25]

Maine's high school graduation rate in the late 1980s was about 78 percent, which is slightly above the national average. Of the 22 percent of ninth graders who do not graduate with their class, about 40 percent of these dropouts eventually obtain their diploma through adult programs. Another concern is that even though the dropout rate has remained rather stable, students were detected to be dropping out earlier than ever. Frank Antonucci, dropout and truancy consultant for the Maine Department of Education, believes that this phenomenon can be explained by such factors as higher graduation requirements, the perception of a strong job market, drug abuse, and family decay. The earlier that students drop out, the fewer skills they possess. Thus, it costs more to train them later, or to support them in a cycle of poverty. State studies also revealed that there are unexplained differences in the dropout rates between similar-sized communities. In the mid-1980s, Eastport and Jackman had dropout rates approaching 10 percent, whereas Rangeley and Falmouth had virtually no dropouts.

Eve Bither, a former teacher and the state's commissioner of education, has established what she regards as acceptable targets for raising student aspirations. She believes that a school should seek a graduation rate of 90 percent by 1993 and a college-bound rate equivalent at least to the national average of 58 percent.[26]

Maine's problems of low aspirations, at least as measured by college attendance, may be partially explained by the rural and geographically isolated nature of the state. Because of out-migration that began after the Civil War, Maine had at one time the "most native" population in the United States. This trend did not begin to change until 1973. (Currently, Maine ranks at about the midpoint among the states in the percentage of its population that is native-born.) Further, one-third of Maine's young people come from very small towns, where fewer than one adult in ten has completed college, and fewer than one in thirty-three has obtained a graduate or professional degree. The lack of role models to stimulate a desire to excel and achieve academic excellence strongly affects students' socialization process. Other evidence from the 1980 census suggests an unevenness in the work force as follows: "While 73 percent of the state's labor force was born in Maine, only 60 percent of the owners, managers, professionals, and technicians are natives. Moreover, of the people with graduate and professional degrees beyond college, about one-third were native Mainers.''[27]

To increase student aspirations, the McKernan administration has undertaken several initiatives. Under one program, schools receive grants as incentives to make changes that are known to affect the learning pattern of students. The specific elements include financial incentives for schools that improve the promotion of stronger families and support from the business community. Some education theorists believe that "unless the dynamics of the school, home and community relations change and become mutually supportive of each other, it will be difficult to achieve the goal of a 90 percent graduation rate (which has been achieved in both Minnesota and North Dakota)."[28]

The McKernan administration has also studied the connection between financial need and college attendance. Maine has had one of the most poorly funded state grant programs for students in the nation, according to the Maine Association of Student Financial Aid Directors. Fewer than half of those eligible receive any aid because of the lack of money available.[29] The state has taken several steps recently to remedy that situation. In 1988, Governor McKernan signed a bill that created a Maine Loan Authority, which makes more money available to students at relatively low interest rates. In 1989 the legislature enacted a measure to consolidate student financial assistance services within the Maine Finance Authority. The intent of that measure is to improve the delivery of financial assistance to Maine students attending postsecondary educational institutions and to their families.

More attention has also been directed at the traditional role of guidance counselors in the schools. Thirty-eight percent of 850 Maine high school juniors surveyed by the Department of Education in 1986 claimed they had received little or no help in selecting a college or vocational school. Guidance counselors report that they are reacting to the demands of their job and, unfortunately, have little time for one-to-one counseling. Successful counselors have used value-clarification approaches, field trips, guest speakers, and other techniques, even in junior high school.

Finally, the Maine Aspirations Compact itself represents a cooperative approach between the Department of Education and the Maine Development Foundation to assure that the school systems and businesses work together to help solve the aspirations riddle. During 1988–90, twelve competitive grants were awarded for model projects in local schools. It is hoped that these strategies will all contribute to raising the aspirations of Maine youth. Realistically, the problem is extensive, with the prospect of change occurring only in the long run. Most of the solutions are experimental, and they are by no means comprehensive.

A report put together by faculty members from the state's public and private colleges in the early 1980s, *Maine: Fifty Years of Change 1940–1990*, identified the key policy questions in this area: How should educational systems respond to the education and training needs of the private sector? Since economic development in Maine depends on the quality of education available, will the quality of elementary, secondary, and postsecondary education in Maine encourage in-migration and business relocation? Will there be adequate educational opportunity for all children in the state? The report concludes:

> Maine people have always been the state's most valuable resource. As we move toward the year 2000 and beyond, it will be the people and their values, and their individual and collective development, that will form the basis for Maine's state government of the future.[30]

CONCLUSION

This chapter has briefly examined five policy areas that currently engage state decision makers. Although virtually every state is concerned with similar problems, many of the solutions that Maine seeks are distinctive. The state insists on maintaining and protecting its physical environment and will encourage the creation of jobs only if they are compatible with preserving the environment. Economic development raised the issue of the "two Maines," although by the late 1980s growth seemed to have alleviated some of the disparities between regions. The McKernan administration has tried to diffuse the issue through a targeting strategy. The rapid increase in real estate development in some areas brought about state efforts to regulate growth, an important need because of the large number of small communities. In its social policies, Maine can be considered fairly generous among the states, especially in light of its residents' traditionally low income. While the state has been effective in maintaining a floor under its citizens' living conditions, it has been less successful in instilling an attitude of achievement in its youth. For its economy to continue to expand, a heightened set of aspirations among its young people will be critical. In all these areas, the weakening of the Maine economy in the early 1990s has presented extraordinarily difficult challenges to Maine policymakers.

CHAPTER ELEVEN

Maine in the Federal System

Maine's relationship to other governments—in particular, the New England states, the U.S. federal government, and the eastern provinces of Canada—has been conditioned by many of the state's special characteristics. Some are mostly physical, such as its large geographic size relative to the other New England states and its isolation from them. Others are cultural. The sense of Maine's being "a place apart" is important in understanding Maine politicians, including its national representatives. Likewise, Maine's rather low-key style of politics is cherished, even as the state's political interests are advanced in collaboration with the goals of other states with different political traditions.[1]

Maine's national politicians have to accommodate themselves to localistic norms when running for office. The strong identification that Maine people have with their communities and their habit of expecting to meet politicians on a personal basis mean that candidates for federal office must travel widely and extensively during a campaign. Support is lined up on a person-to-person basis, and in very small groups. Once in office, members of Congress return most weekends to meet with groups of citizens, usually in different communities each weekend, and to answer questions and address problems in town-meeting fashion. Maine's two U.S. Senators maintained, in 1991, a total of fourteen district offices in Presque Isle, Bangor, Rockland, Waterville, Augusta, Lewiston, Portland, and Biddeford to assist them in this work. Compared to other states, this was an unusually high number of local offices. Approximately one-third of all the staff members working for the congressional delegation (two U.S. Senators and two U.S. Representatives) serve in the district offices.

MAINE IN THE CONGRESS

Maine's congressional delegation has long been strong and effective in bargaining with the federal government on critical issues affecting the state. The delegation has enjoyed a relatively prestigious position in the Congress. In 1986, Maine was the only state to have both of its U.S. Senators (William S. Cohen and George J. Mitchell) named as members of the joint Senate-House committee assigned to investigate the Iran-Contra affair. In 1989, Mitchell was elected Senate majority leader. He became the second leader of the Senate to come from Maine in the post–World War II period (Wallace White, a Republican, was the Senate leader in 1947–48). During that period, Senator Margaret Chase Smith and Senator Edmund S. Muskie were also national spokespersons for their respective parties on various issues.

There was a similar pattern of leadership in the nineteenth century. The state's most prominent politician during this period was probably James G. Blaine, who served in both the U.S. House and Senate and ran several times for his party's presidential nomination, securing the Republican nomination in 1884. In the 1890s, two Maine congressmen played a key role in the U.S. House. One was Thomas B. Reed, who was elected Speaker; the other was Nelson P. Dingley, an expert on tariffs, who served as chairman of the House Ways and Means Committee, as well as the Republican party floor leader.[2]

In accounting for Maine's tradition of influential congresspeople, certain features of the state's political system are relevant. One is that the state has no real career ladder of public offices that a politician can climb to win a congressional seat. There is no statewide elective office other than the governorship. Although many congressional candidates have had state legislative experience, legislative districts are too small to constitute an effective springboard for a congressional race. Moreover, the state offers few other types of structures that a candidate may use to gain support. The state has no large cities; its business organizations are predominantly small; and party organizations tend to be weak. The upshot is that candidates for Congress are unusually dependent on their personal talents and resources, and the most resourceful generally win. Once established in Congress, these members are in a strong position to rise in the congressional hierarchies if they desire a leadership role.

Another aspect of Maine politics that influences its congressional delegation is respect for seniority. Although Maine has always reflected a view that politics is everyone's business, in keeping with its moralistic political culture, it has tended to keep successful politicians in Washington for recurring terms. In the 1890s, Maine's Republican delegation in the U.S. House had substantial seniority in addition to being composed of skillful politicians. More recently, Senator Margaret Chase Smith, who served four terms, and Senator Edmund S. Muskie, who served nearly four terms, gained powerful committee assignments partly because of their seniority.

The tendency of Maine politicians to take a middle-of-the-road stance on pressing public issues, a fundamental characteristic of the state's politics, also influences the state's congressional delegation. While some other northern, moralistic states, such as Wisconsin and North Dakota, were experiencing third-party movements in the early decades of the twentieth century, Maine remained faithful to the Republican party. Closer to home, New Hampshire, like Maine, lacks a "career ladder" of political offices. While New Hampshire regularly injects a great deal of conservative ideology into statewide campaigns, Maine politicians have stuck to "moderate" political appeals.

As the state developed a two-party system, successful candidates in both parties stayed fairly near the center of the political spectrum. The two Republican members of the present delegation (William S. Cohen and Olympia J. Snowe) have compiled voting records more liberal than the voting records of their party cohorts in their respective chambers. The most faithfully conservative Republican in recent years, David Emery, was defeated by a large margin in 1982 by Democrat George Mitchell. Maine Democratic members of Congress have maintained liberal voting records, but their state campaigns have been moderate in tone, as well as related to a variety of issues. Probably the most avowedly liberal member in the delegation in recent decades was Senator William Hathaway, who was defeated for reelection in 1978 by moderate Republican William Cohen.

The small role played by ideology can be partly attributed to the state's economic diversity. Maine's multiple concerns—including agricultural commodities, the fishing industry, tourism, defense installations, shipbuilding, pulp and paper companies, and manufacturing—have generally required its national spokespersons to balance locally competing interests. In addition, the tradition of high citizen participation and a town-meeting approach to politics have usually fostered politicians who relate well to voters on a personal, problem-solving basis. That need tends to force politicians to eschew ideology in favor of finding a solution to a specific concern.

In Washington, then, the members of the Maine delegation generally work well together on Maine issues, and are usually effective in coalition building. They also tend to manifest a strong concern—consistent with the moralistic culture—with the processes of government. In this latter respect, both Margaret Chase Smith and Edmund Muskie distinguished themselves nationally. Senator Smith is perhaps best remembered for her "Declaration of Conscience" speech in June 1950, when she spoke out against McCarthyism and encouraged the nation to find a more rational way to deal with the menace of international communism.[3] Senator Muskie was highly praised in the 1960s for his role in developing the Model Cities program and environmental legislation and in serving as the first chair of the Senate Budget Committee.[4] He was also a strong supporter of the U.S. Advisory Commission on Intergovernmental Relations, an agency that examines, and seeks to improve, the ways in which federal, state, and local governments relate to each other. Muskie served on the commission as a U.S. Senator from December 1959 to March 1977.

More recently, Maine has depended on its congressional delegation to handle several major problems involving the federal government. The issues discussed here include the American Indian land-claims dispute, defense contracting, and grants-in-aid.[5]

American Indian Land Claims

The most dramatic was probably the Indian land-claims controversy of the 1970s, which ended in 1980 with a settlement negotiated by White House representatives. The issue began when the Passamaquoddy Indian tribe, through the federal government, sued the state of Maine to recover lands taken from them in violation of the Non-Intercourse Act of 1790, which declared that no state could acquire any Indian lands unless such action was approved by the Congress. Because of this law, a 1794 treaty between the Indians and Massachusetts (of which Maine was then part) was rendered unconstitutional by the United States government because the treaty had not been ratified by the Congress. The land claims of the Passamaquoddies (and later the Penobscot tribe) eventually amounted to 12.5 million acres, or more than half of the territory of Maine. During the course of the legal dispute, land titles in much of the state were left in question, prompting the Maine Municipal Bank to cancel a $27 million bond sale.

The question facing Maine public officials was whether to seek a negotiated settlement or to contest the Indians' claims in court. State leaders at the time, principally Attorney General Joseph Brennan and Governor James Longley, preferred to pursue the matter in court. Their strong stance undoubtedly helped Brennan in his successful 1978 gubernatorial campaign.

The congressional delegation favored a negotiated settlement, and one was eventually worked out by a presidential task force. Under its terms, Maine was absolved of responsibility, and the federal government agreed to pay the Indians some $81.5 million. The critical step of securing Congress's approval for the funds was accomplished, many observers believed, in large part because of the efforts of Senator Edmund Muskie. He was chair of the Senate Budget Committee and had a close working relationship with the Carter administration. Only a few months after the land-claims issue was settled, Muskie became Carter's Secretary of State.

Defense Contracting

Maine is one of the New England states that is especially dependent on the income and jobs generated by federal defense spending. Defense contracting in Maine has been about as important as the pulp and paper industry. During the 1980s, each added about 8 percent to the state's annual gross product. Members of the congressional delegation protect the state's defense-related industries in part by securing seats on the armed services committees. Senator Margaret Chase Smith (1949–73) was for years the ranking Republican on the Senate unit. Senator William Cohen currently is a senior member. First District Congressman David Emery (1975–83) was a member of the House committee, and Congressman Tom Andrews, who has represented the First District since 1991, now holds a seat on the committee.

The congressional delegation helps the state by combining an advocacy of local interests with its efforts to shape national policy. Cohen, in particular, has become perhaps the chief Republican spokesperson on defense and military policy in the Senate. In 1983, for example, he and others persuaded the administration to accept a build-down proposal in return for congressional support for the MX missile. In Maine, the two largest facilities that Cohen and the rest of the delegation have tried to protect are the Loring Air Force Base in northern Maine and the Bath Iron Works on the southern coast. Both have been threatened in recent years as defense policy has changed. The Bath Iron Works (BIW) lost a major Navy contract in 1970 to the Litton Industries shipyard of Mississippi. However, in 1981, BIW obtained a new $1.2 billion Navy contract. One factor in Maine's favor was that the Defense Department was more inclined in the 1980s to distribute contracts among different shipyards. Republicans also held a majority on the Senate Armed Services Committee in 1981 (which they did not hold in 1970), a fact that undoubtedly aided Cohen's efforts.

Loring Air Force Base has not been as successful. The base, which opened in 1953, was recommended by the Air Force in 1976 to be nearly phased out. Largely due to the efforts of Maine's two senators (Muskie and Cohen), that decision was reversed by Secretary of Defense Harold Brown. President Carter at that time was campaigning for renomination as the Democratic candidate, a struggle in which Maine Democrats played an important role. In 1991, the Air Force again recommended the closure of Loring (by 1993), and this time, despite strenuous objections from the Maine congressional delegation, the decision was upheld. The loss of the base may cost Aroostook County about 20 percent of its economic activity.

Federal Assistance

Another task of the congressional delegation is to help the state secure federal grants-in-aid and other forms of federal assistance. The importance of financial relationships between Maine and the federal government grew between the mid-1960s and the decade of the 1980s. In 1986–87, the state ranked among the top ten states in the nation in the portion of state and local revenues it derived from federal grants.[6] The "terms of trade" that Maine had with Washington were very favorable: in 1982–84, Maine received $130 for every dollar its citizens paid in federal taxes. In 1988, the state was third in federal spending per capita on the Medicaid program. Maine also benefited from other types of federal spending. In 1987, it ranked tenth among the states in the numbers of federally paid civilian employees it had per 10,000 population.

To draw the financial picture differently, one study found that in the early 1980s some 17 percent of Maine citizens depended on federal dollars for income.[7] That figure included recipients of entitlement programs, such as Aid to Families with Dependent Children, food stamps, and social security, and holders of jobs that were wholly or partially federally funded. At that time, it was estimated that federal assistance accounted for 30 percent of the Maine state revenues and for approximately 12 percent of the revenues of local governments.

During the Reagan administration, Maine policymakers were hardpressed to maintain their favorable position with the federal treasury. Administration policy was to reduce aid to state and local governments. The Maine congressional delegation supported some of the reductions that Congress approved at President Reagan's urging in 1981. However, it was an uneasy partner in those efforts and fought to protect programs of special importance to Maine. Senator Cohen criticized administration efforts to reduce the

weatherization program as "unwise and contrary to our national effort to reduce energy consumption," and introduced legislation to expand the program.[8] The delegation also sought to retain funding in the low-income energy assistance and food stamp programs.

In general, the strong economy in Maine in the 1980s helped minimize the
effects of federal budget reductions on state activities. The reduction in defense spending in the late 1980s did reduce the flow of federal dollars into the
state. In 1988, Maine received just over $4 billion from all federal sources,
compared to $4.1 billion in the previous year, with the reduction mainly due
to defense curtailments. If the incomes of Mainers rise in the 1990s, the state
will experience reductions in some federal welfare programs. In that situation, the "terms of agreement" with Washington may not be as favorable as
the terms to which the state became accustomed in the 1980s.

The long-run effects of the Reagan policies seemed generally to put more
responsibilities on state institutions. Maine had to position itself to finance
more fully many of its programs. The state looked harder at its own sources
of revenue, and it began to institute certain reforms in such areas as property-
tax policy. The Reagan administration's block grants provided more power
and resources to the governor and key state department commissioners than
the narrow-based, categorical grants that they replaced.

One example was the reassignment of the management of the small cities
portion of the Community Development Block Grant from the U.S. Department of Housing and Urban Development to the states. In Maine's case, the
program was initially managed by the State Planning Office, but it later became a key part of the new Department of Economic and Community Development. The Reagan years also fostered a greater degree of interaction between Maine state and local officials. Because federal funding was
uncertain, town and city officials began to work more closely with state legislators and state executive agencies to secure the assistance needed for their
communities. Total state aid to local governments nearly doubled between
1982 and 1988 (from $317.5 million to $611.8 million), the sixth-fastest
growing rate in the country.[9] Generally, a degree of state centralization took
place in the 1980s that brought state government more directly into the political life of most of Maine's nearly five hundred localities.

MAINE AND THE PRESIDENCY

As a state with only four electoral votes, Maine does not have a large impact
on presidential contests. However, for many years it enjoyed a reputation as

something of an electoral forecaster, suggested by the slogan "As Maine goes, so goes the nation." Until 1960, Maine held its gubernatorial elections in September of even-numbered years, and its vote was thus known two months prior to a presidential election. The slogan came from the 1840 campaign when Maine, until that time a Democratic-Republican state, surprised most people by supporting the Whig candidate for governor.[10] The vote proved to be prophetic when, two months later, the Whig presidential ticket won nationally. Despite the 1840 elections, the slogan was never very accurate historically.

Between the Civil War and the late 1950s, Maine was an almost solidly Republican state. The state gubernatorial outcome and the national presidential result were in agreement (in party terms) about two-thirds of the time. That fairly high percentage existed only because the nation, as well as the state, was predominantly Republican during the period. In the years since Maine has become a two-party state, its gubernatorial vote has had even less predictive value. In the four closest presidential contests since World War II—1948, 1960, 1968, and 1976—Maine voted for the losing candidate every time (the only state to do so).

The state, nonetheless, has had several of its politicians on national tickets. Hannibal Hamlin was elected vice president in 1860 with Abraham Lincoln, and in 1884, James G. Blaine ran unsuccessfully for president on the Republican ticket. Arthur Sewall in 1896 and Edmund Muskie in 1968 ran for vice president on unsuccessful Democratic tickets. In the cases of Hamlin, Blaine, and Muskie, the route to the national ticket ran through the U.S. Senate, where each man had distinguished himself as a national politician. Muskie, for instance, was well known for his expertise on big-city and environmental problems, and was popular with urban and minority groups both in and outside Washington. Even so, Muskie's 1972 campaign to win the Democratic presidential nomination was not effective.

Two of Maine's recent governors have held positions in the executive branch. President Lyndon Johnson named John Reed (governor, 1959–67) to the National Transportation Safety Board. Through his support of the administration's Vietnam policies, Reed had gained the president's favorable attention. Kenneth Curtis (governor, 1967–75) was an early supporter of President Jimmy Carter, who later appointed him U.S. ambassador to Canada. Both Curtis and Reed were considered political moderates and undoubtedly added to Maine's prestige during their years of service in the national administration. However, the state's primary point of access to the White House is through the Congress.

MAINE AND THE U.S. SUPREME COURT

Another link between Maine and the federal government lies within the court system. How has Maine fared in the U.S. Supreme Court? Since 1930, the U.S. Supreme Court appears to have decided in full opinions six cases that were appealed from the Maine Supreme Judicial Court.[11] The Court upheld the decisions of the Maine justices in four instances, and reversed the other two. A look at several cases helps indicate the extent to which Maine's norms and policy concerns comport with those of the nation, at least in the area of constitutional law.

The most recent of the six cases questioned whether a law affecting plant closings was unconstitutional by virtue of its having been preempted by federal law.[12] In the 1970s, Maine passed a measure stipulating that when a company closes a plant in order to relocate, workers who are not able to move or commute should receive severance pay adjusted according to tenure. The law was challenged on the ground that it violated certain federal statutes, especially the Employee Retirement Income Security Act. The Maine Court upheld the state's statute, and the U.S. Supreme Court agreed in a five-to-four decision. The minority thought that the decision would create a loophole in the federal act unintended by the Congress.

Other cases involved civil rights. In *Maine* v. *Moulton*,[13] the Supreme Court affirmed a Maine decision that the state had violated the defendant's Sixth Amendment right to counsel. Both courts believed that a police informant had unfairly induced the defendant to give incriminating evidence against himself. Another recent case involved the extent of citizens' rights under an 1874 federal civil rights act, which holds that no state action can deprive a person of rights guaranteed under federal law. Maine had computed an individual's Aid to Families with Dependent Children benefits in such a way to reduce the amount to which she was entitled.[14] The Maine Supreme Judicial Court held that the civil rights measure applied to all cooperative federal-state programs (not just to certain ones), and the U.S. Supreme Court agreed, by a six-to-three margin.

The Maine Supreme Judicial Court has been reversed in only two cases in the past several decades. Both involved quite technical matters. In *Maine* v. *Thornton*,[15] the Maine Court believed that police violated a defendant's Fourth Amendment rights when they conducted a search without a warrant on the defendant's posted land and discovered marijuana. The federal Court, however, sustained the conviction on the basis of the "open fields" doctrine (first announced in 1924), which permits police officers to enter and search a field without a permit. The Court took a broader view of the doctrine than did the Maine Court. It distinguished land immediately around a house from land farther away, and maintained that the posting of land did not necessarily safeguard it from warrantless searches.

The other reversal, concerning a Maine tax law, took place during the 1930s.[16] The Maine Supreme Judicial Court had upheld a law making stock in Maine corporations part of the taxed assets of persons who died in other states. The U.S. Supreme Court, believing that the measure violated the due-process clause of the Fourteenth Amendment, overturned Maine's decision.

These six cases, when taken together with the much larger number of cases in which the U.S. Supreme Court denied an appeal from Maine's highest court, permit two tentative generalizations. First, while Maine's political culture and history are distinctive in the federal system, they do not appear to have given rise to policies that bring the state into much conflict with the federal courts. Several of the cases where appeals (certiorari) were denied involved instances in which Maine laws had been upheld in Maine courts over a claim that they violated federal constitutional provisions. Among them were laws involving drunk driving, games of chance, and consumer credit reporting.

Second, where state law or practice does on occasion conflict with federal law or the federal Constitution, the Maine court appears to be careful to follow U.S. Supreme Court guidelines. As chapter 8 pointed out, the Maine Supreme Judicial Court is an appointed court whose members typically have substantial prior experience in the lower courts. That structure probably helps to reinforce the state's already cautious policymaking style.

MAINE AND NEW HAMPSHIRE

Although Maine and New Hampshire were one jurisdiction in very early colonial history, they have separated in more ways than geographically. Because of an increasing number of disputes and differences between the two states, a recent article in *Newsweek* described them as "neighbors, not friends."[17] One area of competition has been over winter tourism. Another has involved fishing rights. A "lobster war" grew so intense in the 1970s that the U.S. Supreme Court was called in to settle it.

A particularly difficult area of conflict has to do with state revenue. Since 1969, Maine has taxed the income of nonresidents who work in the state, many of them from New Hampshire who are employed at the Portsmouth

Naval Shipyard in Kittery. The tax is especially unpopular in New Hampshire, which does not have an income tax. In retaliation, New Hampshire enacted a commuter tax, which was found unconstitutional in 1975 by the U.S. Supreme Court because it taxed nonresidents differently from residents. The tax disputes between the two states erupted again when Maine added a nonresident spousal tax in 1986. This measure sets the rate of the nonresident tax, ranging from 1 to 10 percent of a family's total income. Although Maine does not specifically tax the earnings of a spouse who does not work in the state, it now calculates the income tax based on total family income. In 1988, over three hundred residents of New Hampshire demonstrated against this policy. Later in the year, New Hampshire's attorney general requested a refund of the Maine tax for a New Hampshire couple, resulting in New Hampshire challenging Maine's tax policy in court. In March 1990, the Maine Supreme Judicial Court rejected New Hampshire's claim. Subsequently, the U.S. Supreme Court refused to grant certiorari in the case, allowing that decision to stand.

Reinforcing the economic competition between Maine and New Hampshire are important differences of ideology and political style. While Maine is characteristically moderate in politics, New Hampshire's politics are more polarized and combative. In the past two decades, conservative Republicans have held sway in New Hampshire, in contrast to Maine, where a two-party system has been in place since the 1960s. Officials in the two states, especially members of their congressional delegations, usually cooperate on issues pitting northern New England against other regions. However, competition between the two states over economic development and taxes is likely to persist.

MAINE AND CANADA

Of the three jurisdictions bordering on Maine, only one (New Hampshire) is part of the United States. The other two (Quebec and New Brunswick) are provinces of Canada. Ties to Canada are further strengthened by the ethnic composition of Maine's population. During the latter half of the nineteenth century, about one-quarter of all the French Canadians who migrated to the United States settled in Maine.

In the past two decades, Maine has developed extensive relations with the Canadian provincial governments, and the state's interest in Canadian affairs has, to an extent, shaped its relationship with the U.S. government. Governor Kenneth Curtis (1967–75) was especially active in promoting closer ties between the state and Canada.[18] Under his direction, a state Office of Canadian Relations was established in 1973. (Currently, Canadian affairs are handled by a special assistant to the governor.)

In 1973, the state also signed agreements with several Canadian provinces promoting cooperation in such areas as environmental protection, energy, trade, tourism, fisheries, forestry, and recreation. A study of formal interactions between the American states and Canada showed that, in 1974, Maine had concluded by far the largest number of understandings and agreements of any state, accounting for 110 of the 766 understandings and agreements (14.4 percent) in existence that year between the fifty states and Canadian provinces.[19]

Curtis believed that effective ties with Canada assisted the state in avoiding certain problems during his administration. He cited the example of a business promoter of a northeast oil refinery who suggested to Curtis that he was considering a site in New Brunswick, and who told Premier Richard Hatfield of New Brunswick that he was considering a location in Maine. The two leaders, who knew each other well, discussed the matter and decided that the project was not economically sound. (The refinery was eventually built in another Canadian province and ran into financial difficulties.) As another example, during the OPEC oil-embargo crisis of 1973, Canada sought to protect its supplies by halting exports through a federal order from Ottawa binding on all provinces. A Great Northern Paper Company mill, which at that time obtained its oil from a refinery in New Brunswick, would have had to shut down had not Curtis persuaded Hatfield to intervene. Through Hatfield's work, an exception to the order was obtained.[20]

After Curtis left office in 1975, his successor, independent James Longley, showed less interest in Canadian affairs. The state legislature thereupon established its own office of Canadian affairs, which continues to the present.[21] The existence of many Democratic legislators from French-speaking constituencies was an important factor in the creation of the legislative office, which is unique to Maine. One of its tasks is to assist legislators whose districts border on Canada in working out constituent problems involving Canada. Other problems tackled by this office have included the spruce budworm infestation of forests and the flooding of Maine farmlands caused by excessive amounts of water released by a Canadian dam into an international river.

Observers of relations between Maine and the maritime provinces believe that federal system issues pose both an incentive as well as a barrier to cooperation. The impetus for close relations is in the fairly small size and limited economic power that both Maine and the Canadian provinces have in their respective federal systems.[22] If they can work out a policy agreement, it is at least theoretically possible for them to have added weight in national policymaking. The difficulty is that the place of the legislature is different in the two systems. Maine has a long tradition of legislative strength and independence, whereas legislatures in the parliamentary arrangements of the Canadian provinces are traditionally subordinate to the executive. That difference will probably preclude further formalization of the link established by Maine's legislature.

The more critical policy areas affecting Maine and Canada involve, of course, other states and the U.S. government. Maine is working with New Hampshire and the other New England states to develop a regional energy policy under which they can purchase nuclear and hydroelectric power from New Brunswick and Quebec. The most troublesome issue between Maine and Canada has focused on trade. Maine has sought to prevent Canada from flooding the United States market with such products as fish, lumber, and potatoes that compete at lower prices with Maine products. The state has not enjoyed a great deal of success thus far. On January 1, 1989, the United States adopted a Free Trade Agreement with Canada that was opposed by both of Maine's senators. They believed that the pact leaves important natural resource and agricultural issues unresolved. Later in 1989 their concerns seemed to be justified when a lobster war broke out between the United States and Canada over lobster size. Canada permitted the taking of smaller lobsters than the United States allowed. The conflict especially affected Maine because the state produces about 40 percent of the U.S. catch. The result of the war was an unusually poor year for Maine's lobster industry.

CONCLUSION

Maine has long depended on the federal government to protect its economic interests, even as it has sought to maintain its distinctive way of life. To a large extent, it has been successful. Its greatest battles have been fought in Congress, and its success there has been due to the presence of a very strong congressional delegation, which the state's political system seems able to produce quite regularly. The state is too small to engage in much bargaining in presidential politics, and it has not tried to challenge the U.S. Supreme Court. Competition increasingly seems to characterize the relations between Maine and its only U.S. neighbor, the state of New Hampshire. While this competition is largely based on the economic similarities of the states, it is probably strengthened by their ideological differences. On the other hand, Maine has undertaken to foster close ties with the bordering Canadian provinces, partly because its problems are not always of major interest to the federal government, and perhaps partly because it wishes to strengthen its hand in dealings with the federal government.

CHAPTER TWELVE

Local Government

Maine has a rather large territory (31,886 square miles) for a relatively sparsely populated eastern state. Although its total population in 1990 was only 1,227,928, the state contains a large number of local governmental units, including the following: 434 towns, 22 cities, 35 plantations, 3 Indian reservations, 16 counties, and more than 300 special districts.

A newcomer who travels the state may be struck by the large number of small adjacent communities, and their distance both in miles and in habits from the state and national capitals. There are well over 800 governmental units and 420 unorganized townships, which illustrate the underlying governmental diversity and noncentralization at the state's grass roots. Under Maine law, only cities and towns are considered municipal corporations.

Some longtime critics of Maine's vast landscape of local governments have even classified it as a "jungle" that inevitably forces more centralization. They argue that the weaker units of local government cannot perform adequately, and eventually lose control over some of their service functions.[1] These small governments were challenged in earlier periods as they lost direct control over education services to newly formed school administrative districts in the 1950s and to the State Department of Education (see chapter 13 for a more detailed discussion). During the 1980s, the state government also became more active in local affairs by imposing more mandates in such areas as solid waste disposal, protection of natural resources, and land-use planning. Even more state mandates and additional demands for local tax dollars may be expected because of the withdrawal of funding for key federal programs during the Reagan administration. Maine's system of local government and substate units will surely be tested as the state approaches the twenty-first century.

TOWNS, PLANTATIONS, AND CITIES

Some authorities have contended that the early English parish meeting was the origin of New England town government, while others argue that it evolved from farm meetings in ancient Germany. In New England, town government began only a few years after the initial settlements in the Boston area. The New England town itself averaged twenty to forty square miles in size and usually followed the natural terrain while proceeding with straight lines. However, only a fraction of that area was actually inhabited. Colonists lived in close proximity of the meeting house, schoolhouse, and town center. By the end of the seventeenth century, new settlements were created within the towns as the population often had dispersed. Residents began to insist upon and acquire local rights, as towns were divided into religious parishes, and road, militia, and tax assessment and collection subareas.

Due to an expanding population, the Massachusetts legislature decided that each settlement should be authorized to organize and govern as a town, in the same manner as the English parishes. Weekly or monthly meetings were held to conduct town business. Eventually, the agendas became unwieldly, attendance declined, and decision making was delegated to a committee of "select men" who would act between meetings. Eventually this interim committee made it possible to lengthen the periods between meetings.[2]

Maine has been called a union of towns. Even today, towns remain the most numerous unit, and in terms of area, they continue to dominate the state. There are 434 towns, but about half of them have less than one thousand residents. When formally "incorporated" by a special act of the legislature, a community becomes a "town" under Maine law. As a municipality, it is given certain privileges; it also assumes obligations to perform duties that would not be required of an unorganized township, but that are required of all Maine towns. As a corporation, it may sue and be sued, and it has responsibilities for collecting taxes and supporting a school system.

Within some Maine towns, "village corporations" were also authorized by special acts of the legislature. Historically, most village corporations were established to provide a specific service (e.g., fire protection for the town center) that applied to residents of the village, but not to the more rural residents, who did not use the service and were not taxed for it. The legislature established 124 village corporations from the 1830s to the 1930s; but only a few remain in operation. Most of them exist in a few coastal communities that need additional services for the numerous seasonal residents who may be clustered in a particular part of the town.[3] These village corporations may also be viewed as precursors of special districts, which are discussed in chapter 13.

Plantations originated in the Massachusetts Bay Colony, and are unique to Maine among all the states. First envisioned as a temporary "halfway house" between an unorganized township and an incorporated township, they have continued to flourish as local government units. In 1992, there were still thirty-five plantations in the state. They may even again be considered as an option where town government has become too expensive for the smaller communities.[4] Most are rural and sparsely populated northern and northwestern communities where there is little demand for the variety of services enjoyed in the larger towns. Plantations resemble towns in size and are, therefore, much smaller than counties.

Plantation government resembles town government, with the traditional annual meeting constituting the legislative function. Assessors, rather than selectmen, are elected to carry on the day-to-day operation of government. However, there are several key differences: (1) plantations must be organized by a vote of the county commissioners, while towns are incorporated by a vote of the Maine legislature; and (2) they do not have the powers granted to towns and cities under Maine's home-rule statute. Thus, the chief disadvantage is that they lack discretionary authority in certain governmental matters.[5]

One municipal expert, James Haag, explains their perceived advantages for some communities:

> Plantations are small in population size but tend to be relatively well off in terms of high per capita tax commitment and low effective rates of property taxation—indeed, much better off financially than the average Maine town or city . . . plantations appear to have available all the state aid which is available to Maine towns and cities. In the instance of welfare, plantations receive state aid which is not available to Maine towns and cities.[6]

Maine has twenty-two cities that are incorporated through a charter form of government. The city charter or "local constitution" is a written document that outlines the city's general philosophy and form of local government. Cities are required by state law to adopt a charter stating how local self-government will be established, while towns are not. There are no minimum population requirements for cities, which often confuses newcomers to Maine about their status vis-à-vis towns. Eastport, for example, is a city of

1,965, while Brunswick is a town of 20,906. Still, cities tend to be the largest communities in the state, but are small by national standards.

In cities, representative government replaces the town meeting. City residents elect their representatives to serve on councils and establish the overall policies of the community. Medium-size and larger Maine cities (Portland is the largest with a population of 64,358) tend to be well-run communities with a capacity to administer and deliver a wide array of services. This is due in part to the use of council-manager government in Maine. According to the 1990 U.S. Census, 357,890 Mainers resided in its twenty-two cities. (Projections by state government had predicted 358,000 city residents by 1990.)[7]

FORMS OF LOCAL GOVERNMENT

Maine's 491 plantations, towns, and cities have adopted a variety of different governmental structures. However, there are four basic forms of municipal government: (1) town meeting–selectmen, (2) town meeting–selectmen-manager/council-manager, (3) council-manager, and (4) mayor-council.

Town Meeting–Selectmen

For more than three hundred years, the town meeting has existed in New England, including Maine, and has been praised as a pure form of direct democracy. It is an assembly of the town's eligible voters, usually held in March, where the citizens themselves discuss and act on the issues facing the town.[8] Special town meetings may be held during the year and are called by either the selectmen or a specified number of voters in the town. Issues must be listed in the form of articles on a warrant that announces the time and place of the town meeting. Moderators traditionally have enjoyed broad discretionary powers to run a meeting.[9] At the actual meeting, votes may be taken only on the specific articles placed on the warrant.

The town meeting expresses the legislative function of local government. The townspeople pass the laws needed for town governance, approve a budget, levy taxes, authorize borrowing, and elect the various town officers. A plural executive body of three to seven members, called the board of selectmen, is elected for one-year terms and charged with administering town business, enforcing laws, and implementing the decisions made at the town meeting. Under state statutes, selectmen have specific administrative responsibilities that relate to town meetings, elections, finances, personnel, streets and highways, public safety, human services, public works, and planning. Maine state law also grants them some limited powers to enact laws or ordinances regulating vehicles, public ways, and public property.[10]

Other officials elected at a pure town meeting may include the town clerk, tax collector, road commissioner, board of assessors, and overseers of the poor. All of these officials have duties and responsibilities specified by state law. (If no such officials are elected by the voters or appointed by the selectmen, their duties are assumed by the board.) State law also requires the people to elect a school board (or representatives to a School Administrative District), which appoints the school superintendent.

The town meeting has been praised as the outstanding example of direct democracy. Thomas Jefferson called it "the wisest invention ever devised by the wit of man for the perfect exercise of self government."[11] In the late nineteenth century, James Bryce commented as follows:

> Of the three or four types of systems of local government which I have described, that of the town or township with its primary assembly is admittedly the best. It is the cheapest and the most efficient; it is the most educative of the citizens who bear a part in it. The town meeting has been not only the source but the school of democracy.[12]

While the town meeting has been glorified in the past, it has also been criticized for the following reasons:

1. Citizen apathy and poor turnout, which in turn have often allowed a few well-organized special interests (i.e., volunteer firefighters, teachers, relatives and extended families) to control policymaking.
2. The physical problem in some towns of housing a large turnout of citizens for a meeting.
3. Problems increase as the size of the town population increases, especially beyond 2,500.
4. Problems of whether a part-time executive body (selectmen) can effectively administer town affairs (e.g., in some cases, selectmen lack clear-cut authority over other elected town officials, who have duties and responsibilities specified in state law).
5. The question of whether a citizen forum is capable of adequately deliberating very complex matters in one day (e.g., financial issues).

Indeed, studies of the New England town meeting have provided evidence of poor attendance and relative lack of debate at times for even salient issues. For a number of reasons, a large percentage of townfolk have given up their privilege of participating in this unique institution. However, as Joseph A. Zimmerman concluded about the citizens:

> Their lack of attendance at an open town meeting may be interpreted as a vote in confidence in a de facto representative town meeting. Fortunately, attendance appears to be a function of the importance of the unresolved issues, and voter apathy tends to disappear when a major issue is brought to the open town meeting for resolution. [13]

During the twentieth century, the pure town meeting form has been modified in a number of communities to help cope with socioeconomic changes. Under the name of *Finance*, *Warrant*, or *Budget*, a special committee composed of elected or appointed citizens has been used by a number of Maine communities. First adopted by the town of Brunswick in 1902, this committee either participates in the preparation of the budget or investigates a proposed town budget. After a thorough review, the committee makes its recommendations on the budget to the town meeting.

Another possible modification in the town meeting establishes the "Limited or Representative Town Meeting." However, this reform drastically alters the town meeting as the citizen's legislative body and as an example of pure democracy. Persons are elected from each of several districts to attend the town meeting. Any voter may still speak, but only the elected representatives may vote. This form has been used by three Maine towns: Sanford, Old Orchard Beach, and Caribou. Today, only Sanford uses this town-meeting format with its seven wards and 143 representatives, but it remains very popular in other parts of New England. [14]

Town Meeting–Selectmen-Manager/Council-Manager

Under this form of government, the board of selectmen hires a qualified full-time manager to carry out the various administrative duties of the board. The manager may be given authority to appoint other personnel in the town and serves at the pleasure of the board of selectmen. In theory, the person should be professionally trained in public administration, but in practice, this does not always occur.

This modification of town government became a widely acceptable device in Maine, which effectively maintained the Yankee tradition of the town meeting while incorporating the values of professionalism expressed in the national movement to reform local government by means of the city-manager form of government. By 1970, over 25 percent of town-meeting munic-ipalities had added town managers; in general, most towns over 2,000 in population have adopted this form, while those under 1,000 have not. Most Maine towns adopted the selectmen-manager plan through provisions of the general law—an enabling act passed in 1939 that specifies the manager's du-ties, responsibilities, and powers. In the late 1960s, the town-manager en-abling act was revised to help clarify the roles and duties of selectmen and managers and to provide broader administrative authority to the manager for appointing department heads, subject to confirmation by the selectmen. Several traditionally elected offices, such as town clerk, tax collector, and treasurer, can be discontinued and their roles assumed by the manager or a designee.

In practice, small-town managers have acquired a number of difficult roles and responsibilities, which may vary somewhat from one community to another. Official "hats" of the manager may include serving as purchas-ing agent, treasurer, tax collector, road commissioner, overseer of the poor, clerk, civil defense director, and building inspector. In general, the manager is responsible for administering all of the operations of town government with the exception of the schools. In Maine, managers cannot serve as as-sessors, a practice that can occur in neighboring New Hampshire.

Since the passage of Maine's home-rule statute in 1969, towns and cities have had the authority to adopt, under a local charter, any form of govern-ment that employs a town or city manager. Thus, a town or city may select either the "Statutory Town Manager Plan," or create its own list of duties and responsibilities for the manager and a framework for governance within the context of its own home-rule charter. Even before the town-manager en-abling act, some communities received special authorization from the legis-lature to hire an appointed administrator. In 1925, Camden became the first Maine town to adopt this form of government, followed by Fort Fairfield, Mount Desert, Washburn, Rumford, and Dexter.

A number of hybrid forms of this plan dot the Maine landscape. Forty-five Maine towns, like Farmingdale, adjacent to Augusta, and the island community of North Haven, have hired full-time or part-time "administra-tive assistants." These assistants are hired by the selectmen to advise them on specified matters, often financial. There is no state law providing for ad-ministrative assistants. Therefore, they serve at the pleasure of the selectmen and derive their authority as delegated by the board.[15]

Some of the smaller communities have cooperated to hire a "circuit-riding" manager to save on costs and obtain the services of a professional administrator, which they probably could not afford individually. An example of this cooperative arrangement exists in the towns of Castle Hill, Mapleton, and Chapman, which are located in northern Maine.

A slightly different variation used in sixteen communities is the "town meeting–council-manager" form, whereby legislative functions are typically shared by the town meeting and the council. For example, most legislative functions regarding the budget are reserved for the town meeting, but selected legislative functions regarding ordinances are exercised by the council. Thus, the "council" acts at times in a plural executive capacity as "selectmen" do, and, in addition, exercises legislative functions.

Council-Manager

The tide of municipal reform of the early twentieth century swept into Maine and has had an impact, especially in the adoption of the council-manager plan and the previously discussed town manager plan. At one point, Maine was ranked fifth nationally in the number of managers, trailing only California, Texas, Michigan, and Pennsylvania. However, because of the large number of small towns and the town-meeting tradition, adoption of the pure council-manager plan has been limited.

In 1917, Auburn became the first Maine city to adopt the city-manager form of government. Portland followed suit in 1920. As was often the case nationwide, corruption and inefficiency under the previous weak mayor-council structure accelerated the trend. By 1970, there were twenty-eight council-manager municipalities (cities or towns). By 1988, the number had increased to thirty-one communities, and thus the council-manager has become the most popular form of local government for those communities that have seen fit to eliminate the town meeting. It tends to be most prevalent in communities with a population over 5,000. Unlike the town meeting–selectmen form, this form of government must be adopted through a local charter.

The council-manager form was first adopted by the small town of Staunton, Virginia, in 1906, when a professional was hired to conduct all the executive work of the community. By 1914, Dayton, Ohio, became the first major American city to adopt the plan, which gained rapidly in popularity. By 1987, the International City Management Association listed 1,866 communities with populations over 5,000 that had adopted the plan.[16] The basic features of the plan include (1) a small council, usually elected at large (each member of the council is elected from the entire community) and on a nonpartisan basis; (2) a mayor, usually elected from among the members of a council, who serves as chair and the ceremonial head of the city; and (3) an expert administrator—the city manager—hired by the council to manage the city's business.

This appointed professional can serve for an indefinite length of time. On the other hand, he or she may have a mutually agreed-upon contract with the council for a specific time period. The individual need not be a local person. Indeed, in most cases, an outside expert is hired because of his or her educational background and experience. Typically, the city charter specifies the manager's legal duties and responsibilities to include:

1. preparing the budget for the council
2. appointing and removing department heads
3. overseeing the execution of policy
4. making recommendations to the council

The manager has no vote, but does have influence because of his or her expertise, control of information, and full-time appointed executive status.

In Maine, there are some deviations from the general model. For example, about one-third of the municipal councils are oriented toward a district or combination system (ward and at large), rather than being purely at large. Moreover, council appointment of city officials is fairly widespread. Some Maine managers are even precluded by charter or by historical practice from appointing or dismissing municipal officials (e.g., clerks, tax collectors, treasurers, assessors) whom, in theory, they are supervising.[17] Thus, in the area of personnel management, Maine local executives are often characterized as "weak managers."

The original theory of the city manager plan was patterned after the corporate business model used in the private sector. The council would decide on policy, the manager would execute the policy, and neither would interfere with the function of the other. Thus, the advocates of this plan believed that the manager was to be a "nonpolitical" position, while the council would determine policy and remain as the political body.[18] This dichotomy has been debated and largely debunked elsewhere. The primary difficulty is trying to separate politics and administration.[19] The "gray area" of the plan remains controversial even among proponents of the plan. A major question is the extent to which the manager should be a leader in shaping municipal policies. Indeed, it seems that city managers often evaluate their own success and that of their colleagues on their ability to promote change, initiate policy, and build support mechanisms in the community, and not merely by carrying out the council's will.[20]

Mayor-Council

Although the mayor-council form is the most popular government structure among all U.S. communities, it has very limited application in Maine. As recently as 1970, there were only five mayor-council communities, which together served about 11 percent of all the state's population: Biddeford, Lewiston, Saco, Waterville, and Westbrook. All had adopted mayor-council charters in the latter half of the nineteenth century, which provided for the election of bicameral legislative bodies by wards and a mayor elected at large. Although the mayor was designated the "chief executive," administrative and financial powers also were vested in the legislative body. Each of these cities also used a bicameral arrangement; Waterville was the last to abandon bicameralism in 1967. Mayors and council members serve concurrent terms; voters can thus change all elected officials during each election. With the exception of Lewiston, these cities all have a partisan nomination and election process. They also have substantial Franco-American populations.

The council is the municipal law-making body, and the mayor is the designated chief executive. The council approves the budget, may override the mayor's veto, and may confirm or even make some of the personnel appointments, while the mayor may be vested with authority to preside at council meetings, call special meetings, and cast deciding votes to create or break a tie.

Only two of the above mayor-council municipalities—Waterville and Westbrook —can be classified as "strong mayor" models by national standards. In both, the mayor has authority to appoint department heads and control budget operations. Interestingly, these communities also have added a professional chief administrative officer, who reports to the mayor and is responsible for preparing the budget and supervising most of the department heads.

The city of Lewiston, which had a unique mayor-council system, was once designated by University of Maine political scientist Edward Dow as "a government of 37 legs and no head." Its administrative and finance authority was fragmented among six boards and commissions, each with five members, a seven-member board of aldermen, and a mayor. Like many other weak mayor-council cities, Lewiston eventually altered its government structure. It now has a new city charter and a city administrator, who reports to an elected council and acts as the appointed executive. Thus, perhaps one of Maine's most blatantly political cities joined the ranks of communities with council-manager governments in 1980.

In practice, there are and have been numerous variations over time in the specific structure of Maine's few mayor-council communities and in the actual division of power between the legislative body and elected political executive, the mayor.[21] In general, these communities followed an evolutionary pattern in urban politics associated with larger cities in the United States. Ethnic politics, which in Maine's case involve mainly Franco-American and Irish-American participants, often influenced both the structure and behavior of city governments. These communities resisted the early major prescriptions of twentieth-century reformers, such as nonpartisan elections, the city-manager plan, short ballots, smaller councils, home rule, and professionalism in general. While these parts of the "reform package" became operational in other Maine cities and towns, the ethnic composition within the urban culture of these small cities continued to dominate and often restrict more drastic structural change.

However, these communities began to change incrementally by hiring professionals, even if their form of government remained the same. Pressure for competition with other communities and regions, the impact of economic growth, and the influx of new ideas from newcomers all had an effect. In the 1970s, Lewiston hired a Harvard-educated planner, and Westbrook employed a professionally trained city administrator to provide new leadership, even though not all of the "reform package" was acceptable in those cities. The middle-class reform ideology did not always go over well in these heterogeneous cities, as was the case in Boston, too. The reformers wanted to take politics out of local government and eliminate the boss and machine, which were branded as corrupt, or at best inefficient. Party structure, class, and ethnicity acted as brakes on reform in these cities.

POLITICS FROM SMALL TOWN TO SMALL CITY

As earlier chapters have explained, Maine's history is one of a rural state that has recently experienced selective urban growth along Interstate 95, on the coast, and in its southern sector of York and Cumberland counties. The four Metropolitan Statistical Areas (MSAs) of Portland, Lewiston-Auburn, Bangor, and part of the Portsmouth, New Hampshire, MSA (in York County) contained over 35 percent of the state's population in 1990 and have experienced moderate to rapid growth during the past two decades. Thus, local politics in Maine takes on several basic forms—that of small-town politics, which is characterized by the large number of communities in the state under 5,000 in population, and the urban and suburban politics of Maine's four relatively small metropolitan areas.

Oliver Williams and Charles Adrian have developed a typology for different images of the proper role of government, which is especially useful in analyzing Maine's local governments. They believe that a government's role can be one of an agent of growth (active economic development strategy), a provider of amenities (additional services for a good living environment), a caretaker (basic services, low taxes), or an arbiter (managing conflict among competing interests). These possible roles may help us better understand the relationship between social and economic change, and political changes.[22] In most Maine towns, there has been a longstanding tradition of caretaker government. Only a few cities have fit the role of provider of amenities or, at times, arbiter. More recently, a number of cities and some towns have used their municipal government in an agent-of-growth role.

Small-town politics is usually practiced in relatively homogeneous and stable communities, where relationships are personal and informal. Townsfolk assume that the various community interests are more or less in harmony with each other. As Clarence Stone comments,

> Perhaps because small towns and villages tend to be socially close knit, conflict and open competition are frowned upon. So, village politics is a politics of consensus. Petty squabbling and personal rivalry may be inevitable, but they are nevertheless regarded as improper. Historically small town life has not accommodated competition and dissent, nor have things changed much in the contemporary village.[23]

Small-town politics is usually a matter of obliging friends rather than choosing policy alternatives.[24] All too often salient issues are avoided, and politics revolves around personalities and small irritants. Limited government may be found in the town of Acton, which has a year-round population of 1,900 and one police officer, eighty-three-year-old Frank Gemelli. Still other towns have no local police and must rely on the county sheriff and the state police.

Rural local government has been characterized as being run by part-time actors, as having an amateur style rather than a professional style, and as being perceived by the citizens as "nonpolitical." However, as Roscoe Martin warned in his classic statement on "The Physiology of Little Government":

Table 4: Estimates of Population of Maine's Metropolitan Statistical Areas (MSAS)

	1960 Census	1970 Census	1980 Census	1990 Census
Bangor	—	—	83,919	88,745
Lewiston-Auburn	70,295	72,474	84,864	88,141
Portland	139,122	141,625	193,831	215,281
Portsmouth, N.H.*	—	—	42,011	48,936

Sources: Based on U.S. Bureau of the Census, *Current Population Reports,* Series P-26, No. 85-ME-C, Estimates of the Population of Maine Counties and Metropolitan Areas: July 1, 1981, to 1985, (Washington, D.C.: U.S. Government Printing Office, 1988, p. 7; U.S. Bureau of the Census, *1990 Census of Population and Housing*, Summary Tape File 1A, New England Division: Maine, issued August 1991, Data Users Services Division, Washington, D.C.

MSAS are as defined by the Office of Management and Budget, June 30, 1986.

* Maine population only

> Little government, being personal, intimate, and informal is supposed by some to be free of politics. In simple truth, no concept concerning local government has less merit. The image of politics as an evil art practiced somewhere else by somebody else is, of course, quite unrealistic, for politics is found wherever people debate issues of public import.[25]

In Maine, the small town has dominated because of the historical dispersion of a small population throughout a relatively large area, political noncentralization, a lack of numerous medium-size and large cities, and the early absence of substate regional administrative alternatives. However, population growth in Maine's four metropolitan areas, and along the coast and Interstate 95, is changing political traditions and landscapes. Urbanization as a movement of people into cities and their suburbs is dramatically affecting southern Maine. The Greater Portland area has rapidly expanded to well over one-quarter of a million persons (see tables 4 and 5).

Quite naturally, growth can be a powerful force that overruns the more primitive local governments and their caretaker outlook. New schools have to be built and services expanded. Coastal communities, especially, have experienced soaring property values and taxes that were previously associated only with urban areas to the south. Growth has meant more diversity in town government as natives and newcomers often "square off" for more extended debate on town councils or at traditional town meetings.

GROUPS AND INDIVIDUALS: MOVERS AND SHAKERS

Influentials in Maine community politics are diverse, and range from the interest groups of the larger cities and towns to the churches and service clubs that are sometimes active in smaller towns. In a mail survey, city and town administrators (N = 219) were asked to assess the degree of influence that a list of twenty-seven groups or individuals had on local issues. The administrators answered at an 84 percent response rate.[26] Those groups receiving more than 50 percent in the three highest categories of "moderate," "high," or "very high" influence were as follows:

- Key Individual Citizens   72%
- Local School Board   67%
- Businessmen and Merchants   67%
- Maine Municipal Association   63%
- Fire Department   63%
- Taxpayers, Homeowners Associations   54%

Businesspeople/merchants and taxpayers/homeowners associations are perceived by the Maine managers as being influential, as is the case in other states. In Maine, fire departments rate high in influence because they are staffed with volunteers in many of the smaller communities. These volunteers are very active in the town meetings. The Maine Municipal Association has been one of the most influential interest groups representing communities in Augusta. Because of its substantial staff and credibility with local government administrators, it ranks as one of the most potent and influential organizations.

Groups which were classified by three-fourths or more of the respondents as being in the lowest categories of "none" and "low" influence were the following:

- Civic Groups   85%
- Republican Party Officials   83%
- Democratic Party Officials   83%
- Private Sector Labor Leaders   83%
- Neighborhood Associations   82%
- Lawyers, Legal Associations   82%

– Public Utility Officials	81%
– Groups of Low Income People	80%
– Bankers	79%
– Other Mass Media	78%
– Churches or Religious Groups	77%
– Chamber of Commerce	75%

Many of the above groups are influential in some communities, but they registered low scores on this statewide survey because they do not exist in many small communities. Some have been very active and effective in Maine's larger and medium-sized communities. Interestingly, political parties were seen as being influential in only approximately 17 percent of the communities—mainly in those cities in which the traditional form of urban politics occurs.

Groups that registered some moderate influence on local issues were newspaper editors, police departments, municipal employees or their union or association, contractors and real estate developers, environmental groups, regional planning commissions and councils of government, farmers, and high-income people.

Decision making in Maine's local governments has ranged from elitism to pluralism, where many different groups compete on different issues.[27] Domination of political institutions by a few economic elites, or by the private-sector leadership of a one-industry town, was much easier to accomplish in earlier periods of history than in the present. However, there are still fears of rich out-of-state seasonal owners dominating the politics of Maine's "golden coast."

With the gradual diversification of the economic base in some areas, coupled with the strong acceptance of the town meeting and amateur government, it has been possible for the average citizen to participate in his or her local government. Findings from the Maine managers' survey somewhat strengthen the argument of the pluralists. In most communities, decision making involves different alignments of power, due to the various interests of the different groups that occur within the community on different issues.

CONCLUSION

Since the 1920s, some constructive tension has existed in Maine between the need for modern management of local government and small-town and

small-city cultures and politics. Many groups and individuals do become involved in the political process from time to time and can be influential. Access to the political process is usually high, but participation is high or low
depending on the saliency of the issue. Where elitism exists, it tends to be in
unorganized townships, small towns, and plantations that operate under the
influence of the paper companies.[28]

Most important, much of Maine's growth today is suburban and southern. The outlying towns in both Cumberland and York counties experienced
major growth in the 1970s and 1980s, while the growth of the major core
cities (Portland, Lewiston, and Bangor) remained stable or declined slightly.
Smaller coastal communities also experienced substantial growth in the
1980s because of "newcomers from away" who perceive an opportunity for
a high quality of life in Maine. The impact of these demographic trends on
Maine's local governments will be felt for years to come.

CHAPTER THIRTEEN

Substate Regionalism and State-Local Relations

Filling the gap between local and state government services has been a major concern for the state of Maine. The tension between the desire for local participation and control and a sense of fairness in service delivery and its financial burden has produced an impasse of sorts. This chapter examines the traditional role of county government, the establishment of a regional council system during the last two decades, the programmatic use of special districts, and a number of other specific examples of cooperation between municipalities. The challenge of the property tax for state and local relations will also be explored. North-south rivalries as well as rivalries between communities of different population have heightened conflict between the state's geographic sections and metropolitan areas.

By and large, Maine has chosen not to pursue the type of drastic institutional mechanisms for solving regional problems that have been attempted in other states, such as city-county consolidation, the urban county (either the Lakewood Plan of California or the one-level approach of Miami–Dade County), or the more developed metropolitan councils formed in Minneapolis–St. Paul and in Portland, Oregon, where a great deal of authority and responsibility have been delegated to regional decision makers. Instead, some communities have experimented with cooperative and voluntary ventures in working with each other. County government still remains, and many see it as another "project" with which to tinker. However, the threat to the status quo posed by the perceived need for both economic growth and protection of the environment may cause greater change in the future.

COUNTY GOVERNMENT

In his classic reform text of 1917, *The County: The "Dark Continent" of American Politics*, H. S. Gilbertson called counties creatures of tradition that "once established, acquired a tendency to 'stick' tenaciously to their original form."[1] In some respects, this conclusion remains valid for many aspects of county government in Maine.

County government has posed a particular dilemma to policymakers and analysts for many years. In New England in general, and in Maine specifically, county government has been a weak institution. In Maine, reformers have coalesced into two camps—those who want to abolish counties (as was done in Connecticut), and those who want to strengthen them (as has been done in California and Florida). No one seems pleased with the status quo.

County government came to New England as a part of the English tradition in the British shire model.[2] Massachusetts created four districts in Maine for its courts in 1636. These eventually evolved into nine counties by 1820. The remaining seven counties were added after statehood. The Maine legislature of 1820 maintained the county system it inherited from Massachusetts, and most officials were appointed by the governor and council. The major role of the county was to administer justice rather than provide general services or enforce local policies. Most political responsibilities rested with the executive branch of state government.[3]

In New England, municipalities (towns and cities) emerged as the prime form of local government in the 1700s. Since that time, towns throughout New England have retained their dominant position as service providers, with counties administering only those few services required of them in their respective state constitutions. Traditionally, these mandated services have included the recording of deeds and other real estate transfers, regional law enforcement, and judicial administration.[4] Outside of New England, county government has a history of providing a stronger base that has aided in its evolution toward a general-purpose type government with significant regional responsibilities.[5]

In 1855, the appointive county officers became elective. However, there was relatively little change in the structure of Maine county government between the mid-1800s and the 1970s. The duties of county officials have remained largely administrative and narrowly defined because the county is a subunit of the state that operates under state laws. Therefore, local voters have very limited control over county affairs. Unlike towns and cities, counties were not incorporated, and until recently have not had the opportunity to have charters or legislative powers.

Counties do enjoy considerably more responsibilities in the unorganized territory, where there is an absence of town or city government, and where counties provide all services not provided by the state, such as fire protection and road maintenance. Maine counties do not operate schools, welfare programs, or hospitals, as may occur in other states.

Maine county governments were responsible in the early 1900s for constructing and maintaining bridges. However, since the early 1970s, these responsibilities have shifted to the state and municipal governments. Maine counties also controlled the superior courts until they were reorganized in 1975 and replaced by a more streamlined superior court system (see chapter 8). Thus, during the 1970s, while many counties nationwide were doing more because of demographic and other pressures, Maine counties were doing less. Their major role was maintaining the sheriff's department, probate court, and the county jails. They remained one of the last bastions of partisan politics in local government, where a certain amount of patronage and favoritism could still be found.

In general, Maine's counties are rather typical of counties in other New England states because they never developed, or in some cases have abandoned, the wide array of local services (i.e., roads, schools, welfare administration) found in many counties nationwide. This was due largely to the earlier strength of the town governments and the political culture of New England communities. The town governance structure itself has been made legitimate by Maine statute.[6]

Maine's sixteen counties reflect a diversity of geographic size and population (see table 5 and map 1). The smallest county, Sagadahoc, is only 257 square miles, while the largest county, Aroostook, is the size of a small state—at 6,805 square miles, it is larger than Connecticut and Rhode Island combined! Nine counties have populations of 50,000 or less. In general, the average Maine county is probably too small to become an effective unit of government under its present geographic boundaries.

Maine counties have shared with other New England counties a long history of the absence of a strong chief executive. They also lack any real basis as a unit of self-government. Maine citizens in each county elect three commissioners to be their chief administrators. Moreover, state law has designated the offices of treasurer, sheriff, judge of probate, register of probate, and register of deeds. John Forster, a former regional planning commission executive director, argues that Maine counties derive no powers from the

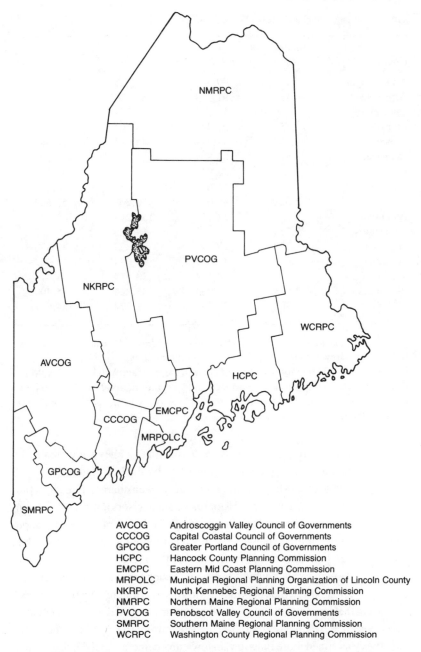

AVCOG	Androscoggin Valley Council of Governments
CCCOG	Capital Coastal Council of Governments
GPCOG	Greater Portland Council of Governments
HCPC	Hancock County Planning Commission
EMCPC	Eastern Mid Coast Planning Commission
MRPOLC	Municipal Regional Planning Organization of Lincoln County
NKRPC	North Kennebec Regional Planning Commission
NMRPC	Northern Maine Regional Planning Commission
PVCOG	Penobscot Valley Council of Governments
SMRPC	Southern Maine Regional Planning Commission
WCRPC	Washington County Regional Planning Commission

Map 1. Maine Counties. (*Source: Annual Register of Maine*, p. 78.)

Table 5: Population and Land Area of Maine Counties

Counties	Square* Miles	1980 (U.S. Census)	1986**	1990 (U.S. Census)***
Androscoggin	496	99,509	101,125	105,259
Aroostook	6,453	91,344	87,901	86,936
Cumberland	853	215,789	228,061	243,135
Franklin	1,789	27,447	29,101	29,008
Hancock	1,522	41,781	44,041	46,948
Kennebec	879	109,889	111,975	115,904
Knox	374	32,941	35,108	36,310
Lincoln	457	26,691	28,331	30,357
Oxford	2,023	49,043	50,208	52,602
Penobscot	3,258	137,015	138,248	146,601
Piscataquis	3,770	17,634	18,006	18,653
Sagadahoc	250	28,795	31,727	33,535
Somerset	3,633	45,049	47,084	49,767
Waldo	724	28,414	30,119	33,018
Washington	2,528	34,963	33,924	35,308
York	989	139,739	158,772	164,587

Sources: *Maine Register, State Yearbook and Legislative Manual*, No. 119 (Portland, Maine: Tower Publishing, 1987). **Population Estimates for Minor Civil Divisions by County*, Maine 1986, (Office of Data, Research, and Vital Statistics, Maine Department of Human Services, Produced under Appropriation No. 1305-1065, October, 1987). ****"Maine's Population Growth Grew 9.2% from 1980 to 1990," *Bangor Daily News*, January 28, 1991.

people, but are entirely creatures of the legislature: "They were created by the Legislature and their powers are controlled by the Legislature."[7]

While counties elsewhere, as in Maine, have been characterized by a plural executive (i.e., county commissioners or supervisors), most other counties nonetheless began to address the pressures of demographic shifts, population increases, cultural change, and the accompanying demands for urban services.[8] Ralph Widner has pointed out that the presence of strong county governments may explain why it has been easier for the southern states to adopt consolidated and metropolitan forms of government than other states.[9]

During the decade of the 1970s, Maine counties faced the prospect of abolition at each legislative session.[10] At the same time, in some instances, they selectively assumed more functions in law enforcement, civil defense, transportation, and social services. For example, Androscoggin County provided a free bus service for elderly, handicapped, and low-income residents because of federal subsidies and local needs. In Lincoln County, a solid-waste program helped to establish a single landfill and a system of collection, disposal, separation, and recycling. County governments also took advantage of federal monies and contracts under the Comprehensive Employment and Training Act (CETA) to provide training and jobs for thousands of Mainers. These regional services, developed during the 1980s and supported by the federal government, provided some needed adrenalin for citizen identification with Maine counties. Because of the geographic diffusion of the population and the state's relative isolation, these pressures came late. Moreover, they were somewhat diverted by the strength of small-town culture, traditional town government, and the legal limits placed on the county as a potentially self-governing body.

However, some changes did come to county government during the 1980s. A 1980 act (L.D. 1038) to provide county self-government amended existing county charter provisions (under 30 M.R.S.A., sec. 1501) and added new provisions to the state statutes. Prior to this act, counties had to submit their budgets to the legislature for approval before they could appropriate funds. Indeed, this cumbersome budget requirement was made more stringent in 1973, when a section (30 M.R.S.A., sec. 253-A) was added to give the legislature the power to "change or alter specific line categories within county estimates." Thus, two of the more significant provisions of the 1980 act provided for a method of appropriating money for county expenditures other than the past statutory method (in 30 M.R.S.A., sections 2, 252, and 253), and provided for the establishment of a finance committee as an alternative method for approving the county budget.[11]

Even with these incremental changes, Maine counties do not possess a pure home-rule option. The legislation enables counties to adopt charters, but unlike under municipal home rule, counties may not adopt a charter granting any power that the legislature has not already granted them. For example, the legislature has not granted counties the power to levy taxes on citizens; therefore, they cannot adopt a charter that would allow them to do so.[12]

There is a perception among many state and municipal officials that county government is rather expensive for the limited services received. In 1980–89, county appropriations increased by 128 percent from $22 million to $51 million. During this period, the portion raised by taxation on municipalities rose by 155 percent, from $14.5 million to $37 million. The balance of dollars was raised by miscellaneous sources and fees, and increased by 77 percent. Some 4 percent of property taxes collected by the municipalities was used to fund county government.[13]

Even though gradual change has occurred regarding county self-government, few Maine counties actually have tried to adopt charters. York, Androscoggin, Hancock, and Aroostook tried unsuccessfully to adopt county charters through referendums. Cumberland County was successful in establishing a charter commission, but when the newly drafted charter proposal went to the voters in 1985, it was defeated.[14]

Recent changes have also been made to provide for the option of a professional county administrator, a reform prescription that has long been suggested by those who have urged the adoption of the county manager form of government.[15] The new Maine statute reads as follows:

> The county administrator shall be the chief administrative official of the county and shall be responsible for the administration of all departments and offices over which the county commissioners have control. He shall act as the clerk of the county. He shall act as purchasing agent for all departments and offices of the county, provided that the county commissioners may require that all purchases greater than a designated amount shall be submitted to sealed bid. He shall attend all meetings of the county commissioners, except when his removal or suspension is being considered. He shall keep the county commissioners and the legislative delegation of the county informed as to the financial condition of the county and shall collect all data necessary for the preparation of the budget.

At the time of this writing, only two counties (York and Aroostook) have adopted the county administrator form. The lack of support can partly be explained by restrictions placed on continuing the salaries of the county commissioners if the plan is adopted: if a county adopts the plan, commissioners lose most of their salary base. In May 1988, the legislature chose to exempt only York and Aroostook counties from the restrictions because the proponents of change argued that their solution would encourage those counties that have already shown some previous initiative, while continuing to compensate the elected commissioners for their participation. As an example of this gradual trend toward appointed leadership, Roland "Danny" Martin, a former town manager and legislator, was appointed county administrator by the Aroostook County commissioners in 1987, while David Adjutant assumed the same position in York County in 1984. However, in November 1989, the voters of Aroostook County approved a charter that established a nine-member finance committee to help implement the home-rule procedure of approving the county budget.

REGIONAL PLANNING COMMISSIONS AND COUNCILS
OF GOVERNMENT

In response to a 1969 Office of Management and Budget (OMB) circular that called for greater federal coordination within substate regions, Governor Kenneth Curtis issued an executive order to establish a uniform system of planning and development districts:

1. Districts should be made large enough to encompass as many state and federal programs as possible, but small enough in geographic size to permit travel from peripheries of the district to the district's service center within a desired one-hour driving time.
2. Each district should have a population base sufficient to finance an adequate regional planning and development technical staff. A 100,000 population base was considered sufficient for adequate local financial support based on present local support of regional planning commissions augmented by federal and state grants.
3. The districts should cover the entire state. Each district should include organized and unorganized territory. Districts should also be balanced in regard to real estate valuation and urban and rural population.
4. In no instance should a district boundary cut through a local governing unit (not applicable to counties or unorganized towns or plantations).
5. Districts should encompass total economic, environmental and human resource areas where possible.[16]

The original eight planning districts were based on the geography of Maine's major river basins. Regional planning districts could not levy taxes or buy or sell property; and in general they were not delegated the legal authority of cities or towns. Instead, they were to develop comprehensive plans for their regions and provide technical assistance to help communities deal with regulations and obtain grants for programs in air and water pollution, solid waste, and shoreland zoning. Their role was to advise municipalities. In general, the regional councils hire staff and focus on activities where they find a demand for services.

In Maine, there are currently eleven regional planning and development districts served by eleven regional councils, which consist of four councils of governments (COGs) (located in Portland, Lewiston-Auburn, Bangor, and Augusta) and seven regional planning commissions (RPCs) (see map 2). One regional council area, previously represented by the Southern Mid-Coast Regional Planning Commission, was without a regional planning

Map 2. Regional Planning Council Boundaries, 1990.
(*Source*: Penobscot Valley Council of Governments).

agency for several years. The State Planning Office filled this gap by using some of its own staff, and by reserving some monies normally allocated to the regional councils for use in the southern mid-coast region. Eventually, a restructured Municipal Regional Planning Organization of Lincoln County was formed.

Regional councils serve 325 dues-paying municipalities within their jurisdictions. It is interesting to note that approximately 170 towns are not active members of a regional council. These towns indirectly receive certain benefits from the regional councils because some funding sources require services that provide benefits to the entire region. Nonmember communities may also derive spillover benefits from transportation and economic development activities in neighboring communities.[17]

Maine's regional councils receive their funding from a variety of sources, including local and regional governments, the state, state-administered federal grants, direct federal grants, and miscellaneous sources. Total funding for all regional councils exceeded $3 million in 1987–88, averaging more than $300,000 for each council. This average is skewed toward the two largest units, the Greater Portland Council of Governments ($1,038,000) and Androscoggin Valley Council of Governments ($668,078). The eight smallest regional councils have average revenues of only $170,000.

Overall, the largest source of revenue (47 percent) is local and regional funding, which includes membership dues and payments for specific services from municipalities. However, there is some disparity because four regional councils have state and federal funds as their largest source of revenue, which makes this the second largest overall category at 30 percent. Specific major programs are the Community Development Block Grant and Coastal Zone Management programs. Both are federally initiated, and the latter program includes state matching funds. The Federal Highway Administration and the Urban Mass Transportation Administration have channeled funds for the councils through the state Department of Transportation's Bureau of Planning and Public Transportation Division.

Direct federal funding is the third largest category at 12 percent. Four regional councils are also designated as Economic Development Districts and rely on funding by the U.S. Economic Development Administration and the Small Business Administration for more than 25 percent of their revenues. Direct state funding of around $194,000 to regional councils has consisted almost entirely of general fund allocations to support the staff provision of technical assistance to municipalities. At first, this increased markedly when the McKernan administration sought to implement its new growth management strategy.

After the 1983 Blaine House Conference on State and Local Relations concluded that regional approaches to delivering public services should be encouraged, and that intergovernmental communications needed to be improved, Governor Joseph E. Brennan issued an executive order encouraging state-local partnerships through regional COGs.[18]

Regional councils were viewed as providing a useful forum for local officials to exchange ideas, express opinions, and work with state and federal officials to (1) improve intergovernmental responsibilities and (2) set priorities for public investments. Regional councils were seen as providers of assistance to local officials and as mechanisms for implementing state programs. The latter reason was debated by many town officials, who valued their local autonomy. In addition, the governor's order stated that the regional councils can assist state and local governments in identifying effective cost-saving measures.

It was further ordered that state agencies would use regional councils, as appropriate, to assist them in planning programs, setting priorities, and delivering services to local governments. Moreover, the regional councils would be defined as "Councils of Governments,"[19] which in Maine means that at least half of the representatives of each member municipality in a regional council must be elected municipal officials. RPCs had been composed of mainly appointed officials. The Penobscot Valley Council of Governments (Greater Bangor Region) moved quickly to take advantage of the COG status.

Thus, in the face of pending and actual federal cutbacks during the 1980s, the governor's order attempted to link the state government to the RPC delivery system more effectively and to strengthen it by further promoting the COG concept. Previously, only the Greater Portland Council of Governments had evolved beyond the RPC status.[20]

SPECIAL DISTRICTS AND SCHOOL DISTRICTS

Special-purpose districts represent a type of government established by law to deliver a specific service. They are designed for a single purpose, as opposed to the general-purpose units, such as towns and cities. Boundaries of special districts may encompass territory within jurisdictional lines of one community, conform to municipal boundaries, or include parts of more than one community. This type of governmental unit is considered here because of its potential and actual use in providing regional services.

Special districts have proliferated both nationwide and in Maine. There are between three and four hundred in Maine, depending on what particular type of substate district classification system is used and whether purely local or state districts are counted.[21] The first known special district in Maine was founded in 1903 when the Augusta Water District was established by special legislation. Until 1941, the "private and special" act was used to form all special districts. However, soil and conservation districts were shortly thereafter authorized by general law. Several other variations have been established since the 1940s, including school districts and housing authorities. These districts were created under general law and must be established by specified procedures for local or regional action, but without legislative participation. The legislature still retains its right to establish any type of special district.[22]

In Maine, these special-purpose districts are legally considered separate local governments with their own authority to levy taxes, deliver services, sign contracts, and sell property. Most have been established in Maine to govern light and power, sanitation, water, and education services. Sanitation and water districts must be established by a special legislative act. Their administrative body or board of directors may be either elected by the voters or appointed by the municipal officials within the boundaries of the district. Light and power districts are also established by legislative special acts, but must be formally approved by the district voters.[23] In the early 1950s, there was a Bangor Recreation Center district, created with its own board of directors, to provide a mechanism for issuing bonds to fund construction of the Bangor Auditorium. In some cases, districts have even been established to satisfy particular interest groups.[24]

Special districts allow communities to charge user fees to those who benefit from the services, which helps to raise additional revenue. Some districts, such as those in the natural resources area, were successful in taking advantage of state and federal aid. Moreover, special district boundaries can often include more than one community, which presents local decision makers with still another option in regional problem solving. This often allows decision makers to bypass the perplexing limits of boundary and taxation problems for service areas. Thus, enabling laws facilitate the creation of the following multimunicipal special districts: lake watershed protection, sanitary, electric, municipal transportation, and refuse disposal.

There is growing evidence that regionalism in Maine had evolved into a new phase by the mid-1980s.[25] Pressure for landfill closures by the Department of Environmental Protection and the passage of Maine's Solid Waste Management Law, which established bold recycling goals, helped to stimulate the exploration of many forms of area-wide service delivery. Regional experimentation included establishing disposal districts (i.e., the Boothbay Regional Refuse Disposal District with four towns and the Penobscot Valley Refuse Disposal District with thirty-three participating member communities). There was an early infatuation with privatization in the latter, multi-member special district in the greater Bangor area. However, eventually tipping fees were increased in midstream of an agreed-upon contract between the privately owned PERC plant and the participating communities. Political fallout included an uproar in most communities and public perceptions of some mistrust and rigidity with this regional approach.

It is important to note that special districts have been criticized on the following grounds:

1. They are often insulated from the citizens, who seldom understand them or have contacts or access to the district government.
2. The degree of citizen apathy is often high, which reduces voting for the directors where elected.
3. Overlapping powers of districts and municipalities can cause inaction, confusion, or delay.
4. Inefficiencies and waste may occur because of duplication of equipment and employees between districts and municipalities.
5. The boards of directors are often unresponsive to the community's elected officials and to citizen input when it does occur.

Why then have special districts been popular in Maine as well as the nation? They facilitate a very flexible response to local government problems with their variable boundaries. Where traditional general-purpose government cannot act, special districts have the capability to help fill this vacuum. Many districts have been established merely to avoid the debt and taxing limits placed on the municipality by the state. Thus, special districts can become a convenient mechanism to perform additional functions.

Others have challenged the basic assumptions of the opponents of special districts. As Robert Hawkins stated: "Our studies lead to two conclusions: (1) that there are few economies of scale to be realized for most governmental services and (2) that where they can be realized it is through variously structured organizations, including special districts." Relying on public choice theory as a framework and reviewing special districts in California, Hawkins concluded that districts are a responsive form of local government. Moreover, a fragmented structure will increase the efficiency and responsiveness of local government because elected officials will compete for scarce public resources, community support, and new ideas about how government should operate.[26] For these proponents, special districts are not seen as illogical units of local government, but instead as organizational choices that may be used when traditional local government experiences operational limits.[27]

Nationwide, districts have been established for virtually every service: fire protection, sanitation, transit, highways, soil conservation, parks and recreation, insect abatement, cemetery, library, irrigation and water conservation, drainage, hospitals, and housing. Clearly natural resources, fire protection, and education have been among the most used districts. Special districts have provided Maine officials with a politically palatable alternative to address some of their growing service-delivery concerns. However, in taking advantage of this option, officials may have postponed the need to explore cooperative regional problem solving, unless there is a regional dimension to the district.

School Administrative Districts and Community School Districts

School districts in Maine are really one more specific application of the special-district concept (although the U.S. Bureau of Census classifies them as a separate form of local government). The school district reorganization movement, which gathered momentum in the 1930s, reduced the number of school districts nationwide. While circumstances often varied from state to state, such contributing factors included changes in social and economic conditions that created demands for new and better services, developments in transportation and communication resulting in population changes, high per-pupil costs of the smaller schools and an inadequate tax base, and declining population in rural areas and movement to larger communities.[28] Subsequently, the number of school districts in the United States declined by about 40 percent in 1942 to 67,346 in 1952, and currently number around 16,000.[29]

It seems likely that Maine's geographic isolation, sizable rural population, and small-town domination contributed to postponing this national trend. However, throughout its history, the organization of Maine's local schools has been in constant flux. An evolutionary pattern developed from its early roots in the Massachusetts Bay Colony, to the district and town systems of the nineteenth century. Additional reorganization efforts occurred with the creation of supervisor unions in 1918 and community school districts in 1947.[30] In order to establish a district, the community school board

within the proposed district must first vote to apply to the state Department
of Education for permission to form a district. Majority votes in each community are required for final approval. School Administrative Districts, or
SADs as they are commonly called, include all grade levels, while Community School Districts may limit the number of grades. The latter districts allow a town to retain its own elementary school and then send its youth to a
regional high school. In both types of school districts, the school board
members are elected in proportion to the populations of the communities that
form the district.

In many respects, the SAD legislation (Sinclair Act) approved during the
Muskie administration in 1957 has been Maine's boldest effort at service delivery beyond town boundaries. As Stephen Bailey's study reported:

> Education may not have been Mr. Muskie's speciality, but Maine
> schools clearly needed help and the Sinclair Bill, unpalatable as
> some of its provisions might be to Yankee localists, was about the
> best help the State had in its power to give.[31]

Because of this significant act, many district mergers occurred between
towns, ending the classic one-room school tradition in some towns and the
school sports' rivalries that reflected a single town's culture. Maine currently
has 73 SADs, 13 community school districts, 34 unions, and 39 cities or
towns with their own individual systems.

Other Cooperative Solutions

Maine citizens ultimately will have to balance the increased costs and demand for services with their traditional values of local participation and control. Informal cooperation between towns, such as regional meetings among
professional administrators (town managers, planners, assessors, etc.), and
formal cooperative arrangements for mutual assistance have a rich history in
Maine. One voluntary, cooperative option that may see more use in the future is the right of local governments to enter into contracts with other towns
and cities as well as counties and the private sector. Under the Interlocal Cooperation Act of 1963, municipalities are allowed to contract for the joint
handling of obligations, but relatively few cases were reported until the
mid-1980s. In some instances, these arrangements have evolved from an informal mutual-aid pact (e.g., especially for police and fire services) to a formal contract between two or more local governments. Because of economies

of scale, many very small communities may be forced to cooperate with larger units, such as towns and cities, COGs, and county governments, for full services. Coastal Lincoln County and the city of Presque Isle in northern Maine serve as different examples of a contracted-host option.

A mail survey of city and town managers (N = 219) was conducted in 1987 and produced an 84 percent response rate.[32] Maine municipal managers (32 percent) felt that entering into joint service or purchasing agreements with other governments has been a "major or moderately used strategy" by their communities. Another 32 percent reported it as a minor strategy, while 35 percent reported it was "not used." Moreover, 27 percent of the managers verified that contracting out services to the private sector was a major or moderately used strategy in their communities, 29 percent reported it as a "minor" strategy, while 45 percent reported not using this technique.

Interlocal agreements such as the Camden/Lincolnville/Hope/Rockport Solid Waste Facility on Maine's coast and the Northern Aroostook Regional Incinerator Facility are examples of the trend toward necessary cooperation among communities. In Maine law, there are several possibilities. One basic interlocal agreement option does not create a separate legal or administrative entity. Thus, major financial or property-related decisions must be approved by the various legislative bodies of the proposed membership. Another more complex type of interlocal arrangement—the "Interlocal Corporation"— creates a separate legal or administrative entity. Regional Waste Systems, Inc. in Portland (twenty members), Mid-Maine Waste Action Corporation in Auburn (twelve members), and Sandy River Waste Recycling Association in Franklin County (seventeen members) fit into this category.[33] While these entities lack the authority to tax, they do provide for local control over the organizational design through a negotiation process among the participants.

PROPERTY TAXES: A STATE AND LOCAL CHALLENGE

During the upsurge in Maine's economy in the 1980s and the accompanying pressures of growth, there has been renewed attention given to overreliance on the real estate property tax. This issue is not really new—it has received the attention of scholars, journalists, and local officials alike for the last three decades.[34] Earlier studies and government reports have pointed out such problems as the regressive nature of the property tax, the need for circuit breakers for the elderly and handicapped (which have been instituted), and the proliferation of exemptions to veterans, churches, fraternal organizations, literary and scientific organizations, government property, and charitable organizations, which all erode the base. Other chronic concerns include poor assessment practices, such as failures to assess at full value, the absence of reevaluations, leading to underassessment, the lack of qualified assessors, and various deficiencies in training assessors. Moreover, more attention should be directed at the lack of regional taxing districts and to the need for more active state involvement and intervention in this process to help assure equity and efficiency.[35]

With the end of the federal revenue-sharing program in 1986, pressure again was felt by local governments to find new sources of revenue and to begin reducing certain programs. Quite naturally, in the vacuum created by the loss of federal funding, new school mandates, and other state mandates for solid waste, salt storage, and road repairs, local officials sought help from the state government. In 1986, a tax study by the Select Committee on Property Tax Reform warned Mainers to get prepared for an $80 million increase in property taxes unless new sources of revenue were found. It recommended that legislation be enacted to allow local communities to propose sales and income taxes, and to levy service fees on tax-exempt property.[36]

A previously cited survey revealed the salient concerns of city and town managers over property taxes. Among revenue-generating alternatives used in the past five years, managers placed a high level of importance on a fiscal strategy of increasing property taxes, obtaining additional federal and state funds, and drawing down surpluses. Indeed, 42 percent of the administrators surveyed reported that increases in property taxes were a major source of new dollars. Moreover, a strong feeling was expressed by 48 percent of the managers that their municipality's total tax burden was high and should be reduced. Only 11 percent of the respondents felt that it should be increased, while 41 percent favored the status quo.[37]

Rising property taxes provoked a sharp reaction in a number of communities, especially where soaring land valuations created a serious threat to the ability of many longtime low- and moderate-income residents to pay their taxes. Citizen reactions have taken numerous forms and serve to illustrate the participatory nature of Maine politics and the presence of group activism.

Rising land values, coupled with uncontrolled development, have provided a common political ground for alliances between environmentalists and advocates of low taxes, such as Freedom Fighters, a group of Waldo County municipal officials who successfully fought mandatory property-tax assessment districts in the late 1970s. In addition, there were increased levels of activity among other property-tax watchdog groups in Monmouth,

Table 6: Per Capita Property Taxes in New England

State	1982	1986	1988
New Hampshire	451	738	927
Connecticut	473	731	911
Rhode Island	413	624	697
Massachusetts	555	601	691
Vermont	377	556	750
Maine	319	478	575

Sources: Tax Foundation, Inc.; *Bangor Daily News*, March 3, 1988; Advisory Commission on Intergovernmental Relations, *Significant Features of Fiscal Federalism*, vol. 2, M-169-11, August 1990, p. 134.

Litchfield, and Freeport, where municipal officials were continuously pressured.

Spending-cap and tax-cap movements developed in the cities of Augusta, Bangor, Bath, and South Portland in 1988. More radical alternatives to property tax reform that parallel California's Proposition 13 (1978) have surfaced, and are being studied by the Freedom Fighters II and other citizen groups. Such initiatives would freeze valuations except for new sales. Some citizens support legislation that would allow towns to assess property at different rates, instead of the current fair-market-value approach. As Bill Terry, a concerned "freedom fighter" who had witnessed considerable increases, protested, "Is it really fair market value when the majority of buyers come from out of state?" He went on to describe the typical scenario: "People from out of state are buying up land at inflated prices, forcing selectmen to increase land values for everyone. Sometimes these developers buy property without site inspections."[38]

The city of Saco passed its own tax cap in 1979 and then rescinded it fifteen months later after completing one of the worst, albeit short-lived, chapters in Maine governmental history. Both the school system and municipal programs were gutted. Indeed, the reputation of the school system, and its ability to attract teachers, will likely suffer damage for years to come. Finally, the city defaulted on a $2 million tax anticipation note. Even ten years later, Saco's City Administrator Harvey Rosenfeld concluded: "We're still behind where we should be, and it's hard to catch up."[39] Some officials breathed a sigh of relief when the voters of Augusta voted down a proposed cap during the summer of 1988, but the issue surfaced in Bangor in November 1988, where the voters also voted down a spending cap.

It is very important to consider both the recent historical trends of the property tax and its relation to other sources of revenue. Property taxes in Maine actually declined as a percentage of personal income between 1976 and 1986, according to the Tax Foundation, Inc., a national organization for tax research. However, in the 1980s, property values were increasing at a rate well ahead of general inflation, especially in the coastal towns and in some scenic rural areas.

Moreover, reorganization efforts have occurred in a few smaller towns and plantations, where high property taxes were a chronic citizen concern. Five plantations and the town of Benedicta have deorganized since 1982. The price for the luxury of a small, personal, yet increasingly costly, form of local government seemed too high for these communities, where citizens reluctantly turned governmental responsibilities over to the county and the state.

Data from the Tax Foundation reveal that Maine residents paid $478 in property taxes for 1986 on a per capita basis, which was $15 above the national average of $463. Maine was ranked twenty-second nationally, with $118 being reported as the lowest amount by Alabama and a high of $1,173 found in Wyoming. A regional analysis, described in table 6, reveals that Maine's per capita property taxes have remained much lower than those of the other New England states.[40] While Maine's per capita property taxes are slightly above the national average, they have actually been increasing at a rate below the national average. From 1976 to 1986, the national per capita average increased from $266 to $463, or by 74 percent, while Maine property taxes went from $297 to $478, or a 61 percent increase.

Although property tax dollars have registered a steady growth, the Tax Foundation studies show them to be decreasing as a percentage of personal income. On a nationwide basis, property taxes per $1,000 of personal income decreased from $45 in 1976 to $34 in 1986. During the same time frame, Maine property taxes per $1,000 of personal income likewise decreased from $63 to $41. Thus, property taxes have not increased as rapidly as personal incomes, but because of their regressive nature, they loom as a constant concern for many citizens, especially those citizens affected by unplanned and uncontrolled growth. The strong desires for local autonomy and community control conflict with the citizenry's concern for equity and fairness, which seems ingrained from the moralistic culture.

It was pointed out at the 1982 Blaine House Conference on State and Local Relations, sponsored by former Governor Brennan, that overreliance on the property tax and its regressive nature have been chronic problems for

Table 7: Relative Progressivity of Maine Sales, Income, and Property Taxes

	Sales Tax	Income Tax	Property Tax
Maine	−0.18	1.41	−0.48
U.S. Average	−0.32	1.64	−0.45
Maine's Rank	7th of 45	6th of 44	41st of 50

Sources: Donald Planes, *Who Pays State and Local Taxes?* (Weston, Mass.: Oelgeschlager, Gunn and Hain Publishers, 1980), pp. 118–26; "State and Local Relations: The Challenge of the Eighties," issues paper for the Blaine House Conference on State and Local Relations, Augusta, Maine, April 28, 1982, p. 25.

Maine state and local officials. (Tax burden was defined as taxes paid as a percentage of income, while progressivity was defined as the increase in tax burden that occurs as income rises.) Thus, table 7 documents negative values for the sales and property taxes, where the burden falls as incomes increase. The state income tax has been very progressive. Most important, Maine's sales tax was the seventh most progressive in the nation, and its income tax was cited as the sixth most progressive. Maine's property tax, by contrast, was cited as the tenth most regressive (forty-first least progressive) property tax. Thus, a Blaine House Conference issues paper argued: "The thesis that overall state tax equity can be increased by shifting the tax burden from property to sales and income taxes appears to be valid for Maine."[41] By 1989, Maine was the thirteenth highest in overall levels of state taxation and eleventh highest in both individual state income taxes and sales taxes.[42]

However, Maine had already decreased its overall dependence on the property tax substantially. In 1988, it accounted for 32 percent of all state and local taxes, which was down from 37 percent in 1980 and 53 percent in 1962. The property tax was the lowest in New England in 1988. Recently, many Maine communities had to raise property-tax rates and rather futilely seek other sources of revenue to meet demands for municipal services. In spite of relatively low rates, however, the burden of the property tax is higher than the national average. In 1988, property taxes in Maine took about 4.3 percent of personal income, compared with the national average of around 3.5 percent. The basic reason for this discrepancy is Maine's below-average per capita income and its above-average reliance on the property tax for local revenues. In Maine, property taxes have traditionally accounted for 99 percent of all purely defined local taxes, whereas for the nation as a whole, they contributed about three-fourths of all local tax revenues.[43]

In 1988, Governor McKernan successfully proposed a property-tax relief package of $19.2 million that increased the funds available to the circuit-breaker program then going into effect. The Democratic-controlled 113th legislature appropriated $28.3 million for property-tax relief in response to increasing public pressure. A poll in 1989 by Capital News Service revealed that Mainers ranked property-tax reform as the second most important issue facing the state, trailing only environmental concerns. Specifically, the legislature expanded its circuit-breaker program for "Elderly Householders or Renters" and established a "General Property Tax or Rent Refund" program for residents with household incomes of $60,000 or less. Refunds are to be given to those whose property tax bill was more than 4.5 percent or whose rent was more than 30 percent of their household income.[44]

Substantial shortfalls in the budget in 1990 and 1991 have limited the ability of the state to contribute more to property-tax reform and other pressing problems. During the summer of 1991, the legislature finally approved a number of revenue-generating solutions (e.g., it increased the sales tax by 1 percent) to help offset the serious financial crisis and partisan deadlock in the legislature. The Circuit Breaker Program was funded by the 115th legislature at $22.8 million in 1992 and $25.3 for 1993.[45] Still, the need to generate new sources of revenue, such as local options for hotel accommodations, entertainment, and consumption taxes, had not been settled at the time of this writing.

CONCLUSION

Regional problem solving continues to emerge around such salient issues as pollution control, public transportation, solid waste management, and health care services. While interlocal agreements seem more politically acceptable for some problems, a substate regional approach (through either the regional councils or county governments) and state assumption of certain local services have been supported by some planners and academicians as more rational alternatives for some services.[46]

The decision as to whether to make county governments truly general purpose in nature and providers of additional services remains as a major policy choice. Meanwhile, Maine continues to use other acceptable mechanisms, such as special districts, contracts, and interlocal corporations, which involve the private sector (e.g., solid-waste disposal plants in southern and central Maine). There is the perception of a heavy reliance on the property tax to pay for services, which accents substate regional differences and issues of equity and economies of scale. Greater state involvement over time appears to be both a given fact and an evolving occurrence.

CHAPTER FOURTEEN

Concluding Observations

One conclusion that emerges from this study of Maine politics is that the state has been something of a political pioneer. As we have seen, its many small communities contain an extraordinarily high number of appointed professional managers. The state government has invested heavily in social welfare, and has led the nation in certain innovative programs for children and the elderly. The court system is one of the best organized among the fifty states. For a small state, it has produced more than its share of national leaders, especially in Congress. Government and politics are important in Maine, even though its picturesque environment and rather isolated location may be its best-known characteristics.

Yet it is the relationship that Maine people have with their environment that has provided the state with so much of its political energy. The state has long been a leader in developing environmental law. By overwhelming margins, Maine citizens insist that the land must be protected even at the expense of economic development. Such a bond between the population and its natural environment probably could not have occurred in many other states. We think its presence is due in part to Maine's political culture. We have argued that the moralistic culture, which stresses a commonwealth view of public affairs and encourages widespread political participation, has helped foster in Maine a consensus about large issues that transcends demographic groupings.

We observed in chapters 2 and 3 that the social and economic changes that took place in Maine in the nineteenth and early twentieth centuries gave rise to some other political characteristics. Among those that have become especially prominent since the 1950s are a tendency toward moderation on the part of the two political parties, and a willingness by citizens to support an activist state government. The 1980s have been described as "a decade that witnessed a truly remarkable diversification in the Maine economy."[1] These most recent changes included a tremendous growth in the service sector— the total number of jobs in Maine grew by about 25 percent, almost all of them in service industries. In some respects, the 1980s were as extraordinary as the early years of Maine's statehood, when the state's population grew rapidly.

These developments are, however, unlikely to create major shifts in the politics of the 1990s. For one thing, population growth is slowing. Maine grew by 13 percent between 1970 and 1980, by slightly over 9 percent between 1980 and 1990, and is estimated to increase by only 5 percent between 1990 and 2000. The values and ideas that shape state government will be predominantly from people who have lived in Maine for a considerable period. In 1991, it was estimated that two-thirds of the state population was native-born.[2] Another factor that tends to militate against major policy change is the economic decline that New England is experiencing in the early 1990s. Maine's budget crisis in 1991 was probably the most serious in its history. The state government will be hard-pressed to meet its commitments, and is unlikely to undertake new programs that entail large new appropriations.

Still, economic modernization has certain political consequences. One of the most significant has been the professionalization and institutionalization of the state government. The changes that have taken place in the past twenty years in the three branches of state government are little short of remarkable. For most of its history, Maine has had a citizen legislature with very high rates of turnover and an inclination to meet only very occasionally during its two-year term. Of late, the house and senate have seen some of their members becoming professional legislators, and the responsibilities for all members have increased with each new legislative session. The members are no longer mostly farmers, barbers, and homemakers who once offered themselves for legislative service for a term or two, after which they retired. Instead, the newer legislators, often young men and women, are individuals whose entire means of earning a living is government-related. They may work as a consultant for an organization with governmental interests between legislative sessions, and may be considering a career in an executive agency after they leave the legislature. These professional legislators are found in growing numbers in Augusta.

Likewise, the executive branch has experienced a rise in professionalism. Many agencies were once directed by boards and commissions dominated by citizens named to those bodies on the basis of their interest in health, or welfare, or education. Maine departed from that system in the early 1970s, creating in its place a cabinet, within which particular functions became the responsibility of a commissioner, usually a career administrator or politician, named by the governor. The courts, too, have revised their arrangements to enhance professional management. In the early 1960s, Maine abolished its municipal courts, largely staffed by citizen judges, and replaced them with the District Court and its career judges. Citizens still find ways to participate in court business, such as in juries and in committees assigned to handle certain functions, but they no longer preside over trials.

Professionalism has not been limited to state government. The number of Maine towns adding managers and other professionals grows steadily. Their work has enabled some communities to continue using town meetings and citizen boards for governance. Yet, an inexorable trend toward state centralization of some local functions seems to be underway. The complex problems that towns must face often impose financial demands that exceed the towns' financial capabilities. Since 1980, several small Maine towns have given up their charters, leaving the state to provide services ranging from tax collection to police protection.

The effects of professionalism are important to notice. All states have shared in the general growth of state and local governments recently experienced by Maine. However, few states have cherished as deeply as Maine has the value of citizen governance. For most of its history, Maine did not just listen to its citizens; citizens directed the government. Now government seems to fall mostly into the hands of a political class of managers, technicians, bureaucrats, and politicians for whom government service is their livelihood.

What are the implications of this change? One probable implication is that political power will increasingly be found within governmental institutions. That statement sounds like a truism, but it speaks to a significant shift in Maine politics from the not-very-distant pattern of private interests having inordinate power over policy. Since the early 1970s, the *Maine Times,* a weekly reform-oriented newspaper, has conducted surveys seeking to determine answers to the question Who Runs Maine? In 1974, it identified the heads of five large companies, including Central Maine Power and the Maine Central Railroad, as constituting a kind of power elite. Their influence extended over a broad array of policies and decisions in the legislature and executive branch. In contrast, when the *Maine Times* examined the issue in 1988, it found the problem harder to resolve. "Today, the answer to the question is: no individual or small group runs the state. Maine has progressed from an individualistic to an institutional power structure.''[3] In particular, the state bureaucracy was seen as a critical force in virtually all areas of public policy.

A second implication of professionalism is that policymaking will likely involve considerable institutional combat. In decades past, the governor was the principal figure in setting policy, largely because the governor commanded most of the technical resources. That situation no longer exists. The legislature is now equipped with staff members who can help provide policy alternatives. Further, some career legislators may believe that their political fortunes are furthered by staking out positions different from those espoused by the chief executive. The shutdown of Maine government during the first sixteen days of July 1991 graphically illustrated the consequences of institutional combat between the governor and legislature. Other parts of the state government, such as the courts and regulatory agencies, have been involved in only somewhat less dramatic battles in recent years.

A third development associated with the rise of government professionalism is the expanded use of the initiative and the referendum. Although Maine has not relied on these devices as extensively as some states, referendums are now seen regularly on the November state election ballot. Likewise, their use has increased in local government. In recent years, several communities, including Augusta, Bangor, Bath, South Portland, and York, have been the scene of referendum battles over the question of whether to limit the taxing and spending authority of municipal officials. Growth in the use of referendums is indicative of efforts by at least some citizens to narrow the gap that they see widening between themselves and public officials.

Public officials seem to be making more effort to meet with citizens throughout the state. In the past few years, all three branches of state government have taken to the road to visit Maine communities. Governor McKernan initiated a ''capital for a day'' program early in his administration. The legislature undertook several bus tours of the state to acquaint its members with regions that were unfamiliar to some legislators. As part of the celebration of the bicentennial of the U.S. Constitution and other special events, the Maine Supreme Judicial Court held sessions in several counties that it normally does not visit. The practice of institutional travel may become fairly common. If Maine citizens no longer serve as members of state government bodies as extensively as they once did, the professionals who now compose the institutions will need to reach out to them somehow.

The recent modifications in the way Maine conducts its governmental business suggest that the state seeks to confirm its cultural and political traditions in the face of economic and technological change. Maine remains a state of many small communities. The most rapidly growing types of communities in the 1980s were towns with populations between 2,500 and 10,000. Mainers continue to be attached to their communities and to the values associated with these communities. Modernization of the state's economy has provided new opportunities, but it has not altered the themes of moderate politics, widespread political participation, and a fairly activist state government. In fact, the new, more diverse economic arrangements may reinforce these themes. Maine will continue to be influenced by the demographic, economic, and political trends touching its New England neighbors. Still, as in the past, its evaluation of these trends will be distinctly on the state's own terms.

CHAPTER FIFTEEN

Maine Documents and Sources

RESEARCH CENTERS

Collections

Maine has a well-established institutional arrangement for maintaining and distributing state documents and records. The State Library, located in Augusta in the State of Maine Cultural Building, which is a short distance from the State House, is the principle depository for all state documents. State departments are required by law to submit copies of their publications to the State Library, which then distributes copies to thirteen depository libraries around the state. These depositories include libraries on campuses throughout the University of Maine System (Orono, Fort Kent, Machias, Presque Isle, Farmington, Gorham, and Portland), as well as libraries of three private colleges (Bates, Bowdoin, and Colby), the Portland Public Library, and the State Law and Legislative Reference Library (hereafter referred to as the State Law Library).

The State Law and Legislative Reference Library is located in the State House in Augusta. Its collections include statutory codes for all fifty states, as well as Canadian and English statutes and court reports. While the Maine legal collection is substantial, the legislative documents are the most comprehensive, going back to 1865 for house documents. The library's collections are also geared to provide information on current legislative issues, such as AIDS and solid-waste management. As a selective U.S. government depository, the library contains collections of congressional bills, reports, and debates. The library also maintains a file of state newspaper clippings listed under a wide range of governmental subject headings, such as "Ethics in Government" and "Municipal Government."

Another major library is the State Archives, located with the State Library in the State of Maine Cultural Building in Augusta. Established in 1965, the State Archives is the principle depository for the working papers of state government. Its Division of Archives Services maintains records transferred to the Maine State Archives by executive branch agencies, and legislative and judicial records administered by the archives under the direction of the legislature and the Supreme Judicial Court, which retain constitutional control. Housed in the same building complex is the Maine State Museum, whose collections and exhibitions depict the natural history of the state.

An additional library of note is the Raymond H. Fogler Library at the University of Maine in Orono, which is another selective U.S. government documents depository. The Special Collections section of Fogler contains an extensive collection of Maine materials, particularly books written by Maine authors. It houses a number of personal collections, such as the papers of James G. Blaine and William Hathaway.

In 1982, the Margaret Chase Smith Library Center was opened at Skowhegan. In addition to the senator's papers, the library contains materials on the politics of Maine and the United States during the time of Smith's congressional service.

Institutes

The University of Maine system has two social science research institutes that are sources of governmental data. The larger of the two is the Edmund S. Muskie Institute of Public Affairs at the University of Southern Maine in Portland. This institute provides both research and teaching programs. The research component is composed of four centers—Health Policy, Aging and Rehabilitation, Child and Family Policy, and Survey Research. The Muskie Institute has particular strength in health and human service policies in both Maine and the nation, and in demonstration projects designed to improve service delivery of programs in those areas. The research centers maintain extensive data files and publish periodic reports in their respective areas.

The other institute is the Margaret Chase Smith Center for Policy Studies at the University of Maine in Orono. This unit investigates a broad range of policy questions. Its staff is especially engaged in interdisciplinary studies with faculties in several fields at the university and other institutions. The institute incorporates the functions of the former Bureau of Public Administration, and publishes pamphlets that describe in some detail Maine's local governmental institutions.

Other research centers are the Maine Historical Society in Portland, which publishes the *Maine Historical Society Quarterly* and occasional bibliographies of various aspects of Maine life, and the Maine Municipal Association in Augusta, which publishes the *Maine Townsman* monthly, as well as other materials for local governments.

GENERAL REFERENCE WORKS

General reference resources regarding Maine government and politics consist of almanacs, checklists, bibliographies, and directories. Also included here are some of the more significant historical resources.

Almanacs

Two almanacs, which are no longer published, are useful in studying recent Maine history. *Maine Almanac*, edited by Jim Brunelle (Augusta: Guy Gannett Publishing, 1979–80), includes data concerning history, biographies, state government, elections, and population by county, town, and city, as well as many other listings. *State O'Maine Facts* (Camden: Down-East Books) is of more limited scope, but it was published annually from the mid-1960s until 1982.

Checklists and Bibliographies

Maine State Library Government Publications Checklist by the Maine State Library lists Maine state agency publications. The *Index to Maine State Documents,* published annually since 1985–86, lists Maine state government items by subject. The Maine section of David W. Parish's *State Government Reference Publications: An Annotated Bibliography* (Littleton, Colo.: Libraries Unlimited, 1981) contains a list of useful references concerning Maine state government. Walter J. Taranko and Dorothy A. Gregory's *Maine Resources: Print and Non-Print* (Augusta: Department of Education and Cultural Services, 1977) is a useful, though sometimes uneven, listing of different materials relating to the study of Maine, in topics that range from government audiovisual materials to biographies and sociopolitical history.

Maine: A Bibliography of Its History, edited by John D. Haskell, Jr. (Hanover, N.H., and London: University Press of New England, 1983), presents historical bibliographic references by county, city, and town, and includes a list of local government documents and publications. A bibliographic source prepared to meet the needs of librarians and researchers is

Bibliography of Maine 1960–1975 (Orono: Maine Library Association Bicentennial Committee, 1976). This collection was compiled from the card catalogues of the Bangor Public Library, Maine State Library, Portland Public Library, and Raymond H. Fogler Library. For a bibliography of Maine bibliographies, see the Maine section in T. D. Seymour Bassett's *A List of New England Bibliographies* (Middletown, Conn.: Committee for a New England Bibliography, 1971).

Directories

The primary source for locating Maine state government officers and their publications is the *Maine State Government Annual Report* (Augusta: Bureau of the Budget). This directory sets forth the location, administrative and financial structure, program description, and publications of each state agency. Some of the materials presented in the report, including telephone numbers and organizational structures, are provided in brief pamphlet form in the *Maine State Government Reference Manual* (Augusta: Bureau of the Budget). The oldest state directory is *The Maine Register, State Yearbook and Legislative Manual* (Portland: Tower Publishing Co., 1870 to present). Published biennially, this source lists the officials of every town in the state and all principal state officials, and it provides much descriptive data on state and local agencies. It is the closest reference Maine has to a "Blue Book."

Historical Resources

Historical research conducted during the nineteenth and twentieth centuries is considerable. The list provided here is designed only to point out some of the more significant sources for background material. The formation of Maine's statehood is undertaken most comprehensively in Ronald F. Banks's *Maine Becomes a State: The Movement to Separate Maine from Massachusetts, 1785–1820* (Middleton, Conn.: Wesleyan University Press, 1970). *Maine: A History*, edited by Louis Hatch (New York: American Historical Society, 1919) probably the best of the pre–World War II histories, traces developments from the state's first settlements. In particular, it is a good source of the state's political history during the nineteenth century and early parts of the twentieth. A recent, and widely used, text on Maine history is *Maine: A History through Selected Readings*, edited by David C. Smith and Edward O. Schrivers (Dubuque, Iowa: Kendall/Hunt Publishing Co., 1985).

In addition, a series of articles in the *Thomas Business Review,* 3 (Fall 1975): 1–42, entitled "The Maine Economy . . . " offers a bicentennial economic history. Another economic history, as readable as it is informative, is Fred Eugene Jewett's *A Financial History of Maine* (New York: Columbia University Press, 1937). There are also a number of specialized treatments of the state's sociopolitical history available among the state's theses and dissertations (see section IV).

MAINE GOVERNMENT TEXTS AND MONOGRAPHS

This section outlines the primary sources on Maine state institutions and political parties. Accompanying these sources are selections of secondary materials. Except in a few instances where there is very little literature on a subject, these selections are in no way meant to be exhaustive, or thoroughly representative. They are included with the intention of helping the student of Maine government get started on a topic of interest.

State Government Overview

A relatively comprehensive text on the Maine state government is *Downeast Politics: The Government of the State of Maine* by James F. Horan et al. (Dubuque, Iowa: Kendall/Hunt Publishing Co., 1975). The focus of the work was on governmental structures and rules; much of the material is still pertinent, though dated. A lively appraisal of the politics and character of Maine from the same period is included in Neil Pierce's *The New England States: People, Power, and Politics* (New York: W. W. Norton, 1976). Pierce's work is in the tradition of Duane Lockard's groundbreaking study of regional politics, *New England State Politics* (Princeton, N.J.: Princeton University Press, 1959), which also contains a chapter on Maine. A recent collection of edited speeches on the state's modifications in politics and policies is *Changing Maine*, edited by Richard Barringer (Portland: University of Southern Maine, 1990). In addition to materials devoted to the state government in general are many works covering specialized topics. For a look at the effects of the Reagan administration on Maine, see Kenneth T. Palmer, Alex N. Pattakos, and Stephen H. Holden's "The New Federalism Downeast: Reaganomics in Maine," *Publius: Annual Review of American Federalism,* edited by Stephen L. Schechter (Lapham, Md.: University Press of America, 1981), pp. 83–91. See also Alex N. Pattakos and Kenneth T. Palmer's "Downeast But

Not Down Under: Maine Responds to the Reagan Challenge," *Publius: The Journal of Federalism* 13 (Spring 1983): 39–49.

Among works on the influence of apportionment on the state government, Eugene A. Mawhinney's *Legislative Apportionment in Maine* (Orono: Bureau of Public Administration, University of Maine, 1969) examines the effect of *Baker* v. *Carr* on the state, and Douglas Hodgkin's "Anti-Gerrymandering Provisions Weakened in Maine," *National Civic Review* 74 (1984): 403–4, reviews the state's 1983 districting plan. For works on the influence of corporations in Maine, see William C. Osborn's *The Paper Plantation: Ralph Nader's Study Group Report on the Pulp and Paper Industry in Maine* (New York: Grossman, 1974), Orren Hormell's *Corrupt Practices Legislation in Maine and How It Works* (Brunswick: Bureau for Research in Municipal Government, Bowdoin College, 1929), and Stephen Munroe's "Power and Politics: Maine's Retention of the Fernald Act," (Honors thesis, University of Maine, 1981), in addition to the Lockard and Pierce works.

The State Constitution

Primary Sources. Maine's constitution is codified every ten years by the state's chief justice, who incorporates amendments added during the preceding time period. The most recent codification was in 1983. In the interim years, the Office of the Secretary of State publishes newly enacted amendments separately. These amendments are inserted in a pocket inside the back cover of copies of the constitution, which are made available in booklet form (free of charge) from the Office of Secretary of State.

Students interested in the framing of the constitution may want to consult the *Debates and Journal of the Constitutional Convention of the State of Maine, 1819–1820* (Augusta: Farmer's Almanac Press, 1894). Maine has had two Constitutional Commissions established to examine the basic document and to propose changes. The most recent commission met in 1961; its work is reported in Samuel Silsby's *Proceedings of the Second Constitutional Commission* (Augusta: Legislative Constitutional Commission to the 101st Legislature, 1963), printed as Legislative Documents nos. 33, 631, 1394, and 1476 of that year. As constitutional amendments are proposed, drafts and debates appear in legislative publications. When the legislature proposes amendments for ratification, the secretary of state prepares a pamphlet, *Referenda Questions and Proposed Constitutional Amendments,* for distribution in advance of the election.

Secondary Sources. There is relatively little literature on the state constitution, perhaps a reflection of the document's stability throughout Maine's history. For a political analysis of the constitution, see Kenneth T. Palmer and Marcus A. LiBrizzi's "Development of the Maine Constitution: The Long Tradition, 1819–1988," *Maine Historical Society Quarterly* 28 (Winter 1989): 126–45. Concerning the constitutional convention of 1819, see Ronald F. Banks's *Maine Becomes a State,* listed under "Historical Resources" in section II. To help explain the work of the 1961 Constitutional Commission, as well as to describe the state's charter, Edward Dow wrote a series of articles for the Portland *Maine Sunday Telegram* published between March 11, 1962, and May 13, 1962. These are held in mimeograph form in major state libraries under the title "Our Unknown Constitution: A Study in Maine's Basic Law." For information on constitutional changes made during the last century, see Peter Neil Barry's "Nineteenth Century Constitutional Amendment in Maine" (Master's thesis, University of Maine, 1965).

The State Legislature

Primary Sources. Maine's legislature maintains a fairly complete record of its proceedings. A verbatim record of all debates and floor proceedings is contained in the *Maine Legislative Record,* which dates from 1897. The day-to-day substantive actions of the legislature are found in the *Journal of the House* and the *Journal of the Senate,* which are available only in the State Law Library. All legislative documents in any form in which they have been considered are annually indexed in *State of Maine History and Final Disposition of Legislative Documents.* A related publication, *Laws of Maine,* publishes the texts of enacted measures. The latter two items are available shortly after the close of each regular session. Copies of bills under consideration in a current legislative session can be found in the Legislative Document Room. Bills of past sessions are kept in loose-leaf notebooks in the State Law Library.

For persons interested in the current business of the legislature, the Legislative Information Office monitors the status of every item introduced before the legislature and maintains its status on a computerized bill status system, which is available through public computer terminals located in the State House Document Room and in the State Law Library. Weekly printouts are also available under the title *Current Bill Status Report.* The reports are arranged by document number, by committee, and by legislative sponsor, and they are the basis of the annual *State of Maine History and Final Disposition of Legislative Documents.* Throughout the year the *Weekly Legislative Calendar,* published by the clerk of the house, lists committee meetings and committee agenda topics. (The standing committees often meet when the legislature is not in session.) Biographical material on state legislators, including their home and business telephone numbers and their standing committee assignments, is provided in the *Senate and House Registers,* a booklet published biennially by the clerk of the house and the secretary of the senate.

The joint standing committees in the legislature do not prepare written reports; they only need to tally the votes of the committee members reporting a bill "ought to pass" or "ought not to pass." Occasionally, however, pieces of legislation are the subject of committee studies. Reference to some orders or acts creating study committees can be found in the bill histories in the *State of Maine History and Final Disposition of Legislative Documents,* and reports are sometimes indicated on the bills themselves. During each session, the Legislative Council publishes a comprehensive list of approved legislative studies. The State Law Library maintains a list of published legislative studies going back to the early 1940s.

Secondary Sources. For a description of the legislature, the most useful guide is a biennial publication, *A Guide for Maine Legislators: Facts, Resources, Procedures* (Augusta: Legislative Office of Policy and Legal Analysis, 1990). See also *A Citizen's Guide to the 115th Legislature,* 1991–92 (Portland: Maine People's Resource Center, 1991). A recent external report on the legislature is *State of Maine: Study of Legislative Structure and Operations* (Augusta: KPMG Peat Marwick, March 1990). Although somewhat outdated, *The Legislative Process in Maine* by Kenneth T. Palmer et al. (Washington, D.C.: American Political Science Association, 1973) provides an overview of the context and operation of the legislature.

The State Courts

Primary Sources. The most complete source of information on Maine courts is *Maine Administrative Office of the Courts: Annual Report.* Published since the mid-1970s, when the office was established, this annual volume contains a brief history of the Maine judiciary, fiscal data about the courts, and statistics, especially caseload data, concerning the three levels of courts. It also lists the judges currently in office. Title 4 of *Maine Revised Statutes Annotated* has the best description of the structure and authority of the several courts. *Maine Rules of Court,* an annual publication of the West Publishing Company since 1959, provides the rules of civil and criminal procedure, rules of evidence, and some material on federal rules, as well as the Maine Bar rules and code of judicial conduct. *The Maine Reporter* contains cases decided by the Supreme Judicial Court.

Secondary Sources. A recent source of general information about the Maine court system is William H. Coogan's *A Citizen's Guide to the Maine Courts* (Portland: Administrative Office of the Courts, 1987). This booklet describes the judicial process and court organization for the would-be litigant. A similar source, somewhat dated but more thorough, is the *Citizens' Handbook on the Maine Courts*, edited by Edward J. Schoenbaum (Washington, D.C.: American Judicature Society and National Center for State Courts, 1976).

In the 1970s, the National Center for State Courts and the Institute for Judicial Administration published several technical reports on the Maine courts. Reference to these items and to a wide range of judicial issues can be found in the *Maine Bar Journal,* based in Augusta, which publishes six issues a year. Examples of fairly recent pieces include Gerald F. Petruccelli and John D. McKay's "The Right to Jury Trial under the Maine Constitution," vol. 1, no. 5 (September 1986), and Kermit V. Lipez's "Adventures and Reflections of a New Judge," vol. 2, no. 1 (November 1987). The *Maine Bar Journal* is indexed by both the *Index to Legal Periodicals* and the *Current Law Index/Legal Resources Index.* A perceptive piece on the Maine Supreme Judicial Court is Edgar Allen Beem's "Invisible But Powerful: A Rare Look at Maine's Supreme Court," *Maine Times,* July 8, 1988.

The State Executive

Primary Sources. A basic source for research on the state executive branch is the *Maine State Government Annual Report* (Augusta: Bureau of the Budget). The annual volume sets forth the administrative structure of each executive department and agency. It also contains a budget summary and a brief description of the functions of each unit, its activities over the preceding year, and publications available from the agency. Names and telephone numbers of senior agency personnel are included in each agency description. Another basic source is the *State of Maine Budget Document,* an annual booklet published by the Governor's Office, which systematically and categorically lists the actual expenditures and requested and recommended appropriations of the state government.

The State Library maintains a complete collection of special studies and reports produced by gubernatorially appointed commissions and committees from 1867 to the present. The State Law Library houses a substantial compilation of the advisory opinions of Maine's attorneys general since 1863. The office of the attorney general has, naturally, the most comprehensive collection of these opinions, although the West Publishing Company's computer-assisted legal research service, called Westlaw, contains a comprehensive collection going back to 1973. In addition, the State Archives, the primary depository for noncurrent working papers of state government, contains papers and documents of recent governors.

Established in 1968, the State Planning Office's duties and publications pertain to planning and development, administrative organization, and some program and grants management. The office is often a valuable source for researchers interested in particular policy areas.

Secondary Sources. A brief description of Maine governors and their impact on the state, from William King in 1820 to Kenneth Curtis in the 1970s, is Jane Radcliff's *150 Years of Maine Governors* (Augusta: Maine State Museum, 1972). There are a number of works devoted to individual governors. For two on former Governor and U.S. Senator Edmund S. Muskie, see Theo Lippman, Jr., and Donald C. Hansen's *Muskie* (New York: W. W. Norton, 1971) and Donald Nevin's *Muskie of Maine* (New York: Random House, 1972). On former governor and U.S. Ambassador to Canada Kenneth Curtis, see *The Curtis Years, 1967–1974*, edited by Allen G. Pease (Augusta: State of Maine Printing Office, 1974), and Kermit Lipez's *Kenneth Curtis of Maine: Profile of a Governor* (Brunswick: Harpwell Press, 1974). On Independent Governor James Longley, see Willis Johnson's *The Year of the Longley* (Stonington: Penobscot Press, 1978).

The State Parties

Primary Sources. Maine's Republican and Democratic state committees are both headquartered in Augusta. At each office, state bylaws and congressional district bylaws are kept, together with some municipal bylaws. Convention programs and party platforms are also on file. The material is mostly current, at best going back only a decade or two. The State Law Library maintains a collection of most of the party platforms adopted since 1920.

For election figures, see *Official Vote for Republican and Democratic Primary Election Candidates and Non-Party Candidates Filing Petitions* published regularly by the Election Division of the Office of the Secretary of State. This is available in pamphlet form from the secretary of state's office and, for somewhat older reports, through the depository library system.

Secondary Sources. Most of the works listed under "Maine Government Overview" above include sections devoted to Maine's political parties. On the growth of the Democratic party, see also Louis Maisel's "Party Reform and Political Participation: The Democrats of Maine," in *The Future of Political Parties*, edited by Louis Maisel and Paul M. Sacks (Beverley Hills, Calif.: Sage Publications, 1975), chapter 6. On the origins of the Republican party, see Richard Rollins Wescott's "A History of Maine Politics 1840–1856: The Formation of the Republican Party" (Ph.D diss., University of Maine, 1966), in addition to selected chapters in the history of Maine edited by Louis Hatch, included under "Historical Resources" in section II above. On the state's transition to bipartisan politics, see David Clayton Smith's "Maine Politics, 1950–1956" (Master's thesis, University of Maine, 1958). A dated, though detailed, analysis of party influence in the legislature is Richard Sawyer and Donald Fowler's *Party Cohesion in the Maine State House of Representatives as a Function of Varying Majority-Minority Party Percentages* (Brunswick: Center for Education in Politics, Bowdoin College, 1963).

THESES AND DISSERTATIONS

The best way to locate doctoral dissertations is to use *Dissertation Abstracts International (DAI)*, which lists works by title, author, and subject. Master's theses in political science and history are held at the University of Maine (in Orono) and the University of Southern Maine (in Portland). The University of Maine System libraries and the libraries of Bates, Bowdoin, and Colby colleges record most of their holdings, including theses, on a single database (URSIS). The State Library will be part of URSIS in 1992.

NEWSPAPERS AND JOURNALS

Several newspapers provide extensive coverage of state government. The *Bangor Daily News* and the *Portland Press Herald* have the largest circulations. In recent years, the *Bangor Daily News* has published biographical sketches of the members of each new legislature. As Augusta's only newspaper, the *Kennebec Journal* has had a long association with Maine politics and government. (One of the state's most famous nineteenth-century politicians, James G. Blaine, served for a time as its editor.) In the early days of statehood, it printed the minutes of the legislature's proceedings. The *Maine*

Times is a weekly paper that often features in-depth articles on state issues and institutions. It has a politically reformist, environmental orientation. An even more reformist, though less widely read, newspaper is *The Maine Progressive*, published in Waterville.

In addition to the files at each paper's central office, major libraries maintain microfilm copies of past editions and have current indexes. Since 1977, the Fogler Library has distributed a regularly updated series of state periodical indexes entitled *Newspapers and Periodicals Indexed* by the Special Collections Department. Journals published in the state are similarly indexed, including ones mentioned previously: the *Maine Historical Society Quarterly*, the *Maine Townsman*, and the *Maine Bar Journal*.

STATISTICAL INFORMATION

Fiscal and Economic Data

The Department of Labor annually publishes a pamphlet entitled *Year-End Economic Overview*, which is similar to but not as comprehensive as *Maine Economy: Year End and Overview*, published by the Maine State Planning Office. A still-useful publication of the State Planning Office is *Economic Distress and the Changing Nature of Rural Maine* (1979), which classifies rural communities according to selected economic distress indicators. The State Planning Office also issues *The Maine Economy: A Forecast to 2000* (current edition, 1989), which analyzes Maine's economy in terms of future trends. The *Directory of Labor Market Information*, published by the Department of Manpower Affairs, describes Maine's labor markets and lists more detailed reports pertaining to the subject. Data concerning state finances are found in the *State of Maine Budget Document*, available through the State Bureau of the Budget, and in the *State of Maine Annual Financial Report*, published by the Legislative Finance Office.

Election Data

The principle source of election and voting data in Maine is the Election Division of the Office of the Secretary of State. The division is responsible for the conduct of elections and publishes a variety of guides to assist citizens and researchers in understanding the state's election process. It regularly publishes voting results in a series of reports, such as *Official Vote for County Officers*; *Official Vote for State Senators and Representatives*; *Official Vote for Republican and Democratic Primary Candidates and Non-Party Candidates Filing Petitions*; and *State of Maine Number of Enrolled and Registered Voters*. The reports are available in pamphlet form from the secretary of state. Also available from this office are state and county referendum results and the financial disclosure data that Maine statutes require from candidates for public office and from registered lobbyists. The *Maine Register* (Portland: Tower Publishing Co.) also contains considerable voting data, as well as profiles of each Maine town and city. Virtually all Maine libraries carry a copy of the *Register*.

Demographics

The best annually updated source for Maine demographic data is the *Statistical Abstracts of the United States*, published by the Bureau of the Census, U.S. Department of Commerce. Census Bureau population reports for most decades from 1790 to present are kept in the Maine State Library and the Fogler Library. For a detailed analysis of Maine's demographics in the early 1980s, see Daniel O'Leary's *Population Characteristics of Maine, 1980* (Bangor: Chancellor's Office, University of Maine System, 1983). More recently, the Commission on Maine's Future, a group of citizens and public officials which assembled during 1988 and 1989 to identify problems and trends likely to affect Maine in the 1990s, developed additional data. Their reports are available from the State Planning Office. See, in particular, *The People of Maine: A Study in Values*, vol. 2 (South Portland: Market Decisions, 1989).

Notes

CHAPTER ONE

1 Gerald C. Wright, Jr., Robert S. Erikson, and John P. McIver, "Public Opinion and Policy Liberalism in the American States," *American Journal of Political Science* 31 (November 1987): 989.

2 Market Decisions, *The People of Maine: A Psychographic Study*, vol. 2 (South Portland: Market Decisions, 1989).

CHAPTER TWO

1 See chap. 5, "The States and the Political Setting," pp. 109–49, in Daniel J. Elazar, *American Federalism: A View from the States*, 3d ed. (New York: Harper and Row, 1984).

2 *State O'Maine Facts* (Camden: Down-East Books, 1982), p. 92.

3 Charles E. Clark, *Maine: A Bicentennial History* (New York: W. W. Norton, 1977), p. 91.

4 Governor Joshua Chamberlain, quoted in Edward Chase Kirkland, *Men, Cities, and Transportation: A Study of New England History, 1820–1900*, vol. 1 (Cambridge, Mass.: Harvard University Press, 1948), p. 466.

5 Neal Peirce, *The New England States: People, Politics, and Power in the Six New England States* (New York: W. W. Norton, 1976), p. 372.

6 Jim Brunelle, ed., *Maine Almanac* (Augusta: Guy Gannett Publishing Co., 1978–79), p. 11.

7 Ray Allen Billington, *The Protestant Crusade, 1800–1860: A Study of the Origins of American Nativism* (New York: Macmillan, 1938), pp. 293–94.

8 *Ibid.*, p. 310.

9 *Ibid.*, p. 294.

10 Samuel Carleton Guptill, "The Grange in Maine from 1874 to 1940" (Ph.D. diss., University of Maine, Orono, 1973), p. 26.

11 David B. Walker, *Politics and Ethnocentrism: The Case of the Franco-Americans* (Brunswick: Bureau for Research in Municipal Government, Bowdoin College, 1961), p. 7.

12 *Ibid.*, p. 16.

13 Norman Sepenuk, "A Profile of Franco-American Political Attitudes in New England," in *A Franco-American Overview*, vol. 3, *New England* (part 1), edited by Madeleine Gigiere (Cambridge, Mass.: Evaluation, Dissemination, and Assessment Center, Lesley College, 1981), p. 221.

14 *Ibid.*, p. 219.

15 David B. Walker, "The Presidential Politics of Franco-Americans," in Gigiere, *A Franco-American Overview*, p. 203.

16 Ronald Larry Bissonnette, "Political Parties as Products of Their Environments: A Case Study of Lewiston, Maine" (Honors thesis, University of Maine, Orono, 1977), p. 51.

17 See *Census Reports*, vol. 1: *12th Census of the U.S., Taken in the Year 1900, Population*, part 1 (Washington, D.C.: U.S. Census Office, 1901), p. 807.

18 David C. Smith, "Towards a Theory of Maine History," in *Maine: A History through Selected Readings*, edited by D. C. Smith and E. U. Shriver (Dubuque, Iowa: Kendall/Hunt Publishing Co., 1985), p. 208.

19 *Ibid.*

20 Edward Bonner Whitney, "The Ku Klux Klan in Maine, 1922–1928: A Study with Particular Emphasis on the City of Portland" (B.S. thesis, Harvard College, Cambridge, Mass., 1966), p. 53.

21 James Hill Parker, *Ethnic Identity: The Case of the Franco-Americans* (Washington, D.C.: University Press of America, 1983), pp. 48–49.

22 *Maine Sunday Telegram,* August 21, 1988, p. 18A.

23 Parker, *Ethnic Identity*, p. 51.

24 Walker, "Presidential Politics," in Gigiere, *Franco-American Overview,* p. 204.

25 Parker, *Ethnic Identity*, p. 37.

26 *Ibid.*

27 Daniel O'Leary, "Population Characteristics of Maine, 1980" (report submitted to Patrick E. McCarthy, Chancellor, University of Maine, 1983), p. 7.

28 Brunelle, *Maine Almanac,* p. 160.

29 See, for example, Louis A. Ploch, "The Reversal in Migration Patterns: Some Rural Developments," *Rural Sociology* 43 (Summer 1978): 293–303.

30 The Commission on Maine's Future, *The People of Maine: A Study in Values,* vol. 1, Executive Summary (Augusta: Maine State Planning Office, 1989), p. 13.

31 Denise Goodman, "Maine Shares Unevenly in Economic Growth," *Boston Globe,* November 9, 1986, pp. 1, 83.

CHAPTER THREE

1 Neal Peirce, *The New England States: People, Politics, and Power in the Six New England States* (New York: W. W. Norton, 1976), p. 379.
2 *Ibid.,* p. 376.
3 David Clayton Smith, "Maine Politics, 1950–1956" (Master's thesis, University of Maine, Orono, 1958), p. 12.
4 Jim Brunelle, ed., *Maine Almanac* (Augusta: Guy Gannett Publishing Co., 1978–79), pp. 11, 240.
5 Smith, "Maine Politics," p. 4.
6 Samuel Eliot Morison, *The Oxford History of the American People* (New York: Oxford University Press, 1965), p. 741.
7 Duane Lockard, *New England State Politics* (Princeton, N.J.: Princeton University Press, 1959), p. 108.
8 Smith, "Maine Politics," p. 3.
9 Lockard, *New England State Politics,* p. 95.
10 *Ibid.,* pp. 99–100.
11 Smith, "Maine Politics," p. 89.
12 *Ibid.,* p. 123.
13 Peirce, *New England States,* p. 376.
14 Smith, "Maine Politics," pp. 94–95.
15 *Ibid.,* p. 106.
16 Cherrill Anson, *Edmund Muskie: Democratic Senator from Maine* (Washington, D.C.: Grossman Publishers, 1972), p. 15.
17 Peirce, *New England States,* p. 378.
18 Smith, "Maine Politics," p. 125.
19 Peirce, *New England States,* p. 378.
20 *Ibid.,* p. 391.
21 James Horan et al., *Downeast Politics: The Government of the State of Maine* (Dubuque, Iowa: Kendall/Hunt Publishing Co., 1975), p. 4.

CHAPTER FOUR

1 Election statistics in this chapter have been drawn from materials furnished by the Maine Office of Secretary of State.
2 Kenneth P. Hayes, "Maine Political Parties," in *New England Political Parties,*

edited by Josephine F. Milburn and William Doyle (Cambridge, Mass.: Schenkman Publishing Co., 1983), pp. 191–203.

3 Howard L. Recter, "Who Voted for Longley: Maine Elects an Independent Governor," *Polity* (Fall 1977): 65–85.

4 John McKernan, Jr., quoted in *Maine Sunday Telegram,* August 21, 1988, p. 18A.

5 *Kennebec Journal,* December 16, 1986.

6 *Portland Press Herald,* October 23, 1988.

7 *Ibid.*

8 Interview with Rep. John Diamond (D., Bangor), Orono, November 1989. Diamond was house majority leader in the 1987–88 session.

9 Duane Lockard, *New England State Politics* (Princeton, N.J.: Princeton University Press, 1959), p. 79.

10 Douglas Hodgkin, "Interest Group Politics in Maine: From Big-Three to Diversity," unpublished paper.

11 Christian P. Potholm II, "As Maine Goes: A Look at Politics in the Pine Tree State," *Bowdoin* (Winter 1990): 21–22.

12 *Ibid.*

13 Scott Allen, "The Utilities Probe," *Maine Times,* January 11, 1985.

14 Hodgkin, "Interest Group Politics," p. 17.

15 *Portland Press Herald,* June 6, 1982.

16 *Waterville Morning Sentinel,* July 28, 1982.

17 Scott Allen, "The Mother's Milk of Politics," *Maine Times,* December 5, 1986.

18 Paul Carrier, "Lobbyists Proliferate in Augusta," *Maine Sunday Telegram,* July 23, 1989.

19 Quoted in Scott Allen, "From Lobbyist to Candidate," *Maine Times,* May 23, 1986.

20 Jadine O'Brien, quoted in Nancy Perry, "Ex-Legislators in Great Demand as Lobbyists," *Kennebec Journal,* April 13, 1988.

21 Quoted in *Portland Press Herald,* April 23, 1988, p. 19.

22 Data drawn from files of the Maine State Law Library.

CHAPTER FIVE

1 The drafting of the Maine Constitution in 1819 is discussed in Ronald F. Banks, *Maine Becomes a State: The Movement to Separate Maine from Massachusetts, 1785–1820* (Middletown, Conn.: Wesleyan University Press, 1970), pp. 167–79.

2 William Pitt Preble, quoted in *Ibid.*, p. 153.

3 Ronald M. Peters, Jr., *The Massachusetts Constitution 1780: A Social Compact* (Amherst, Mass.: University of Massachusetts Press, 1978), pp. 193–94.

4 Daniel J. Elazar, "The Principles and Traditions Underlying State Constitutions," *Publius: The Journal of Federalism* 12 (Winter 1982): 11–26.

5 Fred Eugene Jewett, *Financial History of Maine* (New York: Columbia University Press, 1937), pp. 30–34.

6 Lawrence Lee Pelletier, *The Initiative and Referendum in Maine* (Brunswick: Bureau for Research in Municipal Government, Bowdoin College, 1951), p. 8.

7 Peter Neil Barry, "Nineteenth Century Constitutional Amendment in Maine" (Master's thesis, University of Maine, Orono, 1965), pp. 60–61.

8 Herbert M. Heath, *A Manual of Maine Corporation Law* (Portland: Loring, Short, and Harmon, 1917), pp. 13–14.

9 Herbert Kaufman, *Politics and Policies of State and Local Government* (Englewood Cliffs, N.J.: Prentice-Hall, 1963), chap. 2.

10 See Cabanne Howard, "Civil Constitutional Law: Is the Law Court in the Maine Stream?" *Maine Bar Journal* 3 (May 1988): 134. For the activities of other states in this area, see John Kincaid, "State Court Protections of Individual Rights under State Constitutions: The New Judicial Federalism," *The Journal of State Government* 61 (September-October 1988): 163–69; John Kincaid, ed., "State Constitutions in a Federal System," *Annals of the American Academy of Political and Social Science* 496 (March 1988).

CHAPTER SIX

1 "Lawmakers Finish Busy '89 Session," *Bangor Daily News,* July 3, 1989.

2 John Hale, "Loose Ends in the Legislature," *Bangor Daily News,* July 1, 1989, p. 1.

3 *Maine Sunday Telegram,* March 12, 1989.

4 Conducted by the accounting firm Peat Marwick, the report focused on the way to cut back on the number of bills that the committees have to consider. It recommended the present bill-filing process, under which the committees are supposed to consider all bills filed by legislators and referred to them, be replaced by committee bill drafting. Under the proposed arrangement, legislators would provide the committees with briefly stated concepts for bills, but the committees would be in charge of drafting the ideas into bill form. The intent is to reduce the large volume of bills that the committee is forced to study and reject. See *Lewiston Sunday Sun-Journal,* editorial, April 6, 1990.

5 *Maine Sunday Telegram,* March 6, 1988.

6 Citizens Conference on State Legislatures, *The Sometime Governments* (New York: Bantam Books, 1971), pp. 52–53.

7 Ronald Banks, *Maine Becomes a State* (Middletown, Conn.: Wesleyan University Press, 1970), chap. 8.

8 Glendon Schubert, *Reapportionment* (New York: Charles Scribner's Sons, 1965), pp. 65–82.

9 *Baker* v. *Carr*, 369 U.S. 186 (1962).

10 Allen Pease and Wilfred Richard, eds., *Maine: Fifty Years of Change 1940–1990* (Orono: University of Maine Press, 1983), p. 106.

11 Kenneth T. Palmer et al., *The Legislative Process in Maine* (Washington, D.C.: American Political Science Association, 1973), chap. 3.

12 Legislative biographies for this section have been drawn from the *Bangor Daily News*, January 3–4, 1987.

13 *Connection: New England Journal of Higher Education*, 1 (Fall 1986): 67.

14 *1989 House and Senate Registers* (Augusta: Office of Clerk of the House and Secretary of the Senate, 1989).

15 Scott Allen, "Speaker of the House," *Maine Times*, January 9, 1987.

16 Quoted in *Ibid*.

17 This material is drawn in part from Palmer et al., *Legislative Process*, chap. 4.

18 Quoted in John Diamond, "Mr. Smith Goes to Augusta," *The Washington Monthly* 21 (July-August 1989): 36.

CHAPTER SEVEN

1 Kenneth T. Palmer, "Governmental Reorganization in Maine: A Commentary," *Juncture* 2 (October 1971): 24–27. The arrangement of departments is contained in Legislative Research Committee, *Government Reorganization Phase II—Status Report* (Augusta: State of Maine Printing Office, 1970).

2 The survey considers the fifty-nine governors who served six months or longer. These delimited periods, while fairly arbitrary, seem generally to correspond with those that other studies of Maine's government and politics have found useful. See, for example, Allen Pease and Wilfred Richard, eds., *Maine: Fifty Years of Change 1940–1990* (Orono: University of Maine Press, 1983).

3 Data on Maine governors have been drawn primarily from Joseph E. Kallenbach and Jessamire S. Kallenbach, *American State Governors, 1776–1976*, vol. 2 (Dobbs Ferry, N.Y.: Oceana Publications, 1981).

4 Frank M. Bryan, "The New England Governorships: People, Position, and Power," in *New England Politics*, edited by Josephine F. Milburn and Victoria Schuck (Cambridge, Mass.: Schenkman Publishing Co., 1981), p. 82.

5 Much of the discussion of the McKernan administration is drawn from interviews with members of the governor's staff.

6 *Maine Sunday Telegram*, July 9, 1989.

7 Theo Lippman, Jr., and Donald C. Hansen, *Muskie* (New York: W. W. Norton, 1971), p. 90.

8 Governor's Task Force on Government Reorganization, *Toward a More Responsive and Effective State Government* (Augusta: State of Maine Printing Office, 1969), pp. 2–9.

9 Market Decisions, *The People of Maine: A Study in Values,* vol. 1 (South Portland: Market Decisions, 1989), p. 17.

10 Data in this section are drawn from *Maine State Government Annual Report, 1990– 1991* (Augusta: State of Maine Printing Office, 1987), and from information supplied by the Department of Administration.

CHAPTER EIGHT

1 A good discussion of the history of the Maine courts is found in James F. Horan et al., *Downeast Politics: The Government of the State of Maine* (Dubuque, Iowa: Kendall/Hunt Publishing Co., 1975), chap. 5.

2 Quoted in *Ibid,* p. 168.

3 Statistical information and some descriptive material in this chapter have been drawn from *State of Maine–Judicial Department: 1990 Annual Report* (Portland: Administrative Office of the Courts, 1991). This is a most valuable annual compendium.

4 *Portland* v. *DePaolo,* 531 A.2d 669 (1987).

5 Information drawn from *State Policy Data Book '89* (McConnellsburg, Penn.: Brizius and Foster, 1989), sect. J.

6 Kermit V. Lipez, "Adventures and Reflections of a New Judge," *Maine Bar Journal* 2 (November 1987): 324–36.

7 *Maine Times,* November 30, 1984.

8 *Maine Times,* October 31, 1975.

9 Information on judicial backgrounds has been drawn from newspaper files, Maine State Law Library.

10 Robert A. Kagan, Bobby D. Infelise, and Robert R. Detlefsen, "American State Supreme Court Justices, 1900–1970," *American Bar Foundation Research Journal* (1984): 371–407.

11 *Davies* v. *City of Bath,* 364 A.2d 1269 (1976).

12 *Bell* v. *Wells,* 510 A.2d 509 (1989). The remaining cases are drawn from newspaper files, Maine State Law Library.

13 *State* v. *Events International, Inc.,* 528 A.2d 458 (1987).

14 *Association of Independent Professionals* v. *Maine Labor Relations Board,* 465 A.2d 401 (1983).

15 Cabanne Howard, "Civil Constitutional Law: Is the Law Court in the Maine Stream?" *Maine Bar Journal* 3 (May 1988): 133.

16 *Putnam* v. *Town of Hampdem*, 495 A.2d 785 (1985).

17 Harriet P. Henry, *The Maine District Court: A Quarter Century of Progress* (Brunswick: Tower Publishing Co., 1987), p. 39.

18 Quoted in Edgar Allen Beem, "Invisible But Powerful: A Rare Look at Maine's Supreme Court," *Maine Times*, July 8, 1988, p. 9.

CHAPTER NINE

1 Richard Winters, "Political Choice and Expenditure Change in Vermont and New Hampshire," *Polity: The Journal of the Northeastern Political Science Association* 12 (Summer 1980): 603.

2 *The Book of the States, 1988–89 Edition*, vol. 27 (Lexington, Ky.: Council of State Governments, 1988), p. 225.

3 Interviews with G. William Buker, State Budget Officer, Augusta, June 1988.

4 *Ibid.*

5 *Ibid.*

6 Winters, "Political Choice."

7 *Book of the States*, p. xix.

8 *Ibid.*

9 *Summary of the Program and Budget Proposals for the Fiscal Years 1990–1991* (Augusta: Maine Office of the Governor), p. 7.

10 Quoted in Fred Eugene Jewett, *A Financial History of Maine* (New York: Columbia University Press, 1937), p. 34.

11 *Ibid.*, pp. 120–21.

12 *Summary of the Program and Budget Proposals*, p. 7.

13 Jewett, *Financial History of Maine*, see Appendix, table A.

14 *Ibid.*, pp. 90–94.

15 Neal Peirce, *The New England States: People, Politics, and Power in the Six New England States* (New York: W. W. Norton, 1976), p. 388.

16 The welfare proportion of Maine's budget was somewhat higher in the mid-1980s, before the slowing of federal grants and state revenues led to program cutbacks.

17 Peirce, *New England States*, p. 389.

18 See *Ibid.*, p. 389, for a statement of conservative opposition to the rise in welfare benefits.

19 *Summary of the Program and Budget Proposals*, p. 25.

20 *Lewiston-Auburn Sunday Sun-Journal*, June 18, 1989, p. 1b.

21 *Ibid.*

22 Alex Pattakos and Kenneth T. Palmer, "Downeast But Not Downunder: Maine Responds to the Reagan Challenge," *Publius: The Journal of Federalism* 13 (Spring 1983): 45.

23 *Summary of the Program and Budget Proposals,* p. 1.

CHAPTER TEN

1 Edmund S. Muskie, *Journeys* (Garden City, N.Y.: Doubleday, 1972), p. 80.

2 Richard Saltonstall, Jr., *Maine Pilgrimage* (Boston: Little, Brown, 1974), p. 148.

3 Duane Lockard, *New England State Politics* (Princeton, N.J.: Princeton University Press, 1959), chap. 5.

4 These developments are discussed in Allen Pease and Wilfred Richard, *Maine: Fifty Years of Change, 1940–1990* (Augusta: State of Maine Printing Office, 1983), pp. 121–22.

5 Arthur Lerman Associates, *Evaluation of the Enforcement of Four Maine Environmental Statutes* (Augusta: Arthur Lerman Associates, August 1981), chap. 5.

6 Material on recent legislation is drawn from newspaper files, Maine State Law Library, Augusta.

7 Lerman, *Evaluation,* chap. 2.

8 Quoted in *Bangor Daily News,* February 27–28, 1988.

9 The discussion of economic development policies is drawn from Economic Development Strategy Task Force, *Establishing the Maine Advantage: An Economic Development Strategy for the State of Maine* (Augusta: State of Maine Printing Office, 1987), and interviews with members of the Department of Economic and Community Development.

10 Alex N. Pattakos and Charles E. Morris, "The Maine Experience," in *From Nation to States: The Small Cities Community Development Block Grant Progress,* edited by Edward J. Jennings, Jr., et al. (Albany, N.Y.: State University of New York Press, 1986), pp. 53–69.

11 *Bangor Daily News,* April 13, 1988.

12 John L. Martin, "Adapting to a Changing Economy: Economic Education for Policymaking," *State Government* 60 (July-August, 1987): 179–82.

13 Market Decisions, *The People of Maine: A Psychographic Study,* vol. 2 (South Portland: Market Decisions, 1989).

14 John Hale, "Maine's Economy Enjoys Rapid Growth," *Bangor Daily News,* August 5, 1987.

15 Denise Goodman, "Maine Shares Unevenly in Economic Growth," *Boston Globe,* September 1986.

16 "Guiding Growth," *Maine Sunday Telegram,* March 13, 1988.

17 John McKernan, Jr., quoted in Mal Leary, "Growth in Maine No. 1 Concern in Random Voter Poll," *Bangor Daily News,* July 11, 1988.

18 Tax Turkel, "Maine Enters a New Era," *Maine Sunday Telegram,* April 24, 1988.

19 Carolyn Chute, *The Beans of Egypt, Maine* (New York: Ticknor and Fields, 1985).

20 Maine State Planning Office, *Poverty in Maine 1970–1980,* vol. 1 (Augusta: State Planning Office, 1985), chap. 3.

21 Edith Beaulieu, quoted in *Lewiston Sunday Sun-Journal,* April 4, 1984.

22 *Portland Press Herald,* July 18, 1991.

23 Daphine W. Merrill, *A Salute to Maine* (New York: Vantage Press, 1983), p. 79.

24 Dale McGarrigle, "Unique in the Nation," *Bangor Daily News,* April 20, 1984.

25 See *Accepting the Challenge: Maine Conference on Aspirations Proceedings,* April 27, 1987; Wayne Reilly, "Student Aspirations Key to Economic Future," *Bangor Daily News,* Saturday–Sunday, June 4–5, 1988.

26 Karlene K. Hale, "Bither Urges Better Job Training," *Morning Sentinel,* August 10, 1988.

27 *Ibid,* p. 4.

28 See *Accepting the Challenge*; Reilly, "Student Aspirations."

29 Wayne Reilly, "Maine Schools Battle Dropout Problem," *Bangor Daily News,* June 6, 1988.

30 "Social Development," *Maine: Fifty Years of Change 1940-1990,* p. 68.

CHAPTER ELEVEN

1 See Daniel J. Elazar, *American Federalism: A View from the States,* 3d ed. (New York: Harper and Row, 1984), pp. 14–25.

2 One of the best books on the political history of Maine in the nineteenth century is Louis C. Hatch, ed., *Maine: A History* (New York: American Historical Society, 1919). Chap. 22 describes the Maine congressional delegation of the 1890s.

3 See William C. Lewis, Jr., ed., *Margaret Chase Smith: Declaration of Conscience* (New York: Doubleday, 1972).

4 See David Nevin, *Muskie of Maine* (Brattleboro, Vt.: Book Press, 1972).

5 Material for the following paragraphs has been drawn largely from state newspaper files.

6 Statistics in this paragraph have been drawn from *State Policy Data Book, '89* (McConnellsburg, Penn.: Brizius and Foster, 1989), tables F-1, F-6, F-10, F-22.

7 *Waterville Morning Sentinel,* March 14, 1985.

8 Kenneth T. Palmer, Alex N. Pattakos, and Stephen H. Holden, "The New Federalism Downeast: Reaganomics in Maine," in *Publius: Annual Review of American Federalism,* edited by Stephen L. Schechter (Lapham, Md.: University Press of America, 1981), pp. 83–91.

9 *Bangor Daily News,* January 8, 1990.

10 Claude E. Robinson, "Maine—Political Barometer," *Political Science Quarterly* 47 (June 1932): 161–84.

11 To identify the cases, the West Publishing Company's computer-assisted legal research service, called Westlaw, was utilized.

12 *Fort Halifax Packing Co., Inc.* v. *Coyne,* 107. S.Ct. 2211 (1987).

13 *Maine* v. *Moulton,* 106 S.Ct. 477 (1985).

14 *Maine* v. *Thibout,* 100 S.Ct. 2502 (1980).

15 *Maine* v. *Thornton,* 104 S.Ct. 1735 (1984).

16 *First National Bank of Boston* v. *Maine,* 52 S.Ct. 174 (1932).

17 Mark Starr, "Neighbors, Not Friends: A New England Feud," *Newsweek,* June 5, 1989, p. 27.

18 Kenneth M. Curtis and John C. Carroll, *Canadian-American Relations: The Promise and the Challenge* (Lexington, Mass.: Lexington Books, 1983), chap. 7.

19 Roger F. Swanson, *Intergovernmental Perspectives on the Canada-U.S. Relationship* (New York: New York University Press, 1978), chap. 6.

20 For a general discussion on state involvements in international relations, see John Kincaid, "The American Governors in International Affairs," *Publius: The Journal of Federalism* 14 (Fall 1984): 95–114.

21 Donald K. Alper, "Recent Trends in U.S.–Canada Regional Diplomacy," in *Across Boundaries: Transborder Interaction in Comparative Perspective,* edited by Oscar J. Martinez (El Paso, Texas: Texas Western Press, 1986), 122–28.

22 *Ibid.*

CHAPTER TWELVE

1 Dr. Edward Dow, "The Smothering of Democracy," *Bangor Daily News,* August 17, 1976.

2 Andrew E. Nuquest, *Town Government in Vermont* (Burlington, Vt.: Government Research Center, University of Vermont, 1964), pp. 3–4; Daniel R. Grant and Lloyd B. Omdahl, *State and Local Government in America* (Boston: Allyn and Bacon, 1987), pp. 370–73; Lane W. Lancaster, *Government in Rural America* (Princeton, N.J.: D. Van Nostrand, 1937).

3 Kenneth L. Roberts, *Local Government in Maine* (Augusta: Maine Municipal Association, 1979).

4 Seven towns disincorporated in the 1980s, becoming plantations or unorganized townships. See Tom Weber, "Deciding a Town's Future," *Bangor Daily News,* Saturday–Sunday, March 19–20, 1988.

5 James Haag, *A Study of Plantation Government in Maine* (Orono: Bureau of Public Administration, University of Maine, 1973).

6 *Ibid.,* p. 16.

7 See Maine Department of Human Resources, Office of Data Research and Vital Statistics, *Population Projections by Minor Civil Divisions, Sex, Age and County* by Dale E. Welch, senior researcher, June 1987; "Population Changes for Maine Cities," *Bangor Daily News,* June 24, 1991.

8 For an excellent empirical study of town meetings, see Joseph F. Zimmerman, "The New England Town Meeting: Pure Democracy in Action?" in *The Municipal Yearbook* (Washington, D.C.: International City Management Association, 1984), pp. 102–6.

9 A helpful manual prepared to assist moderators is *Maine Moderator's Manual* (Augusta: Maine Municipal Association, 1974).

10 Roberts, *Local Government,* pp. 26–28.

11 Thomas Jefferson, quoted in James Haag, *Forms of Municipal Government in the United States and Maine* (Orono: Bureau of Public Administration, University of Maine, 1970), pp. 25–27.

12 James Bryce, *The American Commonwealth,* 2d ed., vol. 1 (London: Macmillan, 1881), p. 591.

13 Zimmerman, "New England Town Meeting," p. 105.

14 *Ibid.,* pp. 104–5.

15 Roberts, *Local Government,* p. 30.

16 International City Management Association, *The Municipal Yearbook 1987* (Washington, D.C.: International City Management Association, 1987), p. xv.

17 Haag, *Forms of Municipal Government,* pp. 21–23.

18 For a historical perspective, see Richard S. Childs, *The First Years of the Council–Manager Plan of Municipal Government* (New York: National Municipal League, 1965); Richard J. Stillman, *The Rise of the City Manager: A Public Professional in Local Government* (Albuquerque, N.M.: University of New Mexico Press, 1974), chap. 4; Harold Stone, Don K. Price, and Kathryn H. Stone, *City Manager in the United States* (Chicago: Public Administration Service, 1940).

19 For a recent review, see Daniel W. Martin, "The Fading Legacy of Woodrow Wilson," *Public Administration Review* 48 (March-April 1988): 631–35. See also Richard J. Stillman, "Woodrow Wilson and the Study of Administration: A New Look at an Old Essay," *American Political Science Review* 67 (June 1973): 582–88.

20 For a more complete discussion, see Deil S. Wright, "The City Manager as a Developmental Administrator," chap. 6 in *Comparative Urban Research,* edited by Robert T. Daland (Beverley Hills, Calif.: Sage Publications, 1969), pp. 203–48. Also see Ronald O. Loveridge, *City Managers in Legislative Politics* (Indianapolis, Ind.: Bobbs-Merrill, 1971).

21 See Roberts, *Local Government,* pp. 32–34; Haag, *Forms of Municipal Government,* pp. 30–35.

22 Oliver P. Williams and Charles R. Adrian, *Four Cities* (Philadelphia: University of Pennsylvania Press, 1963), pp. 23–32; Oliver Williams, "A Topology for Comparative Local Government," *Midwest Journal of Political Science* 5 (May 1961): 150–64.

23 Clarence N. Stone, Robert K. Whelan, and William J. Murin, "Village Politics," *Urban Policy and Politics in a Bureaucratic Age* (Englewood Cliffs, N.J.: Prentice Hall, 1986), p. 78.

24 Michael Zuckerman, *Peaceable Kingdoms* (New York: Alfred A. Knopf, 1970), pp. 169–71.

25 Roscoe C. Martin, *Grass Roots* (University, Ala.:University of Alabama Press, 1957), pp. 40–41.

26 For more detail, see G. Thomas Taylor and David Sullivan, "Local Fiscal Conditions and Management: Results of a Survey of City and Town Managers," paper presented at the Western Social Science Association, Denver, Colo., April 1988.

27 See Robert Dahl, *Who Governs* (New Haven, Conn.: Yale University Press, 1961); Floyd Hunter, *Community Power Structure* (Chapel Hill, N.C.: University of North Carolina Press, 1953).

28 William C. Osborn, *The Paper Plantation: Ralph Nader's Report on the Pulp and Paper Industry in Maine* (New York: Grossman Publishers, 1974).

CHAPTER THIRTEEN

1 H. S. Gilbertson, *The County: The "Dark Continent" of American Politics* (New York: National Short Ballot Organization, 1917), p. 23.

2 John C. Bollens, John R. Bayes, and Kathryn L. Utter, *American County Government* (Beverley Hills, Calif.: Sage Publications, 1969); Herbert S. Duncombe, *Modern County Government* (Washington, D.C.: National Association of Counties, 1977).

3 Edward F. Dow, "County Government Should Go," *Bangor Daily News,* August 20, 1976.

4 Duncombe, *Modern County Government,* p. 21.

5 Bollens, Bayes, and Utter, *American County Government*, p. 98; Duncombe, chap. 2.

6 John B. Forster, "Substate Regionalism in Maine" (Master's thesis, University of Maine, Orono, 1976).

7 *Ibid.*, chap. 4.

8 See also "Counties," *Intergovernmental Perspective* 17 (Winter 1991): 5–48.

9 Ralph R. Widner, "Foreword," in Duncombe, *Modern County Government*, p. v.

10 For an extensive account of Maine county government, see Edward F. Dow, *County Government in Maine: Proposals for Reorganization* (Augusta: Maine Legislative Research Committee, October 1952); Maine Intergovernmental Relations Committee, *County Government* (Augusta, 1966); Maine Legislative Research Committee, *County Government*, publication no. 103–9, Augusta, 1967.

11 Maine Municipal Association, Bureau of Public Administration, and Greater Portland Council of Governments, *Maine County Government: The Charter Alternative: A Working Paper*, 1981, p. 4.

12 Maine Municipal Association, *Maine County Government*, p. 3.

13 "County Government Study," *Legislative Bulletin* (Maine Municipal Association) 12 (January 12, 1990): 1–2.

14 Scott W. Seabury, "A Comparison of County Governments in the U.S. and Northern Maine" (University of Maine, 1988, unpublished paper), p. 8.

15 See Gilbertson, *The County*; M.R.S.A. Title 30, sec. 202.

16 Executive Order No. 6 was issued pursuant to Title 30, Chapter 239, Sections 4501–4503 of M.R.S.A.

17 Maine Legislature, Office of Policy and Legal Analysis, "An Overview of Maine's Regional Councils" (unpublished draft, December 1987) pp. 2–6.

18 Executive Order 6FY 83–84 (November 15, 1983), "State Policy on Regional Councils."

19 30 M.R.S.A. (1981–86); for a discussion of COGs' evolution nationally, see Nelson Wickstrom, "Studying Regional Councils: The Quest for Developmental Theory," *Southern Review of Public Administration* 4 (June 1980): 81–98.

20 For a summary of the Portland area's evolution as a council of governments, see James F. Horan and G. Thomas Taylor, Jr., *Experiments in Metropolitan Government* (New York: Praeger, 1977), chap. 7.

21 *A More Responsive Government: The Final Report to the Governor of the Task Force on Regional and District Organizations* (Augusta: State of Maine Printing Office, 1978).

22 Forster, "Substate Regionalism in Maine," chap. 2; Edward Dow, "Plantations Have Powers Similar to Towns," *Bangor Daily News*, August 19, 1976.

23 Kenneth L. Roberts, *Local Government in Maine* (Augusta: Maine Municipal Association, 1979), pp. 67–70.

24 Scott Bollens, "Examining the Link between State Policy and the Creation of Local Special Districts," *State and Local Government Review* (Fall 1986): 117–24; John C. Bollens, *Special District Government in the U.S.* (Berkeley and Los Angeles: University of California Press, 1957).

25 See Jo Josephson, "New Regionalism," *Maine Townsman* 53 (August 1991): 12–19.

26 For a favorable review of the application of public choice theory to special districts, see Robert B. Hawkins, Jr., *Self Government by District, Myth and Reality* (Stanford, Calif.: Hoover Institution Press, Stanford University, 1976), pp. 47 and 120.

27 Robert B. Hawkins, Jr., "Special Districts and Urban Services," in *The Delivery of Urban Services,* edited by Elinor Ostrom, (Beverley Hills, Calif.: Sage Publications, 1976), pp. 171-87.

28 Howard A. Dawson and Floyd W. Reeves, *Report of the National Commission on School District Reorganization: Your School District* (Washington, D.C.: Department of Rural Education, National Education Association, 1948), pp. 26–27.

29 John C. Bollens, "School Districts," *Special District Government,* p. 198.

30 John W. Skeehan, "School District Reorganization in Maine" (Ed.D. diss., George Peabody College, Vanderbilt University, 1981).

31 For a discussion of the landmark s.a.d. legislation, see Stephen K. Bailey, Richard Frost, Paul E. Marsh, and Robert C. Wood, *Schoolmen and Politics: A Study of State Aid to Education in the Northeast* (Syracuse, N.Y.: Syracuse University Press, 1962), pp. 73–81.

32 For more analysis of this survey, see G. Thomas Taylor and David Sullivan, "Local Fiscal Conditions and Management: Results of a Survey of City and Town Managers," paper presented at the Western Social Science Association, Denver, Colo., April 1988.

33 See Geoff Herman, "Interlocal Cooperation: Options Which Are Available," *Maine Townsman* 53 (August 1991): 5–10.

34 Bill Caldwell, "Tax Exemptions More Costly Than You Think—MMA," *Maine Sunday Telegram,* June 8, 1975.

35 See, for example, David Wihry, *Institutional Property Tax Exemptions in Maine* (Orono: Bureau of Public Administration, University of Maine, 1975).

36 "Property Tax Panic," *Bangor Daily News,* July 25, 1986.

37 Taylor and Sullivan, "Local Fiscal Conditions."

38 Wayne Reilly, "Skyrocketing Property Values Revive Tax Revolt," *Bangor Daily News,* June 11–12, 1988.

39 *Ibid.*

40 Carroll Astbury, "Property Taxes in Maine, Per Capita, Lower Than Other New England States," *Bangor Daily News,* March 29, 1988.

41 "State and Local Relations: The Challenges of the Eighties," issues paper for the Blaine House Conference on State and Local Relations, Augusta, April 1982, pp. 25–27.

42 Carroll Astbury, "Maine High in Government Costs: State Ranks 11th Nationwide in Sales, Income Taxes," *Bangor Daily News,* March 16–17, 1991.

43 "Political Trends," in *Maine: Fifty Years of Change 1940–1990* (Orono: University of Maine Press, 1983); "State and Local Relations," p. 16; Advisory Commission on Intergovernmental Relations, *Significant Features of Fiscal Federalism,* vol. 2, August 1990, pp. 114–15, 145.

44 Andrew Kekacs, "50,000 Ask State for Tax Relief, Rent Relief," *Bangor Daily News,* September 20, 1989.

45 *Legislative Bulletin,* vol. 13, no. 24, Maine Municipal Association, July 30, 1991, p. 3.

46 *A More Responsive Government,* pp. 35–42.

CHAPTER FOURTEEN

1 Richard Barringer, "Economy and Government," *Maine Times,* January 12, 1990, p. 16.

2 Jeff Clark, "The Roaring Eighties," *Down East,* vol. 37, no. 6 (January 1991): 53.

3 Phyllis Austin, "Who Runs Maine?" *Maine Times,* July 22, 1988, p. 8.

Index

Natural Resources Council of Maine, 50, 123, 132
New Brunswick, 153, 154
New England, xv, xix, xxi, xxii, 7, 9, 142, 157, 173, 194, 197
New Hampshire, xx, 5, 7, 10, 14, 23, 66, 67, 109, 115, 144, 151–52, 154, 162, 166, 189 (table); and Maine, 10, 151–52, 154
Nicoll, Don, 31
Non-Intercourse Act (1790), 145
Northeast, xviii-xix, xxi, 9, 11, 12, 13
Northeastern Boundary Dispute, 57
North Haven, 162
Northwest, xxi
Nuclear power, 22, 50

O'Brien, Jadine, 48
Office of Comprehensive Planning, 133
Office of Policy and Legal Analysis (OPLA), 75–76
Office of Public Advocate, 91
Old Orchard Beach, 161
Old Town, 21
Ombudsman, 87–88, 138
O'Meara, Edward, 41, 43
Oxford County, 131, 176 (table)

Paradis, Eugene, 73
Passamaquoddies, 10, 20, 21, 145
Paternalism, xxv
Patronage, 25, 28, 29, 30, 32, 35
Payne, Frederick, 29, 81
Penobscot County, 67, 95, 128, 176 (table)
Penobscot River, 125
Penobscots, 10, 20, 145
Penobscot Valley Council of Governments, 182

Perkins, Thomas R., 73
Pine Tree State, xxv
Piscataquis County, 40, 176 (table)
Piscataquis River, 19
Plantations, 156, 158, 171
Poles, 18
Policymaking, 109, 122, 127, 141, 196. See also Budget; Economic development; Education; Environment; Government; Social policies
Political action committees (PACs), 43
Political culture, xiii, xiv, xx, 7, 25; defined, 9; individualistic, xxiii-xxiv, xxv, 9–10, 16, 24; moralistic, xxii, xxiii, xxiv-xxv, 6, 9, 10, 11–12, 19, 23, 24, 26–27, 56, 117, 143, 144, 145, 193; national, xxii-xxiii; traditionalistic, xxiii, xxv, 9, 15, 16. See also Political participation
Political moderation, 5, 19, 23, 33, 34, 41, 56, 64, 144, 197
Political participation, xxiii, xxiv, 4, 9, 23, 27, 36–37, 68, 83, 128, 144, 193, 197; and demographic changes, 6, 13, 32–33, 35; and minority groups, 45
Political parties, xxiv, 13, 60, 109, 166. See also Democratic party; Republican party
Political representation, 11, 67
Political unity, 7
Population, xiii, xv, xix, xxv, 3, 4, 6, 8, 10, 14, 16–17, 18, 23, 24, 79, 155; growth in, 12, 14, 18, 19, 21, 28, 67, 166, 168–69, 185, 194; native-born, 139–40, 194
Portland, xxv, 6, 11, 14, 22, 23, 40, 142, 166, 171, 187; bishop of, 16; District Court, 96; population